M000239512

GOING the DISTANCE

Tales and Tips from 6 Decades of Marathons

GOING the DISTANCE

Tales and Tips from 6 Decades of Marathons

by Kevin Boyle

gatekeeper press™

Columbus, Ohio

Going The Distance: Tales And Tips From Six Decades of Marathons

Published by Gatekeeper Press
2167 Stringtown Rd, Suite 109
Columbus, OH 43123-2989
www.GatekeeperPress.com

Library of Congress Control Number: 2021945329

ISBN (hardcover): 9781662918544
ISBN (paperback): 9781662918551
eISBN: 9781662918568

CONTENTS

Thanks for the inspiration

Then . . . Dad

Now . . . Cam

Forever . . . Heather

FOREWORD

"You should make a TikTok video of getting back in shape for the marathon," was my nephew Patrick's response when I told him in May 2021 that I planned to run the Marine Corps Marathon that fall. My first thought was, Tic Tacs are small, oval mints that make a rattling noise in their clear plastic container, letting everyone around you know you are approaching. Why would I make a video about the marathon and breath mints? Plus, a box of rattling mints would annoy every runner near me in a race. My next thought was, I have not run a marathon in seven years, have barely ran more than a mile in the past three years-- who would watch a video of me jogging and huffing and puffing along the Chesapeake and Ohio Canal towpath? That is, unless I tripped and fell into the canal, making the video instantly go viral.

However, Pat's comment did ignite a spark in me. Years earlier, in the Quarterdeck Restaurant in Arlington, Virginia, just across the Potomac River from Washington, DC, my college coach, friend, mentor, and boss, Matt Centrowitz said to me, "Now that we are older, we have an obligation to pass on what we know to the next generation. For me, it's running knowledge; for you, it's legal knowledge." At the time, I was getting close to retirement after twenty-six years as a lawyer in the Army (yes, like the movie *A Few Good Men*, except I never heard anyone yell "You can't handle the truth!" in a courtroom) and was thinking about what to do next with my life. I did follow Matt's advice and became a professor, but that is getting ahead of ourselves.

Instead of making a "Tic Tac" video, I figured I could follow Matt's advice and pass on some bits of knowledge about the marathon through a book. One can walk into any Barnes and Noble bookstore (if they can find an actual bookstore these days) or click on Amazon and find several books about the marathon or running in general. This book is not like those. Certainly, I could write a book with charts and graphs and magical 16-week marathon training programs, but those already exist and to be honest, they are sort of bland.

Back in the 1970s, my homeroom teacher and junior high school track coach was Mike Byrnes, one of the 1968 USA Olympic Track Team coaches. Even with the guidance of an Olympic coach, I was the worst runner on my junior high school track team. Actually, I was the worst runner in the entire county. That all changed in 1979 when I ran my first marathon in tenth grade. A few years later, I had the opportunity to run at St. John's University with Matt Centrowitz as he was training for his attempt to break the American record for the 5K distance (which he did set in June 1982 with a 13:12 clocking).

Over the past six decades, I have used what I learned from these two coaching legends in my marathon journey. Along the way, I have stumbled, succeeded, taken detours, and endured. It would be easy to write a list of the Ten Things That Worked, The Ten Things That Didn't Work, and The Training Plan I Used. But that's not really helpful; it would be just an Internet link to a web page. It's also not helpful because I don't know you; I don't know your work schedule; I don't know your running background, or your reasons for running. Every training plan, and all training advice, must be tailored to the individual.

Rather than creating a list of lists, I have focused on one marathon per decade to offer tips from these races that you can weave into your own marathon journey.

IN THE BEGINNING

"He's a fake, Frank!" Erich Segal, the ABC TV announcer screamed at marathon race leader Frank Shorter, who appeared bewildered as he trailed a race imposter into the Munich Olympic Stadium in September 1972.

As a nine-year-old age group swimmer, my eyes were fixated on Mark Spitz and his seven gold medals throughout ABC's coverage of the XX Olympiad. However, as Frank Shorter entered the stadium, I couldn't believe that after 26 miles he was still running, especially considering my running was limited to the Catholic Youth Organization (CYO) track team and the 40-yard dash. And, on occasion, the 11-person by 40 yard each relay. Yes, somehow a volunteer track coach was able to corral eleven eight- and nine-year-olds to the proper areas of a 440-yard track to complete a one-circuit of the track relay race. Looking back, the relay was an endless series of missed handoffs and dropped batons. All too often, one misguided runner would forgo all the baton passes and wind up running the entire lap solo.

"How is he still running so fast?"

"Run a marathon and find out for yourself."

My father was not trying to be glib. He was just answering in the typical response of my parents, who took to an entirely new plane the theory of hands-on learning. I knew everything about Fiorello La Guardia for having the nerve as a ten-year-old to ask at one Sunday dinner, "Why name an airport LaGuardia?" The following Sunday, I read a report to my extremely disinterested six brothers and sisters. A complaint that we ate too many fish sticks for dinner as an 11-year-old resulted in my mother deciding that we could best manage the complaint by me writing down what we ate for dinner every night for a full year and then completing a statistical report of our dinner consumption. After one year, I was able to proudly prove that, yes, we did eat lots of fish sticks, as well as too much Kraft macaroni and cheese.

"Why can't they make a bridge from Connecticut to Long Island?" earned my 14-year-old brother and me a full-day swim from the Connecticut shoreline across the Long Island Sound to Hempstead Harbor on Long Island's Gold Coast. The day after I asked my dad how Eddie Feigner, the star softball player for the team The King and His Court, could pitch blindfolded, I was in my backyard with my dad whacking Wiffle balls at me as I hunched over in anticipation of the hard plastic ball smashing into my face. I spent the next two weeks throwing Wiffle balls at our makeshift catcher/strike zone: the backrest of a lime green lawn chair. First, with one eye closed, then with both eyes closed, until I could eventually strike my dad out blindfolded. Growing up in the 1970s, my parents wanted us to see the world with endless possibilities, never setting any limits on us. They also created in us a desire to test our physical and mental limits.

So, it should come as no surprise that at 7:00 a.m. in May 1979, my dad dropped me off at Eisenhower Park on the south shore of Long Island to fend for myself in the Newsday Long Island Marathon.

"See you at mile eight," he reminded me as I stepped out of our cigarette-smoke-filled blue station wagon. Prior to the race, my dad and I had studied the marathon course map, devising a plan where he could hand me cups of 1970s-era marathon hydration – Coca-Cola. Luckily for us, the out-and-back course provided multiple locations to meet up. With a filter-free Pall Mall cigarette in one hand, a cup of Coke in the other, and his trusted swim team volunteer timer stopwatch dangling from his neck, he gave somewhat odd pep talks along the route.

"They're gaining on you!" was shouted at mile 16. I have no idea exactly who was gaining on me, as there were 4,000 runners in the race. There seemed to be lots of people ahead of me and lots of people behind me.

"Kick it in!" was shouted when there was still six miles left in the race.

Four thousand runners filled the park, all there to run the 26-mile event coming on the heels of Jim Fixx's 1977 Best Seller *The Complete Book of Running*. The first running boom was in full swing and this 15-year-old, shy, five-foot-two-inch boy was surrounded by a sea of marathon veterans. As I made my way to the starting line and thought about the 26 miles that lay ahead, I had no idea that I was starting a marathon journey that would span six decades. It was a journey that would take me around the world; a journey that would see tremendous changes in the event and would offer glimpses of the best and the worst the marathon can offer.

I would be disingenuous if I was to say that Frank Shorter's Olympic victory was what inspired me to be on that start line on May 6, 1979. Rather, a series of events and people were the impetus for my crazy idea to run a marathon at such a young age.

Throughout the 1960s and 1970s, our backyard and neighborhood was our own Olympic Village. Fire hydrants served as starting and finish lines for running races along sidewalks. Old pillows became landing mats as we attempted the high jump over a broom handle. Unlike the hurdles one sees on TV, where a hurdle will fall when hit by a runner's foot, our shins learned the hard way that wooden picnic table benches are not good hurdles. Right across the street from our house was Wantagh Elementary School with baseball fields, basketball courts, soccer fields, and lush grass open fields that accommodated all different made-up childhood games. Plus, Wantagh Pool was just a short (sort of) bike ride away. From the time the school bell rang, signifying the end of the school day, until my sister reached out our front door swinging an annoying-sounding dinner bell, all the kids in the neighborhood participated in some sort of athletic event. No refs, no adults-- just kids pretending they were New York Knicks, New York Yankees, or New York Jets depending on the season. After dinner, we were back out there. To this day, I have the oddest basketball shot because of shooting at unseen backboards and rims in the dark. I just chucked the ball in the direction where I figured the hoop was.

Those open fields served as the training grounds for my first running workouts. During the 1970s, the highlight of every gym class was the Presidential Fitness Test. Administered each spring, the test consisted of pull-ups, sit-ups, shuttle run, standing long jump, 50-yard dash, softball throw for distance, and the dreaded 600-yard run or walk. As the test got closer, Mr. Aschum, in his blue gym-teacher shorts and polo shirt with a whistle dangling from his neck, would stress to us the importance of the test and leave us in awe with tales of past students who threw a softball 100 feet or jumped over 29 feet. Looking back, he was obviously confusing Bob Beamon, the Olympian who smashed the long jump world record at the 1968 Olympics, with a former elementary school student of his who at best jumped ten feet. Those who scored high enough on each event received the prestigious Presidential Fitness Test certificate (suitable for framing) presented at the end-of-the-school-year awards ceremony. Mr. Aschum added a twist to this by going a step further and adding a "superior" award status to those who met his higher standards in each event.

The Internet is full of articles today about the dread and anxiety that this test caused thousands of students across the country back in the 1960s and 1970s. And our teacher pumped up the anxiety by creating a tiered caste system: those who didn't achieve an award; those who achieved an award; and those who earned the superior award. And trust me, every kid in school knew what group they were in.

I am not fully sure if Mr. Aschum connected the dots and understood why so many students mysteriously "forgot their sneakers" on the days the test was administered. Coming from a large, hypercompetitive family, "forgetting sneakers" was never an option. My younger brother John and I quickly realized that the one event that prevented so many students from achieving "superior" status and the accompanying bragging rights was the 600-yard walk-run. As ten-year-olds, we had no concept of how far 600 yards was. We knew one length of the pool

4

in swim team was 25 yards. But how far is 600 yards? A half-mile? A quarter mile? We figured we would ask the expert.

"Dad, how far is 600 yards?"

"About as far as the longest hole on a golf course."

That meant absolutely nothing to us, but we could do basic math. Scanning the ditto sheets that contained the required mark in each event, we saw that two minutes and ten seconds was needed for a superior score. So, one evening, my brother and I crossed the street to the big field to train for the 600-yard walk-run. We had absolutely no idea how to train, but we were confident that we could devise some sort of system to get us to the finish line in under two minutes and ten seconds.

Looking back, John and I figured out a lot on our own. Every Tuesday, when he was four and I was five, my mother took us to the Jones Beach East Bathhouse Pool. There, in the shallow end, stood lifeguard legend Hank Daly, providing swim lessons.

"Mom, can we take those lessons?"

"It costs too much money."

Not to be deterred, John and I would sit on the pool's edge and study Hank Daly. Once his lessons were completed, John and I would jump into the pool and copy everything we saw. We were swimming in no time –for free. With a family of nine, it is very understandable that my mother had to be frugal.

Years later, as lifeguards ourselves, we worked with Hank Daly, who lived in our neighborhood. Every night at 5:55 p.m., John and I would fight about who had to drive Hank home from work. Driving Hank home ensured that your commute time would double. Hank insisted that you drive no more than one mile per hour above 25 MPH because the area surrounding the Jones Beach Causeway was a seagull rookery and he did not want to risk injury to even one feather of a seagull.

With our goal of two minutes and ten seconds set in stone, and with misplaced confidence in ourselves as budding track coaches, we began our two-week training program. Each night we would run for one minute more than the night before. Night one was one minute; night two was two minutes; and by the end of week two, we were up to 14 minutes of non-stop running. Yes, extremely basic, but it worked. The same principle can be applied to a marathon. If you have a dream to run a marathon, you must start somewhere. If you can jog in your neighborhood for five minutes, just increase this a little bit each day or week, and in no time, you will be up to an hour of exercise per day and have confidence to wade into the marathon waters.

In addition to our neighborhood sporting events and endurance self-training, we were extremely active in organized sports: Police Boys Club Basketball, Little League Baseball, and CYO Swim Team. My parents had several "guidelines" when it came to organized sports. The first was-- you could do any sport that you wished to participate in. My little sister even played Little League baseball back when it was unheard of for a girl to play on a boys' team. My parents were great because they never steered us in a certain direction for sports. Once while sneaking around in early December trying to find hidden "Santa" presents, we stumbled upon what seemed to us to be a million baseball and bowling trophies in the back of my dad's closet. We had no idea he did these sports nor that he was any good at them. Not once did he try to steer us toward baseball or bowling, although the temptation to do so must have existed. I think he avoided displaying these to not place any indirect pressure on us. My mother was the coordinator of the diocese CYO basketball league, yet she never pushed us to play basketball.

With no pressure, we were free to choose whatever sports interested us. However, once you joined an organized team my parents would not let you quit that team. You had to finish out the season to not let your coaches and teammates down. The lesson to never quit and never give up is best captured from my dad's baseball days. In high school, he tried out as a pitcher for St. John's Prep School in New York City and was quickly cut from the team. The next day, when he showed up again at tryouts, the coach yelled, "Hey, Boyle! I cut you yesterday!"

"Yeah, yesterday you cut me as a pitcher, today I am trying out as a catcher." He made the team and had a very long and successful baseball career, as a catcher.

One hard no-go for my father was participation trophies. Back in the 1970s, participation trophies were extremely rare. My brother and I received them for summer swim team and proudly displayed them to my father. Things took a quick turn south.

"Did anyone else receive a trophy?"

"Yeah, it was really cool. Everyone on the team got one."

"Ok, that trophy has no value, take it down to the stream and throw it away."

Today there would be a dam made up of participation trophies across that stream if my dad had his way. My high school athlete scholar plaque is somewhere at the bottom of that stream because every school in the county handed out the same award. I still remember walking home along that stream in June 1981 after our senior award ceremony clutching the LILCO (Long Island Lighting Company) Athlete Scholar award and throwing it into the stream sidearm, attempting to have it skip like a stone across the surface. The lesson that you must work hard and earn something stuck.

Probably the most important guideline, and the one that actually made sense, as compared to throwing trophies into streams, was the policy that you could not specialize in a sport. My parents wanted us to be well-rounded in sports and feared if we specialized in one sport, we ran the risk of overtraining or mental burnout. Once, a few years ago, my brother John's son, Patrick, was starting out in age groups swimming. The other parents at the swim club kept pestering John about why Patrick, who was all of nine-years-old, was not on the traveling team.

John shut them up with a classic remark.

"Look at that team record board. You see all the kids who have the records for eight-, nine- and ten-years-old? You don't see those same names up there for the age 16-, 17-, and 18-year-old records."

Patrick wound up as a scholarship Division 1 swimmer, setting several collegiate records, even though he had no eight-and-under group swim team records. John was right; pushing a child at such a young age all too often results in a mentally and physically burnt-out athlete full of resentment. And it is not just sports. A child should do what a child wants to do; be it sports, school plays, band, or clubs.

As I entered junior high school, there was a vast array of sports to choose from, however, the level of competition was much more than I was accustomed to. No longer could I just sign up for a Little League team. Junior high carried with it "sports tryouts" and the accompanying embarrassing list posted on the gym door, the day after tryouts, of those cut from the teams. I figured I could do swimming as a winter sport, as I was OK at that sport, although I spent most of the time at youth swim practices hanging out under the hot showers proclaiming I was working out a cramp. I knew my extremely awkward basketball shot would make me an easy cut from basketball. Baseball was out as my dad said, "You swing like a rusty gate." Plus, I was never too good at baseball. Every at bat in Little League I tried to bunt just to avoid striking out. Once, I bunted on the third strike. As the ball rolled off the field I heard, "You're out!" yelled by the ump who knew every esoteric Major League Baseball rule. The entire following weekend, all I heard from my dad, my brother, and even my grandmother. was, "What were you thinking, you had no business even being out there, who bunts on the third strike?" Well, this ten-year-old does, as I had no idea that baseball had such technical rules that applied to Little League. So, baseball was out.

Anything where size was needed was out. Ever since kindergarten, I was the smallest in my class. Every year my mother promised me that my growth spurt was just around the bend. All my brothers were a lot taller than me. My older brother was even tall enough to play basketball. Once, as a retiree in Florida, my dad and I were out by the grill in one of Florida's many adult communities with tropical-sounding names to attract unsuspecting New Yorkers. As we stood by the grill in "The Misty Falls" (a fake rock waterfall in which dyed-bluish water flowed at the entrance of the 55-and-older community), my dad took at drag on his Pall Mall, looked at me, and said, "I never could figure out why you are so short. Maybe your mom smoked too much when she was pregnant with you."

With most sports out of my reach, I looked to running. I did enjoy training for the 600-yard walk-run. One running option was cross country. I had never heard of this sport and actually thought that the team ran from New York across the country to California in some sort of endless relay. I had no interest leaving Long Island, plus I figured I would miss too many days of school running to California and would have way too much schoolwork to catch up on. I envisioned the total hassle it would be with my mother pestering me to catch up on missed schoolwork. So, scratch cross country off the list.

All that was left was track. My homeroom teacher was a gentleman named Mike Brynes. Mr. Byrnes was also our high school's varsity track coach. In 1968, he was one of the USA Olympic Track and Field coaches! Imagine that-- your homeroom teacher, and eventual track coach, was the Olympic track coach. Additionally, he owned one of the first sporting goods stores on Long Island where every student went to purchase their letterman's jacket. My dad was a good friend of Mr. Byrnes. I spend countless evenings and weekends in his small store, filled from floor to ceiling with box upon box of sneakers, as I listened to them come up with crazy ideas like placing a dome over the Wantagh Park Pool to have year-round swimming, or placing a dome over the high school tennis courts to have indoor tennis. If they had their way, the entire town of Wantagh would have been placed under a dome, and we would have had our own little Truman Show like the Jim Carrey movie.

Years later, Mr. Byrnes would create the first-ever high school national track championships. Even in 2007, when I saw him at a meet in Landover, Maryland, he was just as energetic as he was back in the 1970s. What set him apart was the fact that Mr. Byrnes was the "cool" teacher. He had long hair, wore cool hats to school, sat on the desk during class, and even taught us how to organize protests (hey, it was the 1970s). Not that we protested for great social justice changes – we just protested for better pizza in the lunchroom.

I really liked Mr. Byrnes. I was his homeroom attendance monitor, and I was in his social studies class, so I felt being on his track team would be a great fit. One morning in the spring of seventh grade, I told him I wanted to be on the track team. Since I did lots of swimming, I thought I would be best in the distance races (not that I had any idea of how far these races were).

In March 1976, I headed out to our high school athletic fields. Our junior high school and high school were one large building separated by an invisible line that no junior high student dared to cross. Both schools shared athletic fields. Once I got close to the track, I scoped out Mr. Byrnes, who appeared to be a ringmaster in a three-ring circus of sprinters, throwers, jumpers, hurdlers, and various other assorted track and field athletes. The JV team, as well as junior high track teams, were there as well. I somehow thought it was OK to bypass both teams and head straight to the varsity track coach. In my seventh-grade mind this was OK because when I told Mr. Byrnes in homeroom that I was trying out for track he never said anything about a junior high team, so I thought we agreed that I was varsity material. I figured he had heard some sort of buzz about my 600-yard walk-run earning me the superior award in elementary school.

Our school had a rich tradition in track with one national record holder and numerous Penn Relay victories, so I just knew Mr. Byrnes, the 1968 USA Olympic Track Coach, saw talent when a scrawny 12-year-old in Converse basketball sneakers came up to him on a cloudy, cold, windy March afternoon.

"You're late, the distance guys just headed out for a five-mile run along the Wantagh Parkway bike path down to Mill Pond. They are also doing a loop around the pond. Go catch up to them." Wow, I am varsity material! Looking back, I know Mr. Byrnes was testing me to see if I actually wanted to be a distance runner.

I wish I could vividly describe every moment of that run; saying that the wind flowed under my feet, and I was transformed into a marathoner; that I ran gracefully and swiftly like a gazelle and had found my sport. But no. The only wind that day was the brisk gusts blowing across the ocean, picking up cold, March seawater along the way and pushing me backwards at each step as the sea salt caused my eyes to water. My "run" was a combination of sprints, walks, jogs, and curses. Once I made it to Mill Pond two miles into the run, I was having serious doubts about why I was doing this. Plus, I never saw any of the other team members. I could have just turned around at this point and skipped the Mill Pond Loop, cutting the run from five miles to four miles. But Mr. Brynes told me the workout and I was not quitting. Junior high ended at about 3:00 p.m. each day. The sun sets early in March on Long Island. Do the math. It started to get dark on my journey back to the school. Dusk was rushing in, cars on the parkway now had their lights on. I was cold, my eyes were stinging from sea salt, I was exhausted, and I was alone. But at least the wind was now at my back, pushing me towards the school. I continued my jog-walk and arrived back at the school in the dark. Some lights were on in classrooms as well as a few administrative offices. Luckily, the main doors to the junior high school were open but my luck ran out when I arrived at the locker room. Locked! I was able to find a custodian, who at first didn't believe that I had just finished sports practice, and therefore refused to open the locker room. After some negotiation, which included my lunch money for a week and a promise to never ask for help again, I was allowed in to get my clothes and books.

I rode my yellow ten-speed Schwinn bike that I purchased with my lawn-mowing money the mile home, arriving just as my dad was returning home from work. My dad did not in any way find it odd that I was arriving home so late.

"I ran a full five miles today in track practice."

"Just do what Mr. Brynes says and you will be all right."

The next morning in homeroom, I meekly approached Mr. Byrnes and told him I completed the run. He didn't seem shocked at all but did tell me that it would probably be best if I stuck with the junior high team that spring. I was proud that I had passed his test of desire, but deep down knew junior high track was where I belonged.

Over the next few years, I continued on the junior high school team running the half-mile and the mile. Even though I was not on the high school team yet, I turned to Mr. Byrnes daily for advice. Looking back, I remember Mr. Byrne's pre-race strategy was super basic. "Run faster than you have ever run in your life," was the advice he would always give me when we spoke about races out on the playground during recess. He was the lunch monitor and since I wasn't interested in getting hit in the face with soccer balls, I mostly walked around on the blacktop far away from the crazy lunchtime games.

In May 1978, I was walking to the library in our town and through the trees that had not fully grown their spring coat of green leaves I saw hundreds of runners on the Wantagh Parkway just a block away. I walked over and asked a volunteer handing out cups of water what was going on.

"This is the Earth Day Marathon."

I couldn't believe it. How did I not know that there was a race the same distance as Frank Shorter's race going on two blocks from my house! Right then, I thought-- I must do this race next year. I figured I had 14 years of running around the schoolyards playing various sports as a child, years of swim team practices, as well as junior high track under my belt, so my endurance should be OK. I just needed a year to fine-tune things. And I needed a plan, plus a parent to sign the race entry form.

Oh, Dad. Even though my father had played baseball in school, he took an interest in all the sports we participated in and learned as much about them as possible. Fortunately, two of his co-workers were marathoners. My dad was a lawyer for Con Ed, the New York City electric company. Back in the 1970s, during the first running boom, there were weekly 3.5 miles races in Central Park between corporate teams. The team races became hotly competitive with various corporations hiring "summer interns" who happened to run fast. Con Ed fielded a decent team wearing T-shirts emblazoned with "Con Ed We Keep NYC Running."

I was able to cobble together my first marathon plan with the help of those who kept New York City running. The plan began to take shape when I got my first taste of road racing on July 4, 1978 in our town's annual five-mile road race that preceded the town parade. Mr. Brynes organized the race, which was one of the first road races on Long Island, and he did an amazing job both organizing the race and bringing in the top runners from Long Island to compete. I was not one of those top runners. Junior High School spring track ended in mid-May and I made my annual transition from track to swim team. So, when my dad came into my bedroom on the Fourth of July at 7:00 a.m. to wake me for the race, I had not run one step in about six weeks.

"Dad, it's swim season. I'm not in the mood."

"Mister, you get in the mood. You signed up for the race; Mr. Celia is at the start area waiting for you. Front seat of the car, 15 minutes."

After an anger-filled car ride, I arrived at the Wantagh Railroad Station parking lot about 35 minutes prior to the 8:00 a.m. start.

Not having run a step in weeks, I knew five miles would be tough, plus, believe it or not, that first day of track five-mile run was still my longest run ever. The odds of me finishing the race were pretty low, and the odds of me actually enjoying the race were even lower. I found Mr. Celia, plus a newcomer to the Con Ed team, Ed Donlon. I could not understand how excited they both were. It was early, I was tired, and all they could talk about was how running races was the best way to see Long Island on foot and this race would be a great marathon tune-up. On the other hand, I just wanted to get it over with. For the first time in my life, I pinned a race number on. That is, if you could call it a race number. Today race numbers are fitted with a GPS microchip to track times, runners' names are written across the top to attract cheers and sponsors logos fill up any remaining space on the high-tech material. In 1978, I was handed four safety pins and a three by five index card with a handwritten number on it.

The race route started at our town railroad station and headed up Wantagh Avenue, cut over to the street I lived on, Beech Street, then made a few loops on adjoining streets before finishing on a grass field in front of Wantagh Elementary School, my field of dreams as a youth. Mr. Byrnes, always enlightened, made the race route pretty much the same route as the town's Fourth of July Parade, which stepped off right after the race finished. By doing so, he ensured the route was filled with spectators.

As the gun started, my dad hit the start button on his swim team stopwatch, which in no way resembled the watches of today. It was basically a small maroon box that had to weigh at least two pounds, dangling from his neck. "But check it out, I can get splits." The digital format of the watch was the envy of all the parents on the pool deck who were still sporting the ancient round stopwatches with the sweeping hands.

Mr. Celia settled into a nice pace and with each mile that passed by I got more confident that I could finish. And I actually liked the race! On track team, the half-mile and the mile seemed like sprints with finishers gasping for air lying on the infield grass after stumbling across the finish line. As we strode down Beech Street, I could breathe and speak as I ran. Eventually, we turned onto the grass field and picked up our pace as I could see both the finish line and clock come into view. As I crossed the line, I was handed a Popsicle stick with the number 54 on it. I had no idea why I received this and figured it was some weird, twisted joke that I just run five miles and I get the stick but not the cherry popsicle. The clock read 31:21 and later I found out I placed 54th in the race.

"31:23, not bad."

"But Dad the clock said 31:21."

"Oh, that clock is not right."

This was just one of many instances in which my father insisted his stopwatch was the gold standard. He could be sitting in the top row of the bleachers at a swim meet and proclaim his stopwatch was more accurate than the pool electronic timing touchpads.

31:21 or 31:23 didn't really mean much, plus I have no idea if the race was actually five miles. Races back then were measured by the odometer of a car. And I had seen Mr. Byrnes' car in the school parking lot. I highly doubted that his odometer was up to speed. Nevertheless, the race for me was a milestone. First, I figured if I could run five miles with no practices, 26 miles couldn't be too bad if I trained. Second, I liked the longer distances better than track races. But the marathon would have to wait; it was summer and swim team was in full effect.

As the hazy, hot, humid summer of the south shore of Long Island ended, thoughts of fall sports entered my mind. I had finally figured out that cross country running did not mean that you ran across the country. The "country" meant grass and fields. Cross country races were 3.1 miles in high school, and I figured I'd give this sport a try, as the races certainly couldn't be as lung busting as a half-mile sprint. As luck would have it, one boy on the cross country team had run the Earth Day Marathon (now the Newsday Marathon) the previous spring. As an 11th grader, Donny had finished the race in 3:34 and was our school record holder. The record, of course, was his, as he was the first in our school to ever run a marathon. All fall, I peppered Donny with questions about the marathon. He was very polite with his answers, but I am sure I was getting on his nerves with my constant inquiries. I was pretty much the worst on the team, if not the worst in the entire county. At our county meet I came in dead last, close to two full minutes behind the second slowest runner. As I came out of the woods with a half-mile remaining, I received the usual round of pity claps from the parents in attendance who offer encouragement, while at the same time wondering, why is this kid even in the race?

That season our team conducted a six-mile time trial along the bike path that straddles the Wantagh Parkway. Somehow, I was the fastest on my team, finishing in 34 minutes. To me this was extremely odd as I was running my 3.1-mile races in 20 minutes. The math wasn't adding up but looking back I realize I really liked the longer distances and tried so much harder in those events and sort of loafed along in the shorter races.

The day after cross country season ended, I was back in the pool. However, this season my mindset was different. As I swam endless laps looking down at a long thin black line at the bottoms of pools throughout Nassau County, my thoughts were of the marathon. I spent that winter learning as much as I could about the marathon, mostly from reading *Runner's World* purchased each month at Mr. Brynes' sports shop.

In January, I officially signed up for the race. Back in 1979, race sign-up was an extremely easy process. You just picked up a race flyer at any local sporting goods store. The top half of the flyer contained all the race information, location, start times, course, etc. Towards the bottom there was a dotted line indicating where to cut off the section of the flyer in which you placed your name, age, and address. You simply filled out the form, mailed it in with the race registration fee, and you were in! Race registration fee in 1979 - four dollars! For that, you received a T-shirt, a race number, and a finisher's medal. Today, marathon registration is an extremely complicated and expensive process. Registration must be done months in advance, often by a lottery system, and fees can be in the hundreds of dollars. Additionally, today's marathon races have become weekend events with accompanying 5-kilometer races, 10-kilometer races and half-marathons. In addition to having to sign-up months in advance, runners today are given several options of races and can even complete several races in the same weekend running festival. Complete the 10-kilometer race on Saturday and the marathon on Sunday and get a special mega-runner medal. Complete the 5-kilometer, the half-marathon and the marathon and get a super mega-runner medal. Although these running festivals are great for encouraging people to get fit and challenge themselves, the à la carte menu of races dilutes the competition angle of the sport. How can you possibly run a fast all-out 10-kilometer race and then do well in a marathon the next day? Back in 1979, there was one option, the marathon. Take it or leave it. In 1979, 4,000 runners took the only option offered, mailing in a registration form and paying the four dollars entry fee.

One of those 4,000 was my swim team coach. Like me, he was attempting his first marathon. Unlike me, though, this was his first running race ever. Coach Bongornio spent that entire swim season training for the marathon on the pool deck as we swam. Our high school did not have a swimming pool, so each day we took a bus a few miles to a pool affectionately known as "The Pit." Calling it "The Pit" was putting it nicely. The pool was designed for scuba lessons and the owner had no interest in pool upkeep. I think he preferred the murky pool water. The waters off Long Island are cloudy so his scuba clients could practice in the real thing. As you entered the complex, you were greeted by an overwhelming smell of various gases and chemicals. After walking past scuba tanks, regulators, wetsuits, and other scuba gear haphazardly scattered throughout the "showroom," you entered a dingy room of rusty lockers set upon a cement floor that at one time may have held tiles. The moldy cement floor guaranteed that you would get some sort of planter's wart during the season. After exiting the locker room, swimmers came upon the most uninspiring pool setting in history. The pool was only four lanes wide by 25 yards long, tiles regularly fell from the dimly lit ceiling, and the cement pool deck was only two feet wide on each side of the pool. Not once do I recall being able to see the bottom of the pool.

And in this marvelous facility, Coach trained for the marathon. As we swam for two hours, he ran countless laps around the pool on the deck. Each circuit of the pool deck was 70 yards. I honestly have no idea how he did it. Not only was the cement surface horrible for running, but the air was also filled with chemicals, and his loop certainly had to be boring. And he only ran in one direction, so his hips had to be totally out of whack after months of running this way. Every time I finished a lap and lifted my head from the pool, he would remind me that as I was swimming, he was marathon training and therefore he would beat me come May. He was right, but I wasn't too concerned. I was trying to enjoy my last season of swim team. I knew that this year would be my last. I had been on swim team ever since John and I taught each other to swim at the Jones Beach pool and although I enjoyed it, I knew it was time to move on.

Our final weekend of swimming was the first weekend of March. On Friday night, preliminary rounds were held with the finals for each event on Saturday. For some reason, the week before our county championship, I got into a bet about shaving my head for the meet. The bet was pretty much me against the whole team. If I shaved my head, they would give me a six-pack of Coca-Cola. If I didn't shave my head, I had to buy the entire team a case of beer. I was up against a wall on this one. First, I don't like to lose in anything. Anything. Second, I wasn't exactly sure how as a 15-year-old I could purchase a case of beer if I lost the bet. I considered my options. On one hand, no shy 15-year-old in the history of the world wants to walk into the teen angst filled hallways of a high school with a shaved head. On the other hand, I figured I could get the beer by stealing a beer a day from my Dad's Schmidt's Beer supply in the basement and pay off my beer debt over time. The stealing issue didn't bother me too much; it was the potential of losing that bothered me. So, Thursday night, I sat in the barber chair at Wantagh Barber Shop, right next door to Mr. Byrnes' Sporting Goods Shop, as the entire team laughed while my head was shaved. Once the barber was finished, I pulled a green wool cap over my head, vowing to not take it off for a month. We then walked into Becks Deli, and I collected my Coke.

Years later, I would have another head-shaving incident. After law school, I joined the Army as a judge advocate. The day before I left for training, my brother said "Shave your head now. You will be ahead of the game when you get to Fort Lee and will have some free time when everyone else has to go to the barber." So that Saturday afternoon, I shaved my head. On Monday at Fort Lee, Virginia, I quickly noticed that every other individual had much longer hair than me. I asked the first sergeant what was going on and he explained "This isn't the 1940s. You can have hair in the Army. There is a haircut regulation, but a shaved head is not required." I think John knew this already; I spent the first month in the Army looking like the over ambitious go-getter.

But that is better than I felt and looked as I walked into first period math class in March of 1979. My green wool cap still covered my head as I took my seat. "Mr. Boyle, no hats in school!" bellowed Mr. Bergman. My face was scarlet-red as the class erupted in laughter when I slowly pulled the cap up. Mr. Bergman, a retired navy officer, just commented, "Nice crew cut, sailor." I am not sure what bothered me the most, the laughter, that the teacher joined in, or the fact that several members of the swim team were in that class and didn't step up to defend me. It's probably a tie between my teammates and Mr. Bergman. I really liked the guy. He inspired me to like math; to the point that I won the Long Island Math Fair. My topic: How to Use Math To Win Money at the Horse Racetrack. Ever since my parents took us to the "Breakfast at Belmont" event at Belmont Racetrack when I was ten-years-old, I was hooked. I think getting people hooked on horse racing was the whole point of the "Breakfast at Belmont" thing. The racetrack allowed you to eat breakfast while watching the horses train and thereby hopefully become a race fan (and of course bettor). I was fascinated and read everything I could about the Triple Crown, how horses trained, and how they raced. In addition to *Runner's World*, I devoured the *Daily Racing Form*. Seniors in high school would take me on Friday nights to Roosevelt Raceway and Yonkers Raceway when I was 13 years old to help them pick winners. For some reason, my parents never saw this as odd.

There I was at Dix Hills High School with every math "genius" from Long Island. They were giving presentations about complicated stuff like rhombuses and how to solve Pi, things I never even heard of. I felt like the episode in which Bart Simpson was mistakenly placed in the smart kids' class. I nervously walked up to the mic in front of a room filled with math wizards and math professors serving as judges and said, "Let me tell you how you can make money with math . . ." Somehow, I won. Was it because my presentation was so out of whack compared to the others? Was it because the judges were taking notes and planning trips to Roosevelt Raceway? Who knows? What I do know is that math can come in handy; so handy, in fact, that a large bet on 1985 Kentucky Derby winner Spend a Buck paid for my first year of law school.

That weekend, I swam my final swim races. On Friday night, one event was the medley relay. My teammates and I figured that if we each did our best time, we could set the school record. I was the anchor leg, swimming freestyle. My dilemma was that the individuals swimming the other legs were among the math students jeering me hours ago that day. As each leg was completed, I could see our overall time on the large overhead scoreboard and knew we were well ahead of school record pace. As I stood on the starting block getting ready to bring it home, all I could think of was math class. The last 25 yards of my swim I purposely swam slow. You make fun of me; you don't get your name of the school record board. My teammates were furious when I explained why my split was so slow. We qualified for the finals the next evening and I felt terrible. By swimming slow, I didn't erase the laughter in class; all I did was act like a jerk. The next night in finals, I swam as fast as I could. Of course, there were disputes with my father about my split. Did I swim the 50-yard freestyle in what the official electronic pool timing recorded me, or did I swim the time my father's stopwatch read? None of that mattered; our team did set the school record. But it did matter. I was way out of line for swimming slowly. Yes, I was only 15 years old, but I should have known better. From this, I learned-- don't be petty, be it with family, teammates, neighbors, or co-workers. Always take the higher road.

On Monday morning during first period math class, the school announcements mentioned our relay team record. Did it alleviate the sting from Friday? Maybe. All I knew was that I was now fully in marathon-training mode.

Swim season ended on Saturday evening with the medley relay; marathon training began on Sunday morning. However, the transition from one sport to the next did take some planning. All winter, I had to endure my swim coach's taunts to the point where I had enough and made him a bet. Winner gets a six-pack of Coke, or beer, in his case. I read as much as I could about running, but running books were scarce in the 1970s and the Internet was non-existent. I continued to stalk Donny in the hallways to seek advice. I also spent a lot of Saturday afternoons that winter in Mr. Byrnes' store asking him questions. However, Mr. Byrnes was at a whole higher level than me in this area. He coached Olympians, he coached national champions, he coached Penn Relays champions, he single-handedly created the High School National Championships in track, and he organized the first road race on Long Island.

"What you want to do is four times the five miles on the track with ten-minute breaks between each. Run it at faster than marathon pace. Stick with the leaders for as long as you can."

Slow your roll, Mr. Byrnes. I was a 15-years-old and my most recent running race was dead last in our cross country county championship by two minutes. I just wanted to finish this thing.

His advice may have been too ambitious for me, but his running shoes were great. Up to that point, my running footwear was whatever my mother could get cheapest at Sneaker Circus in Bellmore, the town next to ours. I trained in basketball sneakers, tennis sneakers, whatever my mother could get a two for one deal for John and me. We once got sneakers that cost 49 cents!!! When we showed my dad he said, "Can't go wrong for 49 cents." Actually, you can go wrong, as the sneakers fell apart the next day. For races, our school had a supply of running spikes that you could use for a season and return. Not only were these racing spikes factories for athlete's foot, but they were also made of extremely thin leather, and you could feel every single pebble on the soles of your feet. To top it off, each pair of shoes had half-inch sharp spikes as we ran on either grass for cross country or on cinder tracks. After every junior high school and high school race you could see bloody shins, on every distance runner, the aftermath of "getting spiked" in a race. Getting spiked meant you ran too closely to the feet of the runner in front of you and their half-inch medal spikes tore into your shins.

Realizing I could not run a marathon in 49-cent Sneaker Circus shoes or in leather spikes, I invested some of my horse-betting winnings in my first pair of actual running shoes-- the Nike Waffle Trainer. Prior to the Nike's foray into running shoes, the main companies were Puma, Tiger (now Asics) and Adidas. Our school had a huge cardboard box full of spikes from these brands. All the spikes in those days had a flat leather sole. Sneakers you wore for everyday running had a flat sole with small ridges. Enter the Waffle Trainer. This classic light blue sneaker with the golden Nike swoosh had a sole that looked exactly like a black rubber waffle. Not only did these sneakers have a better feel on the pavement, but they also looked awesome.

Now that I was wrapping up swimming season; armed with as much advice as possible from *Runner's World*, Mr. Brynes, and Donny; and sporting my new Waffle Trainers, it was time for an actual training plan. About a week before swim season ended, my dad arrived home from work and handed me an eight-week training plan. It was written out on an index card. The first week read as

S	M	T	W	Th	F	S	Total
6	2	8	4	2	12	2	34

Looking at the first week, I realized that within that week I would have to complete my two longest runs ever, one of which was twice as far as I had ever ran in my life. Each week, the daily runs progressed a bit to the point that the Sunday run was 15 miles, and the Friday run was 20 miles. The beauty of this program was its simplicity. No interval workouts, just an easy run each day. To this day, I still believe this simple schedule is best. Certainly, the days of the week could vary, especially the long run, depending on work schedules and such. I have no idea how my dad devised this schedule. Was he reading *Runner's World* on the sly? Was he meeting up with Mr. Brynes? All I knew was that the schedule worked.

The final piece to the puzzle was: where would I run these miles? Most of our track practices were on the track or around our school's athletic fields, where we had to avoid face planting each time we ran past the baseball diamond because the players on the bench purposely stuck their legs out to trip runners. I didn't want to run 20 miles on a track or spend time avoiding getting tripped by individuals who envisioned themselves as the next Reggie Jackson. On occasion, we ran a one-mile loop repeatedly around Mill Pond up the road from our school. All these seemed limiting to me.

Fortunately, I had two aces up my sleeve. One was the Jones Beach bike path. Growing up, we lived about one mile from Cedar Creek Park located on Merrick Road on the south shore of Long Island. We also lived about six miles from Jones Beach, also on the south shore of the Island. From Merrick Road heading south toward the beach was a long, flat, six-lane stretch of road called the Jones Beach Causeway or Wantagh Parkway. This road brought beachgoers from the Island along a thin strip of land that traversed channels, bays, and marshland. Tall, green, or brown reeds, depending on the season, bordered each side of the road. Every mile or so, a small bridge crossed over a portion of the bay. In the early 1970s, there was a push to put a bike path along this causeway. One fall afternoon when I was about ten years old, a bike protest closed the causeway as thousands of cyclists took to the road demanding cyclers' rights. Of course, my brother and I took part signing various petitions along the way. This protest actually worked, and the following summer there appeared an asphalt 11-foot-wide bike path from Cedar Creek Park to Jones Beach. This became not only my training ground, but also where I learned so much about where I lived. I learned about tides, I saw birds I never saw before, and observed the beauty of the back bays as I ran across the several bridges.

The other ace I had was my dad's car odometer. In the era before GPS, everything we measured was based on my dad's blue station wagon purchased from Rupps Chevrolet in Rockville Center. My dad would swear up and down about the accuracy of his odometer. Once he got into a beef with our local Catholic School. My older brothers and sisters attended St. Francis Elementary School. Students who lived a mile away from the school got to ride the school bus. Those within a mile of the school walked or rode bikes. The school told my dad that our house was just inside the mile radius, hence, no bus rides. He spent an entire weekend driving back and forth to the school measuring every possible route. Each route he found was over a mile according to his trusted odometer. The school wasn't buying it, so my family was bike riders and walkers.

Why he was fighting about bus versus bike is beyond me because he made us bike everywhere. When John and I were eight- and nine-years-old, we informed my dad that we wanted to play Little League. "Better get lights for your bikes; it will be dark by the time games end." He then measured the distance to Mandalay Field-- the site of our games; it was three miles exactly. Wantagh Pool was three miles on the dot. Newbridge Pool, once again, was three miles. In his mind, these were all easy biking distances to swim team practice for eight-year-old swimmers. I knew the distance to about every place we visited. Once, my brother biked from our house to Montauk Point, the easternmost point on the island. As he arrived tired and sweaty at Hither Hills State Park after a full day of biking along Sunrise Highway, he proclaimed, "I made it, 100 miles!"

"Actually not, I clocked it on my odometer on the way here. It's 99.3 miles. Do a few loops around the parking lot to meet your 100-mile goal."

Since I knew the distance to just about every landmark in my town, I figured I could just do my runs to various places. Six-mile run, no problem, run to Newbridge Pool and back. Two-mile run, just go to St. Francis and back. For long runs, I could explore the somewhat-new Wantagh Parkway bike path.

Now that swim season ended, I had my sneakers, I had my training plan, I was ready to go on March 11, 1979-- eight weeks exactly to race day. Eight weeks may seem short for a marathon training plan, but I had been continually training with running and swim team for a few years, so I really wasn't starting from scratch.

The month of March conjures up thoughts of spring with crocus flowers blooming to signal the end of a long, hard winter. However, on Long Island, winter does not yield based on a change of calendar pages. Winter lingers as long as it wants, till winter decides it is time to exit stage left. This attitude brings blustery, cold, grey days, and often snowy St. Patrick's Day Parades. As an island surrounded by the Atlantic Ocean on the south shore and the Long Island Sound on the other, frigid winter water mixed with winds from any direction adds an additional chill to the air. On such a cold, grey, windy March Sunday, I began my marathon training program. It was the kind of day where the sides of the roads still have leftover sand and gravel tossed from plows from the latest snowstorm.

High-tech winter running apparel did not exist in 1979. Gore-Tex, Dri-Fit, and an array of other clothing options were not even on the horizon. Winter running clothing consisted of baggie sweatpants, a thick cotton sweatshirt, white painters' gloves, and a nylon windbreaker. I donned the uniform of the day as well as my new Nike Waffle Trainers and headed to Newbridge Pool-- three miles there, three miles back. The red brick school across the street from our house held a huge clock on its white facade, a black octagon with long golden hands. I used that clock to time every run for years.

As I ran past the storefronts on Merrick Road, noticing my reflection in the huge panes of glass, I didn't see myself as the last-place runner in cross country. I was now a marathoner. I really had no idea of pace; I just ran comfortably, enjoying the sensation of moving quickly along the sidewalks. Time was irrelevant, as I had never considered a time goal when I signed up for the marathon. Finishing would be enough.

After I finished that first run, I placed a big 'X' across the six on my training plan. I also started keeping a notebook noting how far I ran, where I ran, the weather conditions, and how I felt. Over the years, I continued to add pages to that binder, and it served as a great reference for creating training plans. I could look back and see what worked well and what didn't work so well. Today, there are a wide array of print running logs, digital running logs as well as computer programs allowing a runner to attach a GPS watch through a USB port to download daily runs. Whatever systems you use, make sure you track both your progress and use this material for future reference. Maybe you noticed you did too many long runs or ran too fast in practice and were exhausted come race day.

The next morning, my legs felt horrible. I had forgotten the stiffness that accompanies the first few days back to running after a long lull during swim season. However, I powered through, and on Tuesday completed an 8-mile run, my new personal record. For the next few days, I fretted the upcoming big 12-miler. I decided that I would run along the bike path to Jones Beach and back. The weather had quickly changed from just a few days prior, and I could comfortably wear shorts.

I didn't know it as I set out for the run, but that day I would meet an individual who would transform my vision of the marathon. I was headed south along the bike path, about three miles into my six miles in each direction run, when I saw headed towards me a short, stocky runner. As we got closer, I noticed that he was much older than me and his running attire was even worse than mine. It looked like he obtained his shorts, sweatshirt, and sneakers from the gift shop in some sort of museum of ancient running. "How ya doing, I'm Vinny," he greeted me with a huge grin as we were within a few feet of each other. I usually ran with my track team in a large group. Running solo along a deserted bike path, I really didn't know the protocol for introductions when meeting other runners. Do I wave and keep going? Do I stop and chat?

Vinny solved that problem as he quickly turned around and started running with me. Over the next few miles, I realized that I was running with the kindest and most generous person I ever met. Vinny was Vincent McAvoy, a volunteer firefighter in our town who worked the early morning shift at various newspapers; hence, his ability to be out running at around three o'clock in the afternoon. Every time we passed a person on the bike path, they yelled out, "Hi, Champ!" Even though runners were few and far between on the long stretch of path, they all seemed to know each other, and they all seemed to be running at relatively fast paces, especially for folks who seemed to be about my dad's age.

By the time we made it to Jones Beach and were heading back north, I learned that "Vinny" (I could never call him Vinny as he was my dad's age, so I always called him Mr. McAvoy) had run the Boston Marathon, the New York City Marathon, and several others; all under three hours, and he was in his fifties!

The miles flew by as he regaled me with tales of Heartbreak Hill and the old New York City Marathon around Central Park. He answered all my questions about pacing, about race day hydration, and about the dreaded marathon "wall" at 20 miles. By the time we parted ways at Cedar Creek Park, I was in awe of the man. He had been running these marathons for years. Maybe this 1979 marathon wouldn't be a one-time thing for me. Also, he appeared to be headed home on his run and took the time to turn around and run nine miles with me. Maybe people can run further than I had previously thought. My confidence soared. I had just run my longest run ever with a sub three-hour marathoner!

That night I told my dad about the encounter. "Oh yeah, Vinny is always at 6:00 a.m. mass at St. Francis." First off, how did my dad know who attends 6:00 a.m. mass? My mom had recently been diagnosed with cancer. Was my dad sneaking out to 6:00 a.m. mass searching for a miracle? And second, why hadn't he ever told me we had a marathon "champ" in our town?

"I figured you'd run into him eventually on the bike path."

Over the next several weeks, I followed my dad's training program to a T. I ran into Mr. McAvoy often on the bike path during my Sunday longish runs. He also introduced me to another individual from our neighborhood training for the marathon, Mr. Devlin. I'd often join them, pestering them with questions, and they freely gave their advice. Mr. Devlin also was a sub three-hour marathoner. It seemed that every person we ran into on the bike path had run several marathons under three hours. It got to the point where I thought every person who ran a marathon ran it under three hours. I really had no concept of time when it came to a marathon. I knew Bill Rodgers would run about two hours, ten minutes in his winning marathons. I just figured the other 4,000 people behind him finished between two hours and ten minutes to three hours.

Days turned into weeks, and I felt more confident as my long run progressed from 12 to 14 to 16 to 18 to 20 miles. At home, my marathon aspirations were not a big deal. I have three brothers and four sisters, and everyone was involved in some sort of sport, school play, or school concert. And my parents were there for every event. So, my marathon was just one of many things going on in my house in the Spring of 1979. The biggest, though, was my mother's cancer. From 1978 through 1981 she was in an endless cycle of chemo, remission, and new diagnosis. But she never let it get her down. I never heard, "Why me?" She made sure we were on top of schoolwork, made our dinners, and came to all our events. I have no idea how my parents managed through that period.

As race day approached, I had to make final preparations. *Runner's World* had a huge back-page ad, "Break Through the Wall with Nike Elites." The Elites were Nike's new racing shoes, and if they were going to get me through the wall, I needed a pair. They looked and felt very much like the Waffle Trainer only lighter. I purchased a pair the day before my 20-mile run, to break them in.

My 20-mile run was going to be my big test physically, mentally, and tactically. I planned to test my new shoes and also try to have a drink for the first time on a run. My drink of choice was Coke. There was also a new running drink on the market called E.R.G. – Electrolyte Replacement with Glucose, which was a lime-green powder mixed with water. I figured I would give that a try as well.

By now, it was mid-April and winter had finally left for good. I could run in cotton shorts and a cotton shirt each day. I never gave any thought to what the weather would be on race day. I guess I gave it no thought, because it wasn't something I really had any control over, so why worry about it? Over the years, I have found that fall marathons are generally better weatherwise. You train in the long, hot summer and by fall the weather cools, your runs are easier, and your confidence soars. The reverse is true for spring marathons. You train in winter and as you run your body heats up to a comfortable temperature. Then race days come and spring has instantly arrived and it's 75 degrees and sunny and your body is not used to that temperature. Either way, weather is something out of your control; all you can do on race day is adjust. I have seen people stare at the weather channel for days fretting about the weather forecast for race day. By the time race day comes, they are already mentally exhausted. Save your nervous energy for something useful. On the flip side, there are the excuses that flow after races in bad weather-- "it was rainy," or "it was windy." What, you've never run in the rain or wind before? Weather is beyond your control, but you can physically and mentally prepare yourself for it. If you know there is a good chance it will be hot in the month of your intended marathon, make sure you go for some runs when it is hot outside.

My plan for my long run was to do a few of my dad's trusted car odometer loops in town for about eight miles, stop quickly at the high school softball field so my older sister could give me a cup of Coke, then head down to the beach and back. The first eight miles were perfect. The hitch in the plan came when I arrived at the softball field and my sister was behind home plate catching. I guess I didn't factor in the fact that she would be playing a game when I wanted my drink. I had to wait around for what seemed like hours until the inning ended and my extremely-annoyed sister handed me my Coke.

"Why are you bothering me, and why did I get chosen for this task?"

"Thanks a lot," I said as I headed to uncharted waters, miles 19 and 20.

Mission accomplished. I didn't get blisters from my new Nike Elites and didn't get any cramps from the Coke. But I still had that nagging feeling that I really didn't run 20 miles non-stop, as I had to wait at the softball game. I was very tempted to do the whole thing over the next day, but wisely did not. Often, you will have a subpar run or subpar workout. You must let it go. Don't fall into the temptation to redo the workout, as you will just dig a bigger hole for yourself. No one run is the key to a good race. It is the constant, continual building blocks that create the foundation for a good race. Have confidence in all the training you have done and will do, and let the one bad run fade from memory, quickly! The same for races. No one race defines a running career. If you have a bad race, the beauty is you get to go out and race again soon. Analyze what you did wrong, i.e., went out too fast, ate too much the night before, whatever. Then move on. Dwelling on a bad race will create an endless cycle of self-doubt.

Even though my 20-mile run went great, except for the drink stop, I still had one more long run left-- an 18-mile run ten days before race day. I have no idea how my dad came up with this. Every marathon-training plan I have seen over the years has a 20-mile run two weeks out from race day. But, seeing as how at the time I had not seen any of these training plans, I didn't doubt my dad. Everything he had told me thus far had worked, so why tinker with anything?

Luckily, I timed my drink stop better for this run. I placed a cup of E.R.G. under a tree in my front yard and grabbed it as I flew past my house at mile nine of my run. Like the Coke, the E.R.G. didn't in any way cause cramps or other issues. Lesson learned: never try anything in a race that you have not tried in practice.

With my final long run down, it was time to taper, just a week of easy short running. One week before race day I ran into Mr. McAvoy on the bike path, and he greeted me with his usual smile. "You ready?"

"I think so," was my meek reply.

As a seasoned veteran, he could sense some self-doubt from a first-time marathoner, so he jogged with me a bit and after about ten minutes he had me convinced that I would break three hours the next weekend.

One thing I had been reading about in *Runner's World* was carbo-loading. Back in the 1970s, the theory was for three days you ate no carbs at all, just protein. Then for the three days before the race, you just ate carbs. I have no idea of the science behind this. My mother had enough on her hands with her chemo treatment and taking care of us that I didn't even think once about asking her to adjust my meal plans that week. I figured that I had done a 20-mile run and an 18-mile run off of whatever we usually ate, so why adjust anything? However, my mother did let me eat some extra cookies the day before the race.

The night before the race, I chose my race outfit of thick white cotton shorts with a yellow winged-foot that read 'Wantagh Track Team,' and a yellow Bethpage GO Cross Country T-shirt. The previous fall, my team had won the Bethpage Student Government Organization (GO) cross-country invitational team title. Across the back the shirt read "Team Champions." Not that I in any way helped us win that championship. But the shirt was thin, and I figured it if got hot, the thinner the better. As I pinned my number on the shirt, I realized what the shirt said was irrelevant as the number covered up all the words except GO Bethpage. As I ran the next morning every cheer for me was GO Bethpage. I suspect everyone thought I was from the town of Bethpage. I should've worn a Wantagh shirt. The number I pinned on my shirt was much fancier and larger than the one from my Fourth of July adventure. Additionally, the number had arrived in the mail a few days earlier. Yes, back in 1979 there were no big marathon expos. Your number and race T-shirt came to you in the mail.

Another thing that did not exist in the 1970s were sports drink bottles. Therefore, I had to improvise for my Coke and E.R.G. The morning before race day I walked up Wantagh Avenue to the Carvel Ice Cream Store and requested three large empty soda cups with lids and straws. The manager, who may have been all of 16 years old, was extremely confused by my request and appeared even less enlightened when I explained what the cups were for. Finally, I just offered to pay for three drinks just so I could get the cups. "Can't do that, it's against company policy." What company policy? All I knew about the company was that the owner ran weird ads on channel 11 and channel 9 about odd-sounding ice cream cakes called Cookie Puss and Fudgie the Whale. I wound up buying three cokes, dumping them out and then rinsing out the cups. To this day I will not step foot in a Carvel, even if they were to offer me a free Cookie Puss.

I filled two of these cups with E.R.G. and one with Coke and placed them in the fridge before heading off to bed. I set my alarm for 4:00 a.m. on my clock radio set to WGGB, hits of the 1970s. I tossed and turned a lot that night and before I knew it Blondie's 'Heart of Glass' was blaring over my radio.

I quickly shut it off, but not before I woke my brother. He was going to meet me with E.R.G. at mile eight of the race so I figured he had to get up anyway. I headed downstairs to eat two pieces of toast and a cup of Tang. Tang was the orange powdered drink of the astronauts. If it was good enough for Neil Armstrong, it was good enough for me. I wanted to get some food in my system but didn't want to eat too close to the 8:00 a.m. start time. After this, I headed out my door for a short walk to loosen up. I still follow this routine today. Once you find your pre-race routine, stick to it. It helps reduce any pre-race anxiety if you do the same thing each time. Also, being at home helped keep everything normal for me the days leading up to the race. This is helpful, but not always possible. If you do have to travel for a race, try to keep things simple. Limit sightseeing and limit time on your feet at the expo.

After my short walk, I put on my race outfit and headed to the front lawn for a pre-race photo. We then hopped into our station wagon for the ride to Eisenhower Park. Of course, since we were headed to a marathon my dad lit a cigarette for the drive over. The smoke didn't bother me; I was so used to it. The smoke was part of who he was, and I was in the car headed to my marathon because of him. Him, telling us to pick a sport we liked. Him, telling us to never quit. Him, a baseball player at heart, somehow creating the perfect marathon training plan.

"See you at mile eight," he yelled as I stepped out of the car. Race time was an hour away and I now had to set out to find Mr. Donlon amongst the 4,000 runners crowding the park. To this day, I like to get to the start area at least an hour in advance. This gives you time to relax, make any last-minute bathroom stops, stretch, and think. A race is stressful enough without the added pressure of a late arrival causing you to scramble to fit in all your pre-race issues. The more you can fall into a routine on race morning the better your performance will be.

However, as I scanned the fields for Mr. Donlon, I realized my efforts were futile. There were a lot more runners than I had expected and for some reason we never set up a meeting spot. Texting was out, as cell phones didn't even exist. My plan had been to run with Mr. Donlon since he had a few marathons under his belt, but now I realized I was on my own.

I headed over to the start line, which was an arch of multi-colored balloons. This was pretty cool as all my high school races started with a call to either a track starting line or a white line in the grass at the Bethpage Park Polo fields. The PA announcer called, "All marathoners to the start." This was much more comforting than what I heard in the fall at cross-country meets, "Varsity race to the start," followed by "Scrubs to the start." Yes, in the 1970s Nassau County had a division called scrubs. Imagine the embarrassment of going home and telling your parents you ran in the scrub division.

The start line of 4,000 runners was surprisingly well-organized. Runners lined up based on their anticipated finish time, using the honor system. Unlike races of today, there was no need for roped-off areas designating start zones with monitors scouring bib numbers to ensure runners enter the proper zone. I started towards the front, figuring I would run slowly at first and Mr. Donlon, who I assumed was starting behind me, would eventually catch up.

Both lanes of traffic on aptly named Park Boulevard were filled with runners. I looked back and the line of runners seemed to extend forever. Back in 1979 there was no such thing as chip timing which is used today. The gun went off, you started to run, and whatever the clock said at the finish was your time, no matter how long it took you to get the actual start line, even if you had begun at the back of the pack. You could certainly start your own individual watch when you actually crossed the start line, but your finishers' certificate read gun time to finish line clock time. Even under this system, people did not crowd to the front of the pack in order to cross the start line sooner than those in the back. Everyone knew their pace, everyone knew where to start, and believe it or not it worked well – with no angry monitors and start corrals.

I didn't run with a watch. I preferred to run by feel. At the sound of the starter pistol we were off. Four-thousand marathoners storming down Park Blvd for a mile before we exited the park and meandered through some neighborhoods before arriving at the Wantagh Parkway for the trek to Jones Beach and back to the park. Within a mile Mr. Donlon caught up to me and for the next five miles or so he kept reminding me to slow down. I couldn't contain my excitement and energy and I am glad he was there otherwise my first marathon would have been a 'Did Not Finish.'

As we wandered through East Meadow, then Merrick, and then Bellmore the sparse crowds yelled "Go Bethpage!" I think they had sympathy for me, as I was by far the youngest runner to pass by the spectators lining Merrick Avenue and Sunrise Highway. Eventually, we entered the Wantagh Parkway. It looked so much different from the road as compared to the view on the bike path. But it was still comforting to be on a familiar route.

By now, the crowds of runners had thinned out substantially and I knew soon I would see my dad and brother. The race sponsor Newsday had published a course map and my dad had scouted out hydration stations. Our plan was for him to park at Cedar Creek Park and walk down the bike path a bit to hand me a cup of E.R.G. at mile eight and then again on the return trip at mile 14. He would then jump in his car and drive up to Wantagh High school to be there to hand me some Coke for the final push.

As we approached the first bridge on the parkway, I could see my dad and brother standing alone. Somehow, my dad juggled a cigarette, a Carvel cup full of E.R.G. and a camera to get a shot of me. My shaved head had grown back in so the photo does not look horrendous.

The thing about the actual race is that is goes by pretty fast. You train for weeks and months, then race day arrives and by mile eight you are already a third of the way done. By the time Mr. Donlon and I arrived at Jones Beach, I couldn't believe this was half over. I savored very minute running on the wooden boardwalk; the same boardwalk we walked barefoot on all summer to get to snack bars. We had to run through a short, dark tunnel before we proceeded back north on the Wantagh Parkway. I had been in this tunnel a million times as a kid. Just like each previous tunnel passage, I shouted to hear the echoes bounce off the wet walls of the tunnel. Some older runners glared at me. But hey, I'm a kid, that's what kids do, they shout in tunnels.

Before I knew it, I met up with my dad again. "You're just over three-hour pace." How in the world did he know my race pace? I had no idea of my time. I never saw any clocks along the course. And he was standing on the side of a parkway with not a clock in sight. Then I saw it, the maroon swim team stopwatch. Even though he was nowhere near the park at the start, he must have started it exactly at 8:00 a.m. Who knows if the race started exactly at 8:00 a.m.? But I do know there would be a huge dispute at the finish line between the time on the official race clock and the time on his stopwatch.

I looked back as I saw my brother and Dad racing to the car to meet up at the next checkpoint. As the next few miles passed, Mr. Donlon's pace began to falter, and I knew I was on my own. I felt bad leaving him, but he assured me it was OK to forge ahead without him.

Mile 20 was exactly at my high school, which was located right on the side of the Parkway. I spent most of my school years looking out the classroom window at either the parkway or at King Kullen, the supermarket next to school.

"Kick it in!" he shouted with a filter-free Pall Mall cigarette in one hand, a cup of coke in the other, his trusted swim team volunteer stopwatch dangling from his neck. "Kick it in?" Did he have any idea how far this race was? I had six miles to go! I gulped down the de-fizzled Coke and carried on.

About a mile later it hit me. I had heard of 'The Wall' in the marathon. At mile 21, I hit the wall, or at least some version of it. And I think everyone around smashed into the same wall as me. No longer were runners smiling, chatting to each other, and high-fiving spectators. Runners were now walkers on what appeared to be the Wantagh Parkway version of the Bataan Death March. By now the sun was high in the sky to increase the suffering.

My mind began to play tricks on me, and any sense of logic was gone. Two weeks ago, I had run 20 miles, felt fine and then played basketball with my brother. How was it possible now at mile 21 I was tempted to join the walking brigade? My running went from a run to a jog then to an extremely slow jog. I was barely lifting me feet. Nike Elites, you were supposed to break through this wall. I was thinking of suing Nike and *Runner's World* for false advertising.

Recall just a few pages ago I proclaimed that the marathon race goes by too quickly. Tear those pages out of your book. Miles 20 to 26 go on forever. After an extremely slow slog, we climbed an steep grass hill off the parkway onto the road that bordered Eisenhower Park. What demon designed the racecourse that had us climb this hill so late in the race? Couldn't we just find a nice, smooth, and easy exit ramp?

As soon as I reached the park, my energy was renewed. The final mile was a long, twisting path through the park's golf course. If this had been a regular Sunday, the path would be filled with golf carts and gleeful golfers chasing par. Now, the path was littered with joggers chasing the immortality of finishing a marathon. This mile didn't feel too bad, but it must have felt horrible to the runner in front of me. About 300 yards from the finish line, he collapsed right in front of me-- like, out cold, collapsed. Fortunately, we were close to the finish line so medical personnel could quickly respond.

As we exited the golf course path, we ran behind a red wooden warehouse for about 50 yards, then turned right and the finish line was in sight! I wish I could say the final 200 yards were some sort of magical moments for me, but they weren't. I just wanted to sit down. As I crossed the line on a grassy field the clock read 3:04:51.

I finished in 200th place out of 4,000, and there went my theory that everyone ran under three hours. The finish line area was excruciating anticlimactic. The grass was brown with many bare patches and the type of fences keeping dunes intact at the beach surrounded the area to keep spectators at bay. I assume my dad was amongst those spectators, but I didn't see or hear him. Once I crossed the finish line, I was handed a cup of water and a tin medal the size of a quarter that said, "I finished the Newsday Long Island Marathon." I was quickly ushered out of the area. I still have that medal and show it to people to compare how medal sizes have increased exponentially although the race distance is the same. I quickly spotted an empty picnic table under the greenest pine tree I have ever seen in my life. I sat alone of top of the table for what seemed like hours but must have been minutes. Shortly after, my dad found me and said, "3:05:20."

"That's not what the clock at the finish line read."

"Who you going to trust?"

I wasn't going to get into a dispute over such a minor point. His time was amazingly close seeing as he was in a car about eight miles away when the starter gun was fired. A few minutes later, Mr. Donlon joined us.

"Hey, you got the school record."

Yes, technically I ran faster than Donny, but I figured more than two people must do an event for record-keeping purposes.

"You going to try again?" was my dad's first question on the drive home.

"Maybe."

As we drove home, I am not sure that it had sunk in that I had just run 26 miles. Maybe I was too young and naïve. To me, it seemed like I signed up for the race, trained for the race, and ran the race. It never crossed my mind that I wouldn't finish. And I think even today that philosophy should hold true. First, you can do anything you set your mind to. Second, once you have that goal, don't over think it. Do the training, have confidence, and always have positive thoughts. Self-doubt is a recipe for disaster. As soon as a doubt creeps into your head, get it out immediately, otherwise it will just grow and grow and snowball. If the only thought you have is that you will finish, then more likely than not you will actually finish the race.

The next day, my legs ached more than any part of my body ever ached before or since. I could barely walk downstairs. I couldn't tie my shoes. It took double the amount of time to walk to school. When I got to math class, there was no parade, there was no announcement. My shaved head got more of a reaction than finishing a marathon. I just dove into parallelograms and the race was a memory, until that night when I scoured the results in Newsday. The Champ ran 2:55. Mr. Devlin ran 2:58. Then I had to scroll past runner after runner to get to my name. I was sort of upset. I ran with these guys all the time and they wrecked me, plus they were like my dad's age. If my answer yesterday was maybe, my answer today was a resounding YES!

But that had to wait. Swim season was starting. Even though I vowed in March it was time to move on, I changed no more winter swim team to yes to summer swim team. As the weeks passed, the marathon faded a bit, but I did wear my marathon T-shirt every day in gym class. Occasionally, a marathon reminder would arrive in the mail, such as my finisher's certificate with the official race time from the race clock, not from my dad's stopwatch. Today, the day after a marathon, runners receive an email link to whatever photography company was at the event. This link will take racers to a wide array of race photos of themselves and they can order a variety of post-race photos. In 1979, there were no computers, no Internet, and no email link to a dazzling display of your accomplishment. In 1979, about two weeks after the race, a race photography company would send in the mail one sheet of paper affixed with several one-inch by one-inch glossy sample photos of yourself; of course, with an accompanying order form. These photos were so small you could barely recognize yourself. As you studied the photos with a magnifying lens, often you realized that many of the photos were not even of you. Often, you received sample photos of individuals who ran sort of close to you. Technology was nowhere near today's standards. These companies did the very best they could given the circumstances of trying to quickly snap photos of 4,000 runners, process those photos, sort them, then cross-reference race numbers to home addresses. I'm surprised I even got one clear shot of myself.

One Friday night in June, I walked with a friend to the Wantagh Theater to catch Rocky II. On the way home, we decided to stop over at the house of one of the seniors from the cross country team who was headed off to Brown University the next fall. As we approached the house, all we could hear was loud music and loud talking. A party! I had never been to any parties since like ten-year-old birthday parties, and now this was a senior party! I walked around to the backyard like McLovin from Superbad. My blue platform shoes, bell-bottom pants, and button-down shirt with a large Elvis-like collar were so out of place that I just froze when I saw the crowd of seniors. Then from over by the keg I heard, "Hey kid, get over here." My mind raced about what type hazing I was about to undergo. Was I about to be held upside down by my feet with my head dunked down into the icy water keeping the keg cold? I slowly walked over, making sure to not make any eye contact. There at the keg was our school's All-American football player. Yes, our All-Long Island, All-State, All-American wide receiver heading to Penn State in the fall. I dreaded whatever type punishment I was about to receive for daring to show up at a senior party. "Aren't you the kid who ran the marathon? Tell me about it," he said, as he handed me a large cup of beer that to me appeared to be more foam than beer. I had sipped a few of my dad's Schmidt's beer with him present. I think he did that so we would not like the bitter taste and be turned off from beer.

But this was no Schmidt's with my dad in our yard. This was keg beer with an All- American hero, totally different taste and vibe. And he was treating me as an equal. We sat on a bench under a tree. I rambled on and on and he was genuinely interested. I was and am extremely shy, but I think that first beer, and the two more he gave me, got me talking.

I had no idea of how beer affected the brain until I stood up to leave. My mile walk home was just as challenging as the final five miles of the marathon but in a different way. I was talking to myself. I was seeing three stop signs where there was one. I was stumbling all over the street. As I got closer to home, I just kept saying to myself, 'play it cool, play it cool.' Luckily, no one was awake except my dad. He could see I was drunk a mile away, but he was the one playing it cool. "Stick to Coke till you're 18, and by the way when you lie down in your bed tonight, your bed will not be actually spinning. Good luck in the morning."

Summer swim team turned into fall cross country. The training I had done for the marathon helped me as a cross country runner and I performed much better than the year before. As I was doing much better, I figured why not combine the two? Run cross country with the team during the week; on Sundays, do a long run on my own; and then do a marathon after the season ends. And this was one of those rare occasions where a plan came together. After my season ended, I entered the Jersey Shore Marathon down on Asbury Park. Just like Long Island, the registration process was easy and cheap. A few days before the race, my shirt and number arrived by mail. Mr. Donlon and I drove down the morning of the race. My dad said he could not make the trip as it was CYO basketball season for my sisters.

The race attracted fewer runners than those on Long Island, but seeing how this was early December, all those on the start line were there to race. Unlike today's marathons, there were no pace groups back in the 1970s. People did form informal groups based on chatter at the start line. As I took my place on the line, I saw an individual who had written down on his race number all the splits needed to run a 2:50 marathon. "Mind if I run with you?" I asked. He said sure, but I am not so sure he thought this 16-year-old was being realistic. It was a cold and windy day on the flat double out and back course: 6.5 miles into the wind, 6.5 with the wind, 6.5 miles into the wind, 6.5 miles with the wind. I felt much better in this race, probably because I had been doing fast cross country races all fall, so this marathon pace felt easy. Back in the spring, I had done no prep races, partly because I only had eight weeks to train, and partly because my goal was just to finish. I recommend that if you wish to do your best time in a marathon that you do a few prep races at a faster pace so that on race day your marathon pace will feel easy to you.

Even with the wind changes, we stayed on pace the entire race. With about 200 yards to go, I heard, "Kick it in, you can qualify for Boston." Did he sneak down here? I looked to my right and there on the sidewalk was my dad, Pall Mall in hand. He knew deep down I was upset with my time in Long Island and was looking to run faster here but did not want to have me feel any pressure from his presence.

"Hey, you got to be 18 to run Boston," I joked back.

Back in 1979, the Boston Marathon qualifying time was 2:50 for the 18-34 male category. Over the years, that time has flocculated upwards. I crossed the line in 2:50:29 and in lieu of a medal I was handed a Jersey Shore Marathon mug that I still use today. Generally, Boston will allow a runner in if they are within one minute of the standard. So, maybe I qualified, but it didn't matter. I was too young. It would take me ten years from that race to stand on the start line in Hopkinton. In those ten years, a lot changed . . .

BOSTON BOUND

First held in 1897, the Boston Marathon is not only the granddaddy of all marathons, but also the one race that marathoners around the world dream of and aspire to compete in. Not only is it recognized as the oldest marathon in the world with its fabled course from Hopkinton to Boston with its infamous Heartbreak Hill luring 30,000 runners a year, but strict qualifying times add to its siren's call.

Fifteen runners toed the line back in 1897 and over a century later, 30,000 runners per year trace the same route. Over the years, as I have run in Boston, I have seen the best of the city and the towns along the route. I also saw that same city come back to life after I ran the 2013 Boston Marathon, marred by the bombings.

However, it was my first Boston Marathon in 1989 that I remember the most; probably because that race was ten years in the making for me. There is an expression today that is overused. Why didn't you write that novel? Why didn't you sail around the world? Why didn't you visit the Eiffel Tower? The response is always, "Life happened." Other priorities took precedence-- working, raising a family, lack of money, etc. In my case: Why didn't you run the Boston Marathon after you ran 2:50 in the Jersey Marathon? The answer: track and cross country happened.

Both the Long Island Marathon and Jersey Shore Marathon gave me tremendous confidence in my running. I am not sure if it was physical because of the high mileage I was doing, or it was mental knowing that I could accomplish something in the sport. Probably a bit of both. With this new-found confidence, I had a laser focus on both the two-mile track race as well as five-kilometer cross country events. Even today, forty years later, I can close my eyes and visualize every step of the Bethpage cross country course, starting with the mad dash of 150 high schoolers sprinting from the start line across a seldom-used grass polo field. After 400 yards, the mad dash becomes more controlled as runners exit the green grass of the polo fields and run 200 yards on an old tar road, the sound of metal spikes clicking on the asphalt becoming more distant as the leaders separate themselves from the pack. A sharp 90-degree left turn takes runners off the road onto a flat two-mile winding path through pine trees and oak tress. Each fall, the green of the pine trees is juxtaposed with the bright red leaves of the oaks. The light brown dirt path, oddly interspersed with white sand, was heaven to me. I could run alone freely on this path.

From ninth grade through my first year of college my mother courageously fought cancer. It was an endless cycle of chemo treatments and the accompanying side effects, remissions, followed by more bad news from doctors. It seemed to be an emotional roller coaster for the entire family, except for my parents. They both wore masks of bravery, never letting my mother's condition get in the way of our school, our sports, our plays, our band concerts.

On the two-mile wooded stretch on Bethpage's cross country course, there were no coaches, no spectators, no thoughts of chemotherapy-- just me running alone as fast as I could under cloudless blue skies in the cool and crisp fall air. As quickly as one entered the woods you exited. A quick left turn had runners heading up a slight incline next to the park's entrance road. After 200 yards, a quick 50-yard jaunt through a patch of trees took us back to the polo fields. As runners exited the polo fields, one could hear "It's a red shirt," "It's JFK kid," as spectators identified the runners returning to the fields. The race concluded with a half-mile loop around the exterior of the polo fields.

In Thornton Wilder's play *Our Town*-- set in Groves Corner, New Hampshire-- following her death, Emily Webb was allowed to return to Earth to relive one day in her life, so that she could observe the simple joys of everyday life. She chose her twelfth birthday as the day to relive.

Given Emily Webb's opportunity, I would choose the day of my eleventh grade cross country county championship and state championship-qualifying meet. The same race I had come in dead last the previous year. The race was held on a cold, rainy Saturday morning at my favorite venue, Bethpage State Park. In every sport, qualifying for the state championship was a cherished accomplishment in Nassau County. In swimming, the top two in each event made it, and the same with track. In cross country, both the top teams and top few individuals qualify. I remember a couple of years ago the pride in my brother John's eyes when Patrick, the non-record holding eight-year-old, qualified to swim the 500-yard event in the New York State Championships.

The previous fall, my team failed to qualify for the state meet, even though we were the favorites beforehand, and certainly they were not taking the last place runner, so I did not take the trip upstate for the championships. In fall of 1979, there were several teams in contention, as well as a few individuals, none of whom I knew. When you come in last place the year before you really don't get to know and socialize with the top runners. They have begun their cooldown before you even finish. Throughout that fall, I continued to improve with each race, although my school competed in the small school division so I never really had run against the top teams and runners. I did know that Mepham High School and Bellmore JFK were amongst the top teams, as they often ran at Mill Pond at the same time as my team.

The race began with the usual dash across the polo fields; however, these runners were much faster than those I usually competed against in league dual meets. As we entered the woods, I had to be in about 100th place. Over the next two miles, I ran through cold muddy puddles as I passed runner after runner with no idea who they were. As we entered the polo fields, I saw my mom sitting in a foldup lawn chair under an umbrella in the wet grass. "Run faster, Kevin!" It wasn't in the rah-rah tone of most spectators. It was the same tone of, "Clean up your room!" For a second, I felt like I was getting in trouble. As we rounded the polo fields, my younger sister sprinted across the field and tried to run next to me for a few strides. Somehow, as we entered the final 200-yard straightaway, I had moved up to third place. And the Rocky-like story ends here. I didn't pass any more runners, but I did qualify for the state meet. As soon as I crossed the line, my dad came over in his maroon jacket, stopwatch dangling but still running; he was so excited he never turned it off. So not only did I qualify, but for the first time in my life there was no dispute about my race time. As he wrapped me up in a hug, he screamed, "We made it!" Yes, WE made it! If I could relive one moment of my life, it would be that hug.

At the awards ceremony minutes later, I met the Nassau County Cross Country Coordinator as he handed me my award and instruction letter for the state meet. Little did I know at the time, Mr. Bob Baratta, who recently was inducted into the Nassau County Sports Hall of Fame, would become my boss, friend, role model, and tremendous mentor.

Cross country turned to winter track, then spring track. My parents came to each meet. My mom set her lawn chair in lane five at each meet, screaming at me to run faster. My dad stood at the finish line billowing secondhand Pall Mall cigarette smoke into each runner's face on each lap.

The marathon was becoming a distant memory, but I continued to read every thing I could about Bill Rodgers as he dominated both the Boston and New York City Marathons. Con Ed was a sponsor of the New York City Marathon, so one year my dad was able to get me finish line seats and I was able to meet my idol, Bill. Years later, I met him again a few days before the Honolulu Marathon as I was living there at the time. He was extremely patient, gracious, and kind.

As I entered twelfth grade, I had to start thinking about college. I figured all along I would go to college, but never really did much to prepare for it. I hadn't taken the SAT, nor was I even signed up for them for that fall. In August, my dad pressed the issue so I said I would go "Wherever." My dad went to St. John's for both undergraduate studies and law school. My mom attended St. John's, too, so I just figured St. Johns was in the cards for me. Plus, I wanted to be a lawyer. Not that I had lofty ideals like wanting to change our justice system. To me it was simple: Mr. Donlon and Mr. Celia were both lawyers, they ran marathons, so being a lawyer must be a good job that allowed you to run. Aside from that, I knew nothing about the law. To me, practicing law equaled time to run. I also wanted to go to the same school for all seven years-- four years undergraduate and three years law school. St. John's had the best law school in New York and had the highest pass rate for the bar exam, so I figured I would go to law school there and may as well go to undergraduate there. Like I said, I really didn't do any research into college. Also, St. John's was close to home. My mother was gravely ill, and I wanted to be around to help her and my father. At the time, St. John's was a huge sports school. Eventual Cy Young Award winners Frank Viola and John Franco lead St. John's to the College World Series; the track team had recently been top-15 in the NCAA championships; and the basketball team did, and still does, have amongst the most wins in college basketball history.

We grew up as St. John's basketball fans. My Dad blasted every game on the radio. It was so loud you would think our house was Madison Square Garden, with Frankie Alagia, St. John's star point guard, shooting from behind our living room couch and Coach Lou Carnesecca pacing along our blue and white checkered rug, calling out plays. Every night, as we played Nerf basketball in our bedroom, we heard tales of former SJU stars, Sonny Dove and Frank McGuire. My Dad would dunk on us, doing his best to imitate St. John's center Bob Zawoluk shouting, "Zeke would do it lefty!" as he dunked over John and me, tearing our makeshift wire-coat-hanger rim off its hinges.

As I entered the polo fields at Bethpage cross country course one chilly, yet sunny, October Saturday morning my senior year, my dad shouted, "Pick it up St. John's is here!" College coaches did, and still do, regularly attend high school meets for recruiting purposes and my dad had seen the St. John's coach in the crowd.

After my race, a tall, thin, twenty-something-year-old with a big, brown moustache approached me and said something along the lines of, "Nice win, but you really didn't beat anyone good; you're like the champion of your own backyard," as he handed me a thick manila folder with my name written across the top. "I'm Matt and I coach at St. John's. I'll give you a call sometime," he added as he walked away. I was like, whatever. Hadn't this Matt guy just seen my race-- how I won by a minute? That had to be the single worst recruiting pitch and response ever. I had no idea who this "Matt" was. But my dad did. As I tore into the envelope to read the letter from the head coach and browse through the glossy St. John's Sports Department magazine, my dad told me everything about Matt Centrowitz, his New York State high school mile-record time (that still stands today), his two Olympic teams, etc. My dad was like Wikipedia before Wikipedia even existed. "You call him Mr. Centrowitz if you are lucky enough for him to call. You don't say 'yeah.' You say 'yes.'" And thus began my over forty-year coach, mentor, boss, and friend relationship with Matt Centrowitz.

Today, Matt is better known as the father of Rio Olympic Gold Medalist, Matthew Centrowitz. However, as I dug through old editions of *Track & Field News,* I found out that he had run for famed University of Oregon, although at time the only Oregon runner I was focused on was Alberto Salazar, winner of the New York City Marathon. I read that he had qualified for two Olympic teams and that he had recently become St. John's distance coach. By the way, every time I have interacted with his son Matthew, he has been extremely kind, humble, and gracious.

I didn't have to wait long for a call. I took Matt's advice and started traveling into New York City's famed Van Cortlandt Park (VCP) to race against people "Not from my own backyard." If Bethpage Park was heaven, VCP was super heaven. Like Bethpage, runners traversed a large grass field during the early part of the race. Unlike the polo matches of Bethpage's field, the fields of VCP hosted every game imaginable: Football games; soccer games; cricket matches; and baseball games, with picnics and BBQ grills interspersed. Those in the infield were oblivious of the championship races circling the fields. We were equally disinterested in their games, except when an errant soccer ball would come shooting across a pack of runners. Once in college, at the Metropolitan Cross Country Championship, a soccer ball rolled in front of the lead pack. I witnessed eventual race winner, Pat Petersen, give that ball a kick that Pelé would be in awe of, all without missing a step. A few years later, Pat would go on to set the American record in the marathon. Tragically, he died too young.

After rounding the fields, runners entered the stretch of the course known as the cow path. Three-hundred-fifty runners would try to funnel into a path about eight feet wide. And many of these were rough and tumble kids who would not give an inch as elbows flew for positioning. After a short stretch on the cow path, runners hit the first hill on the course, Freshman Hill, which took all of about ten seconds to summit. A sharp turn across a bridge over the Henry Hudson Parkway and runners were now headed to "the backwoods," a thin path going up and down a series of short steep hills. Today, the backwoods are finely manicured with cinders, and the course is extremely smooth. In the late 1970s, the course was full of rocks, roots, broken glass, and huge ruts caused by rainwater rushing down hills. Every step was an adventure. Poking out from behind the large graffiti-coated rocks were the rusted, burned-out chassis of abandoned automobiles. I have no idea how these cars arrived at this automobile graveyard since the trails were only about six feet wide. I could only assume they were stolen, stripped for parts, and left to languish in the dismal landscape of the park.

Old timers like to debate what times the greats of the 1970s could run on this well-manicured course of today. Such debates continue as track surfaces have improved from the cinders Jim Ryan ran on in the 1960s. Modern technology has also improved shoes vastly, with carbon plates embedded in the soles now producing faster times. Would I have liked running in today's high-tech shoes rather than my Nike Elites in 1979? Probably. But such shoes didn't exist. I ran the best that I could with what existed at the time and was happy. People can debate on and on "It's the shoes," "It's the pacing lights," "It's the track surfaces." It makes for good barstool fodder, but at the end of the day different eras have different technology. Do your best in your era.

Out of the backwoods, runners re-crossed the highway overpass and made a sharp right turn to head down a steep downhill leading them back to the open fields and the finish line. Once runners reached these fields, there remained an endless lung-busting 500-meter sprint on a cinder path running parallel to Broadway-- the same bright lights Broadway of the Theater District miles to the south in Manhattan. Unlike the handful of parents and coaches who greeted finishers at Bethpage, the finish line area of VCP was jam-packed every Saturday in the fall. Some invitational meets hosted up to 10,000 runners across a full day slate of races.

Not only did I love the course and competition, but I was also thrilled to be in the city, albeit at the northernmost part of New York City's Bronx borough. If Bethpage was as calm and relaxed as a Tim McGraw song with a few hundred local runners on the venue at any one time, VCP was an overcrowded disco; it was Studio 54. Broadway was always lined with buses from schools throughout the tri-state area. After a race at Bethpage a cup of water from a huge orange plastic bucket served as post-race refreshment. Broadway had Burger King and a deli right across the street from the finish line! I always ran with a few bucks in my shorts pocket and like Monopoly's "Do not pass go, go directly to jail," as soon as I crossed the finish line I was "Do not pass go, go directly to deli." The deli aisles were always full of runners as I jockeyed for position to get a can of Coke and Pepperidge Farm cookies.

I just loved the energy of the crowds and the city. And I loved hanging out with Matt. Yes, our first meeting was quick, but after that initial meeting Matt was at a series of VPC races including our State Meet and the Northeast Regional Meet. But I did notice he paid way more attention to my dad than me. On those VCP fields Matt and my dad created a unique bond that lasted for years. I still get calls from Matt to this day on Father's Day saying that he is thinking of my dad. It was almost as if he was recruiting my dad rather than me. It was all good with me. I loved hearing Matt and my dad's New York City banter. "Neil, there were a few kids ahead of him today."

"Matt, there were a heck of a lot more kids behind him."

As fall turned to winter, I made it a point to race as much as possible at New York City's Armory Track. Today the Armory is the mecca of indoor track in the country with its banked Mondo-surfaced 200-meter track. In the 1970s and 1980s the Armory was the place to race in the tri-state area, but the track left much to be desired. The "track" was a flat wooden floor with faded white painted lines indicating the lanes . . . not that lanes mattered. Two-mile races in the Armory were just a jumble of 50 runners racing in circles for 16 laps, pushing each other along the way. It was mayhem, but fun. Unless you fell. Falls on the Armory track required the steady hands of a team manager with tweezers to carefully dislodge hundreds of splinters.

Ask any runners from that era what they remember most about the Armory. Some might say the splinter-filled wooden floor, some may say the overwhelming odor of BenGay and others will recall the loud cheers as relay races came down to the wire. I will always remember the music. One Saturday at the Armory I heard "Rapper's Delight" by The Sugarhill Gang and spent the next week at home scanning the radio dial on my clock radio to hear that song and others like it, slowly rotating the knob to not miss any stations.

That winter I attended every St. John's home basketball game. I took the train and Q43 Bus to St. John's as often as possible to walk around the school, talk to Matt, and meet the team. During those high school trips into Queens, I met my future roommate Mike Regan (a first-year student at SJU at the time), who was, and still is today, the funniest person I have ever met. He was also a heck of a runner, running four minutes even for the mile. He is in the education field today in Connecticut. Once at a New York Mets game, thirty years after graduation, we called Matt and it was as if we had spoken to him the day before. The bond between coach and athlete never ends. I did visit a few other schools, but none of them could match the energy of St. John's with its location in the city. I also liked the fact that at the time St. John's had no dorms. As a commuter school, most students lived at home, worked part-time, and took classes in between shifts as servers, movie theater ticket takers, or whatever job they could find. I really didn't like the prospect of living in a college dorm because I'd heard horror stories of late-night parties and horrible roommates from my friends, brother, and sisters.

In April, I made my final decision so my dad met with Matt to work out the financial logistics. That June, I met with Matt, who told me he would be sending me summer training schedules, and that he saw me as possibly top-ten on the cross country team, maybe even on the JV squad. To say I was upset is an understatement. I trained so hard that summer just to prove him wrong and was our number-one runner from day one. I was first on the team by a twist of fate—actually, a twist of an ankle. Mike Regan, our projected top runner, was involved in a softball accident over the summer and arrived at campus that fall in a cast. His punishment from Matt for participating in non-running sports over the summer: serving as timer for all our practices. His cast came off a few weeks later and he was able to run at our Big East Championship meet at Franklin Park in Boston. We were running together at mile four in that race when all of a sudden, he fell into a hole. The guy couldn't catch a break.

Years later, in 2012, I was with Matt at the Quarterdeck Bar in Arlington, Virginia, just outside of DC at 1:00 a.m. At the time I was living in Charlottesville, Virginia, and was still in the Army. Looking at the clock, I thought, I must be at PT (physical training) in five hours, two hours down the road down in Charlottesville. I did make it to PT on time, stopping at every Sheetz gas station on Route 29 to buy another Coke to keep me awake. For some reason I said, "You know, Matt, I am still pissed at you. Back in 1981, you told me I would be tenth man on the team. You knew I was better than that. Why?"

He smiled and simply said, "You operate on fear of failure. If I told you that, I knew you would train harder." People can say what they want about Matt, but he knows what makes people tick and how to motivate them, without them even realizing it.

And he really cares about his team not just as runners but also as people. Once I was at American University and we were sitting at Starbucks. A senior on the team stopped in and Matt asked, "What is your plan when you graduate?"

"I don't know."

"What's your major?"

"Math."

"Hang on a minute."

Next thing I knew, Matt called the head of the Math Department and got the student an internship. He cares. Even if you don't notice it right away. Matt knows everybody and is comfortable talking to anyone . . . be it Flavor Flav in a casino, or a jogger in lane eight of the American University track asking for advice.

Although I was focused on track and cross country, I knew that my future was in the marathon. I continued to keep up with race results and kept a sharp eye on my TV every Patriots Day. Even though I had never run in Boston I felt as I knew the course and its New England towns already. Any thoughts of running a marathon in college ended quickly during my first week. I asked Matt if maybe since I was in college I should do some swimming to get in some extra endurance work. "You plan on doing the back float at the Big East meet?" Message received. Stick to cross country training.

Even though I never ran a marathon during college, Matt provided two important lessons that carried over to the marathon. Every Monday morning it was our responsibility to head over to the track office. Right outside the door in the basement of Alumni Hall was a huge white piece of paper with the workouts for the week. It was pretty much the same every week. Monday, Wednesday, Friday – two easy runs on your own. Tuesday, Thursday – track 3:00 p.m. Saturday – race. Sunday – long run. We only saw Matt three days a week. That is, officially. I saw Matt running constantly around campus on his own, day and night. My dad and I would walk out of a St. Johns basketball game at 10:00 p.m. As we left the warm gym and were struck by the cold January night air, Matt would yell out "Did we win?" while he ran endless loops around the sports center parking lot.

Matt wanted us to run on our own as many days as possible so that we would learn how to make decisions and how to take ownership of our running careers. Certainly, he could run an easy five miles with us every Monday, Wednesday, and Friday, but what good would that do us in the long run? He wanted us to make decisions such as: what time should I run based on my school schedule; where should I run; should I stretch out beforehand; or how fast should I run. All too often I see coaches micromanage their teams. The coach controls every single detail. Stretch exactly this way for five minutes, run exactly this route on this day, etc. The athlete has no say in the decision-making process. And when it comes time to decide they are lost-- for example, in a race where things may not go as planned, they are incapable of adjusting. These athletes often don't run after college because they have no idea how to train without a coach telling them exactly what to do each second of the day and they are incapable of creating their own training plan. Matt's plan of teaching us to make decisions on our own extended beyond running. He taught us to make decisions in every facet of our lives that carries on to this day with my job, family, and running.

It is the same with children. Even at a young age, you must let children make decisions for themselves. Otherwise, by the time they get to college and must live on their own they will be lost. Cam was once about sever years old when he asked, "Why do you let me choose if I should climb that tall tree or not?"

I said, "Even though you are seven, I trust you will make the right decision. If I don't let you decide a simple thing like whether or not to climb a tree, by the time you are a teenager you will have no decision-making skills if I constantly tell you what you can and can't do."

Once, I was preparing to go whitewater rafting in Switzerland. Before you board the raft, the guide goes over everything bad that can happen on the rapids. The list is endless, yet every potential scenario ends with you submerged under freezing water with a foot stuck under a rock. After this long-winded scary talk, my buddy Erik Dotson summed it up best, "If you fall overboard, don't just lay in the water expecting someone to jump in to save you. You have to be an active participant in your own rescue." Erik was a fantastic lawyer and an even nicer person. Had I fallen overboard I am sure he would have jumped in after me. Our whitewater-rafting trip went on without incident and a few months later Erik and I would travel together for the Dublin Marathon. I had the chance to tour the city of my grandparents on foot.

Matt wanted us to be active participants in our running careers. Matt didn't run our races, Matt didn't run our morning runs for us, and Matt didn't feel if our ankle hurt. You need to be involved with the process and have two-way communication with your coach. When it came time to race, Matt let us race. I don't ever recall seeing Matt on the infield of a race yelling splits and telling us to run faster, nor do I remember seeing him out on the cross country course at various checkpoints. We trusted Matt that he had prepared us; Matt trusted us to race and react to what was happening in the race. Years later, when I coached high school cross country and track; I followed Matt's lead on this. I would take my team to the start line, gather up their sweats, and tell them to run their best and then head to the finish line area. I would sit on the top row on the bleachers at New York Tech football field and track with a great a view of the course, watching and waiting for them to head down the home stretch. Not once did I go out on the course yelling "Go faster!" First off, they will not run faster just because you yell at them to do so. That must come from them and their own desire. The number of runners who have run faster in a race because their coach yelled, "Run faster!" is probably zero. Secondly, I truly believe that runners appreciate it and work harder when they know that you have confidence in them.

The same holds true in the workplace. Nobody likes the micro-manager. People appreciate being valued and knowing their boss believes in them. Decades later when I was a supervisor of several attorneys, not once did I go into the courtroom to slip them notes of what to say. I knew that they were prepared for court, and they knew that it was their case, not mine, and that they, rather than I, would have to jump up and yell "Objection!"

In addition to teaching us to think and make decisions on our own, Matt also taught one other valuable lesson. Don't have a long-term training schedule. Certainly, have a vision; certainly, have goals; but, as an example, don't have a 16-week training plan with every day preplanned for the next four months.

I asked him about this one evening at Pizzeria Piola in Rosslyn, Virginia, in 2012. I asked if he could write up a 16-week plan for me, because I wanted to run the 2013 Boston Marathon. His response was short and sweet "Nope." In my mind I am like, dude, what is your problem? Then he says, "I'll give you a one-week training schedule," and I am thinking, I need to prepare for more than one week. He continued, "And each week, I will give you another one-week schedule for the next 16 weeks." To me, it seemed easier to just knock it out in one shot. His explanation made perfect sense. "I can write out a 16-week plan right now, but it would be useless. I have no idea what the weather will be like in ten weeks, I have no idea if you will have a minor injury in six weeks, and I have no idea what your work schedule will be like in 12 weeks. Let's go week by week and adjust along the way."

Over the years, I have seen too many runners obsessed with the latest 16-week training plan found in a magazine or on the Internet. They think if they miss one day or don't do the exact mileage written on that schedule that their marathon dreams will be dashed. Running magazines or the Internet do not have crystal balls. A few years ago, three individuals I knew were training for the Richmond Marathon. Every Friday morning, they did the required long run on their training plan and every Friday morning they were lying on the floor in one individual's office exhausted and proclaiming they were still tired from the previous week's long run. I asked them to print out their training plan so I could take a look at it. They printed it out and handed it to me. Without even glancing at it I tore it up and threw it in the trashcan.

"Sir, what are you doing! That's the top-rated training plan I could find on the Internet."

"Let me ask you a few questions, does the person who wrote that plan know your heights and weights? Does the person who wrote that plan know your job schedules? Does the person who wrote that plan know that you are all exhausted every Friday?"

"Ah, no."

"OK, let's do this. To start, every Friday you are making yourselves more tired, so you are taking one step forward and two steps backwards. From now on, do your long run every ten days so you can recover between sessions. Also, every ten days come to my office and let's figure out what to do for the next ten days."

A couple of months later, they all finished the Richmond Marathon.

Yes, a schedule is a good guide but keep it as a guide, not an absolute. Be flexible. If the wind outside is 25 MPH do your long run the next day. If your boss needs you to finish a project, run a bit less that day.

Active participation in your training plan and flexibility are two key ingredients in the recipe for marathon success. Matt did a fantastic job instilling these in me. Not only did he teach these, I saw him use this philosophy himself as he trained in the spring of 1982 in preparation for his American record in the 5,000 meters. As I said earlier, every time I saw Matt he was running, mostly running loops of some sort. Today elite runners carefully choose their races and often space out the time between races. In the spring of 1982 not only was Matt running all the time, but he was also racing a lot.

Two days before the Big East Track Championships, I was walking over to the Citibank on the corner of Utopia Parkway and Union Turnpike just off campus to get a few hundred gambling dollars for the upcoming Kentucky Derby. Matt approached me and asked if he could walk with me. He told me about a race called the Trevira Twosome 10-Mile Run in Central Park. "I got invited to a race this Sunday in The Park, but if I race, I will miss your 10,000-meter race. Just say the word and I will skip the race."

My reply was simple, "Matt, even if you are at Villanova on Sunday morning, you aren't going to run those 25 laps for me; you taught me what to do. Go do your race and we can talk about how my race went when you get down to Nova."

"Are you sure?"

"Yes."

"OK, now just remember to adjust for the weather and react to what happens in the race." Matt's race plans were simple-- react and think on your feet. He didn't have set splits for us; he didn't run around the track yelling at us to run faster.

Matt wound up winning that race in 46 minutes, just beating Geoff Smith, who later went on to win the Boston Marathon twice. Right after that ten-mile race Matt and Geoff leapt into Matt's car and sped down to Villanova. Geoff, who was running for Providence College at the time, jumped out of Matt's car and won the 1,500 meters! I saw him lie on that infield forever after the race, exhausted (with stiff legs since Matt's car didn't have much leg room). I don't know if Matt would have skipped the ten-mile race if I asked him to, but I do know that I appreciated him asking for my input.

A few weeks later Matt won the 1,500 meters at the Metropolitan Outdoor Track & Field Championships at St. John's University. Shortly thereafter he set the American record for 5,000 meters.

The principles I learned from Matt helped me throughout my college years and beyond. Unfortunately, during those college years my mother died. The first person I called when I got the news was Matt. Every single Monday after that Matt took me to a deli on Union Turnpike for lunch. I had the exact same American cheese sandwich on white bread every week, while he listened to and comforted me.

Throughout college my plan was to go straight to law school after graduation. However, I realized I needed Plan B in case I didn't get into law school or didn't like law. My Plan B was to get my secondary-school teaching degree. I never thought I would be a teacher but got it "just in case." "Just in case" came relatively quickly.

"Dad, I got into St. John's Law School."

"How are you going to pay for it?"

"I'll get loans."

"Nope, no loans. Call the dean and have him transfer you to night school and get a job to pay for school." Get a job as what?

I mentioned Mr. Bob Baratta handing me my cross country award in eleventh grade. His son had run for Matt at St. John's and was good, like 1:46 in 800 meters good. In addition to being the county cross country coordinator, he was track coach and athletic director at Great Neck South High School about ten minutes away from St. John's. He was also a good friend of Matt's. I saw Mr. Barrata at a track meet my senior year and he asked me about my plans for the next year. I mumbled something about law school and jobs. He said, "I am thinking of stepping back a bit from coaching. Come to Great Neck and I will make you a teacher and coach." Plan B was now Plan A. I suspect Matt was somehow involved in me getting a job so quickly.

As I prepared for law school, I heard tale after tale about how much schoolwork it entailed. I wondered how I could continue run at all, let alone run a marathon. Within a week I realized it was all tales. Law school students like to brag about how many hours they study as some sort of badge of honor. I have no idea what they were studying. To me it seemed like the day students complained the most about studying. They took just one more class than the night students, had no jobs, but seemed to be in the library constantly. To this day I have no idea what they were reading and studying. I just purchased the CliffsNotes version of all our textbooks and read those when I got a few minutes.

Everyone in my night school class had a full-time job. The first night of law school I looked down and over to the student on my right. There on his ankle pointing straight at me was a pistol. Turns out he was a New York City detective attending law school at night after cracking cases during the day. I spent four years of law school hoping an accidental discharge wouldn't blast into my leg. We had teachers in my class, office workers, and even a surgeon. The professors were very understanding as many of them were adjuncts at night and practicing attorneys during the day. I remember one saying, "We understand you all have jobs but remember you have to pass the same bar exam as the day students."

Pass the bar exam? "Dad do you get a grade on the bar exam?"

"Nope all you have to do to be a lawyer is pass your classes and pass the bar exam."

Passing is like a "D." Law school was awesome. I figured I could get a D on the bar exam and be all set. I had no idea what type of law I wanted to do but knew I didn't want to work a lot of hours or do anything boring like reading contracts or doing mergers all day. I would figure out a plan for that later. Now I had to start teaching, coaching, and figure a way to still run.

My coaching philosophy was very similar to what I learned from Matt and what we followed at St. John's for the distance runners. I had to learn sprints and field events so I solved that problem by making each senior an "event mentor," responsible for guiding those under them. Mr. Baratta was fantastic. He let me run the show and not once did he step in to tell me to change a workout. Not once. The team was successful and the kids had fun. One season we even had the fastest high school miler in the country on our team. He also ran the fastest

1,000 meters in the entire country as well. Years later his nephew, who had the second fastest high school 800-meter time in the US, would come to American University where I was then coaching. Coaching two generations made me feel rather old.

One thing I learned very early on as a coach was you need to separate your running from the team's running. It would be very tempting to run with the distance runners but that would create several problems. One is pacing. Do you run their pace or your pace, and would your pace be too fast for them? The second is that you can't just focus on one set of runners; the sprinters and field events need your help. Lastly, the kids need time away from the coach to talk about prom dates and make fun of the coach . . .all things they would not feel comfortable doing with the coach around.

I also learned not to project personal reasons for running on them. Not every runner joins the track team to win races. Some join for the camaraderie, some join to have something on their resume for college applications, and some even run for health. I had one runner who just was content jogging alone each day way behind the others. I once asked why he didn't want to go faster. It turned out there was a history of heart disease in his family, and he was concerned about his health.

I loved coaching and even considered continuing at Great Neck after law school. Law school itself was not too bad. People say law school is a lot of reading. It is a lot of reading only if you do it. It's no reading at all if you skip your homework. Plus, I had no time for reading. How was I supposed to read a law book while refereeing a dodge ball game in gym class? It was hard enough to get to class, let alone read anything. Track practice usually ended at about 5:30 p.m. and law school classes started at 6:15 p.m. and went until 9:25 p.m.

As soon as the students got on the 5:30 p.m. bus to take them home after practice, I jumped into my car, turned on WFAN's Mike and the Mad Dog sports radio show, and drove along the Northern State Parkway. I honked my way through rush hour traffic, arriving at school shortly after 6:00 p.m. My brother John, who I lived with during law school, was also attending night school and working during the day. He greeted me each night the same way, "Here is a dollar, buy your Coke, buy your Baby Ruth candy bar and leave me alone. I have 50 pages to read." I would buy my dinner of Coke and a Baby Ruth and tell him to shut his book as there was no way he was going to read 50 pages.

After class ended, I would arrive home about 10:15 p.m. and head out the door for my run. I don't like running on roads at night so every night I would run endless loops in the dark on the same grass field that a year ago helped prepare me for the 600-yard walk-run. Some nights I would run all out for 60 seconds or 2:00 minutes figuring those were 400-meters and 800-meters repeats. Other nights I would run for an hour or so, lap after lap. During these often-frigid runs during the winter semester, I started wearing a Walkman for some of my runs. Terminator X blasted in my ears, keeping me awake as I ran loop after loop. That was the only period in my life when I ran to music. I think the Walkman, which was about the size of a brick, felt too awkward for me to carry. Today the options are endless from earbuds to the Apple shuffle.

Weekends were much better for my running. I could run in the daylight on Saturday early in the mornings before taking my team to track or cross country meets. On Sundays I ran either road races or cross country races at VCP with the New York Athletic Club (NYAC). My times were not horrible considering my training regime.

In September of my fourth year of law school I was offered a position as a judge advocate in the Army. Two months before this I didn't even know the Army even had lawyers. During the summer heading into our last year of law school students started going on job interviews. I had spent every summer since high school as a lifeguard down at the beach. Lifeguard plus track coach is not the best legal resume but I did get an interview with a firm in Brooklyn. Before the interview, my dad explained billable hours to me (how lawyers in firms are paid). Most firms required 2,500 billable hours a year at the time. That didn't seem too bad to me-- five days a week, ten hours a day. I was already putting more hours in with teaching coaching and school.

"Billable hours are hours you are actually working for a client, it doesn't include reading the *New York Post*, eating lunch . . ."

Aside from horse racing, I am not good at math, so this was starting to take a turn for the worse. The turn for the worse turned into a drive off the cliff at my job interview. I had to take a train, then the subway, and then walk a few blocks to the law firm's office. I was exhausted by the time I arrived, and thinking I can't do this every day, I'll be dead by the time I am 30. I hadn't even entered the building yet. Things only got worse. I hadn't researched exactly what type of law the firm practiced. "So, you're interested in contracts?" the counsel assigned to interview asked. Contracts? I got a C in contracts and hated that subject the most in law school. Then he patted his large stomach and said, "I see you ran at St. John's," as he glanced over my resume with distain. I assume he may have seen my law school GPA on there somewhere. "I used to run the mile for Fordham. No time to run these days with 14 hours in the office a day, including weekends." Wow, this billable hour thing was worse than Dad said.

"Ok, let's be honest. You aren't going to hire me. I have no interest in working these kinds of hours, so let's call it a day," and I stood up and left.

That night as I recapped my interview with my dad, he told me to join the Army. We were in our backyard patio with the small outdoor TV playing a Mets game. My dad had remarried since my mother's death. My stepmom is wonderful. I looked to her for help. "That's a great idea, I wish I had joined the service after nursing school." For the next half hour, they peppered me with 1940s-era military terms. "You have an office but may have to go out on maneuvers. You'll get liberty every month. You may get to see Bob Hope on a USO tour."

My dad had been in the Army during the Korean War when there was a draft. Every Saturday he still put on his old Army uniform when mowing our lawn. When he was in charge of dinner, he gave us all military ranks and we had to line up mess hall-style by rank in our kitchen. He would toss Sloppy Joes on our plates saying, "Take all you want but eat all you take." I'm surprised he never told us, "Smoke 'em, if you got 'em," the Army phrase for a cigarette break.

"You'll be an officer, you'll eat at the Officer's Club every night, you'll go golfing every day at 3:00 p.m., you can run on the Army track team."

I am not sure what 1940s-era war movie my dad got his impression of military officers from. Yes, I was an officer. No, I didn't eat at the Officer's Club every night. During my entire military career, I only ate at Officer's Clubs when he came to visit and insisted that we go.

"This food is great, and the price-- I can't get a steak like this in Florida for ten dollars. Why aren't you here every night?"

"Ah, because I have a house, a family, and a kitchen."

No, I didn't play golf every day. I played once my entire 26-year career and it was pitch and putt 60-yard holes. As a formerly-enlisted soldier, my dad had a very warped view of the officer corps.

But the Army running team interested me. I applied and was accepted shortly thereafter with a report date six months after law school graduation and the bar exam.

With a job offer in hand, I knew I could do even less at school that fall and have a bit more time to run. Heck, I could skate by and still have a job. And the bar exam couldn't be too hard. They tell you everything you needed to know for the test during classes. With my misguided academic mindset, I found myself playing football one Sunday evening. Yes, on the same Wantagh Elementary fields. Dusk was setting in and it was that first cool fall evening after a long hot Summer. As John and I were throwing the ball around I told him that I was thinking of running Boston that Spring. "You going to use your Jersey Shore Marathon from '79 for your qualifier?" Darn it, my plan was foiled within a minute, as qualification times had to be accomplished within the previous year.

64

Enter Plan B. Donny, yes, the same Donny from the Earth Day Marathon, was living in my neighborhood and I ran with him on occasion along the bike path to the beach. The past Summer we had done a race series at all the New York State Parks on Long Island. We discovered Long Island over the course of ten Monday night races. Since school was not in session over the summer, I also had done some long runs with him as he was preparing for the Marine Corps Marathon in DC.

I quickly called Donny and asked about the race date and where he was staying. The race was toward the end of October, four weeks away. He was staying in a place called Vienna, Virginia, at his uncle's house and I was welcome to stay with him.

Donny also had an extra race flyer that I ran over to his house to grab. This may seem crazy today with marathons getting sold months in advance, but in the fall of 1988, you could register for the Marine Corps Marathon rather easily, even up to the day prior to the race.

I looked through *Runner's World* to determine that the current qualifying standard was three hours. My next call was to California. A few years earlier I had run a St. Patrick's Day race. Later that day my stepbrother Patrick, who is a few years older than I, stopped over our house for dinner. Pat was a super baseball player in high school but was never a runner until that day. He started asking me about the race and then declared he was going to start running. Six months later he was on the start line for the New York City (NYC) Marathon.

My dad knew every single subway line and stop in the city. Somehow in his mind he envisioned where the subway lines ran under the marathon course. In his head he pictured the city on two levels, street level and subway level, and combined the two. Prior to chip timing and runner tracking on computers, he got my stepmom, himself, and me to six spots on the course to cheer for Patrick. We would walk up the stairs from the subway in Brooklyn and within two minutes Patrick would run by. We would board another subway and at our next stop see Pat within minutes. I have no idea how my dad predicted Pat's pace and got to every stop at the exactly perfect time. Amazing. More impressive, dad was just as proud of Patrick as he was of me. The word 'step' was not in dad's vocabulary.

New York City was terribly hot that year. I jumped in at mile 18 and continued to hand Pat water along First Avenue, into the Bronx, and back down to Central Park. He did fantastic and continued to run after that race. Shortly thereafter he moved to California. When I would visit he would take me on runs up in the hills of Palos Verde or along the strand from Manhattan Beach to Hermosa Beach to Redondo Beach and back. I loved those evening runs, trading barbs with Pat as the sun set over the Pacific Ocean. I had never seen an ocean sunset till those runs as Jones Beach faces southward and the sun sets over land toward the west of Long Island.

If I was going to run Boston, Pat was coming with me. I called him and told him to find a marathon pronto to get a qualifying time. A few weeks later he drove down to San Diego, slept in his car next to the beach the night before a race and qualified with a 2:58. His car was tiny. I could barely sit in it, so I have no idea how he got a good pre-marathon night's sleep.

On the other hand, I loved my first Marine Corps Marathon. I continued to do loops in the dark after school and did one 20-mile run on a Sunday a few weeks before the race. I could not join Donny for the drive down to DC on Friday evening before the race as my cross country team had their league championship that Saturday morning. I took the Amtrak down to DC from Penn Station later that afternoon. From Union Station in DC to Vienna, Virginia, I took my first ride on the Metro. I was in awe. It was so much cleaner than the subway. Each station was shaped like a tunnel with an arched ceiling-- to me it looked like Disney's Space Mountain.

Donny, his aunt, and uncle met me at the Metro station in Vienna. We quickly arrived at their townhouse for dinner. "I brought down my dad's famous lasagna," Donny said when I asked what was for dinner. Donny and his entire family are super nice, but chefs they are not. I was at a Fourth of July Party at his house where every single person got sick, including the dog. I didn't want to risk my Boston Marathon so I picked at the food and went to bed hungry, having not eaten anything since a Coke and pretzel on the café car on Amtrak. I woke up even hungrier the next morning in a strange house with no Tang or toast. We got a lift over to Iwo Jima close to the start point. There were less than 10,000 runners in the race. Today there is no way anyone could drive so close the start point with over 30,000 runners taking part in the race.

We walked over to the start point. Again, the honor system was used. I lined up towards the front as without chip timing, gun time would be used for official times, and I didn't want to risk anything. It was a beautiful day, cool, and sunny. The course was somewhat like today's course. To me it was all fantastic. I had never really seen DC before, so like Mr. Celia said years ago about seeing Long Island on foot, I enjoyed seeing DC on foot. Running through Georgetown was a highlight for me as I wondered, why can't there be towns like this on Long Island?

We ran on a small path under a tunnel of golden leaves right next to the reflecting pool heading west toward the Lincoln Memorial as the Marine Corps Band played. With the field now at 30,000, this path is no longer used. Both in 1988 and 1994 that was my favorite part of the race.

We finished on a grass field next to the Iwo Jima Memorial overlooking the city we had just run through. I ran 2:48 and had my Boston qualifying time. Donny finished a bit later. His aunt picked us up and drove me to the Amtrak station and handed me a bag of cookies; my first food in 24 hours. I should have used the three hours on the train to read a law book. Instead, as we rolled through Baltimore, Philly, and Trenton, I stared out the train window thinking of Boston.

As the calendar flipped from 1988 to 1989, I registered for the Boston Marathon. Like my previous marathons the registration process was relatively simple compared to today. The one difference was that the Boston Marathon required proof of completion of a marathon within the time standard. A photocopy of my Marine Corps Marathon time was used for that purpose.

As I started my preparations, I realized that this would probably be my last marathon that I would train for along the Jones Beach bike path. Yes, I loved training in Central Park and VCP. I loved racing in the city. But the Jones Beach bike path was where it all began. Even today, 40 years later, I can close my eyes and smell the salty air, hear the seagulls, and see the brown reeds waving in the ocean breezes. On clear days you could look across the back bay and see the Twin Towers, dark silhouettes against orange sunsets.

I already had my military orders to report to Fort Lee, Virginia, the following January, assuming I passed the upcoming July Bar Exam. Each Saturday when I drove along the Northern State parkway to Great Neck South for a meet with the team, I realized I was coming closer to leaving everything behind-- all my running routes, my friends, my family, and the comforts of being on the same campus for eight straight years. That spring I wanted to savor every last run: runs to Newbridge Pool; runs to Jones Beach; even endless midnight loops on the elementary school fields.

Although I had never run the Boston Marathon, I was familiar with the course, at least from the vantage of the TV crew following the race leaders each April. My main concern was the lack of hills on Long Island to prepare for Heartbreak Hill and the other Newton Hills that strike from miles 16 to 20. Then I made a classic rookie Boston mistake. I disregarded any hill training. I figured they can't be anything worse than Cardiac Hill at the Sunken Meadow cross country course or Cemetery Hill at VCP. In April I learned that the hills of Boston were much worse. Looking back, even if I had devised a plan to drive to a reasonably hilly place each Sunday for a long hilly run, executing that plan would've been impossible.

In January, my seafoam metallic Buick Le Sabre was kaput. Tommy Texaco's, our family's mechanic for years, diagnosis was bleak. "I can replace the entire engine, but it will be expensive and will take some time." I gave him the go-ahead and for the next few months (it took a lot of time including one total redo with a second new engine installed), I was on foot patrol. When I was on high school swim team Great Neck South was our most distant rival. My dad even used his trusty odometer to determine exactly how distant their school was from our house-- eighteen miles. Runs to work early in the morning became my Boston training program. Over the course January and February, I figured out every possible way to reduce the distance. I now know every single parking lot between Wantagh and Great Neck and how to angle across each one. Three days a week I would run to work, and John would pick me up at 5:30 p.m. We would drive into St. John's for class and then drive home together after class. Two days a week I would bike to work and at 5:30 p.m. John and I would jam my bike into his tiny red Honda civic. And every night he would complain. Great Neck was on the way to St. John's. Literally all he had to do was pull off the highway for two minutes. Every night it was, "Get your darn car fixed."

By March I was on the road again. For these final six weeks I combined my dad's original training plan with the flexibility Matt had instilled in me. Back in 1979 my long runs were on Fridays, and I shifted these to weekend.

Two weeks before Boston was strike two. I ran a twenty-mile race at Eisenhower Park. It was four five-mile loops around the park paced by a Nassau County Parks Department pickup truck. I intended to use it as an easy long run that had the added benefit of water stops along the way. After loop two my competitive spirit got the best of me, and I continued to up the pace. I won the twenty-mile race, but although I didn't know it at the time, I'd left my Boston race out there on the sidewalks of Hempstead Turnpike that surrounded the park.

My stepmother, stepsister Mary, and I took the Amtrak up to Boston on the Saturday before the race and met Patrick at the Marriott hotel close to the race finish line. We all shared one room with two queen beds. It was like a family reunion and party all rolled into one, as we hadn't seen Pat in months. That Saturday night was rainy, cold, and windy. I had no idea what the forecast for Monday was, as I hadn't even checked.

Sunday was just as cold and miserable. We headed over to the race Expo early that morning to pick up our race numbers and shirts. This was all new to me as in all my previous marathons a decade ago, this was sent to runners through the mail. As we walked into the convention center, I was in shock. It was huge, it was crowded, and there was booth after booth of running gear, gear that even a decade ago was unimaginable. It was if the entire sport had changed in the decade I had been away. The painters' gloves that I had to walk to the Wantagh Hardware store to purchase, the water bottles I walked to and had to beg for at Carvel, the Nike sneakers I walked to Mr. Brynes store to purchase were all under one roof. And then there were the new products. Booth after booth was filled with carnival barkers, "Use our magic massage stick to get you to the finish line," and "Our energy drink outlasts the competition." This bothered me on so many levels. To me it was all hocus-pocus. First, ten years ago 4,000 runners had finished the Newsday Marathon without a magic massage stick. I am all for technological improvements in sports, but at the right time and place. Thirty-six hours before a marathon at the Expo is not the right time and place to play on people's self-doubts about finishing the race by offering them a magic potion. Secondly, how will people be able to test these products on a training run prior to the race? I pity the person who tested out a new energy drink during a marathon because they had never tried that drink on a long run to see how their body reacted to it. Certainly, go to the race expo and enjoy the energy, and enjoy the guest speakers. Purchase any gadget that catches your eye. Just don't use that gadget on race day. Test it out in practice and if works then use it at your next race. If it doesn't work in practice, you have saved yourself the heartache of an upset stomach or sore muscle during your race.

I wanted to get my race packet and leave. My stepmom, on the other hand, is the friendliest person on Earth. She was talking to every runner she bumped into at the Expo. She even somehow found, and signed us up for, a bus tour of the race route and scored us tickets to the pre-race pasta dinner. The next hour the four of use were boarding a big coach tour bus headed out to Hopkinton. As we headed out of Boston our tour guide said "Yes, its raining, but as they say in Boston if you don't like the weather, wait a minute." I had no idea what he was talking about. It's been raining, freezing cold, and windy since last night. That's a lot of minutes and nothing is changing.

We arrived in Hopkinton and the bus driver allowed us to exit the bus to walk around the start area for a while. I felt like I had walked onto a movie set. I recognized everything: every house, the white church on Main Street just to the left of the start line, the town square with its' white-domed gazebo. I had seen these images a thousand times in photos or on ESPN's airing of the marathon each Patriots Day, the third Monday in April. Now I was experiencing them in person.

There, across Main Street painted in blue and gold with the Boston Athletic Association's Gold Unicorn, was the start line. As I walked across the line in the cold rain, I could imagine myself finally arriving on that line 24 hours later. Just behind the start line I noticed a big shamrock painted on the ground with the number 58 written in its center. I knew enough about the Boston Marathon to know that this shamrock designated the starting point for Johnny Kelley, two-time race winner, who would be running his 58th Boston Marathon the following day.

What struck me most about the start was how narrow the road was. Massachusetts Route 135, called Main Street as it travels through Hopkinton, consists of two lanes. Not two lanes in each direction-- two lanes total! One lane going in each direction, with each lane having an extremely narrow shoulder. The start line measures 30 feet across. The following day over 5,000 runners would have to cram their way through that narrow passage. Years later upwards of 30,000 runners (36,000 in 1996 for the 100th Anniversary Race) would weave their way across that line. As field sizes increased, race organizers broke the field into waves of runners starting in 30-minute intervals.

The tour followed the exact course route on the return trip to Boston, with our guide pointing out every town and landmarks along the way. Hopkinton, Ashland, Framingham, Natick, Wellesley, Newton, Brookline, as well as Heartbreak Hill, were noted. As the bus drove up Heartbreak Hill in the rain it was difficult to ascertain exactly how long and steep it was. I would find out the next day.

That evening Pat and I went for an easy run in the dark chilly rain, passing the famous bar Cheers from the TV series of the same name along the way. Later the four of us entered a large hall filled with long tables covered by white tablecloths. This was the pre- race pasta dinner, the final chance to carbo load. Runners lined up Army mess hall-style and walked in a line as chefs scooped heaps of ziti noodles and red sauce onto paper plates. Was the pasta the best I ever ate? I don't remember, but I do know I felt much more comfortable eating it as compared to "Donny's famous lasagna." Pat and I ate quietly as my stepmom worked the room, cheerfully talking to every runner, many of whom were alone. Her friendly disposition helped calm their pre-race nerves as they ate in solitude. What was noticeably absent from the crowd was the prestigious Boston Marathon race jacket. This status symbol worn proudly by Boston Marathon runners did not come out until 1991.

Pat is much more nutrition-conscious than me. Notice how much I have mentioned Coke thus far? Every year that I have run the New York City (NYC) Marathon I run with a twenty-dollar bill in my pocket. As soon as I finish, I politely decline the big red apple (symbolizing "The Big Apple") handed to all finishers and the bottles of Poland Springs water tossed our way by cheering volunteers. Instead, I exit Central Park as quickly as possible and seek out the nearest hot dog vendor to buy an ice-cold can of Coke and a dirty water dog, simply the best post-marathon meal.

Years later while visiting my parents in Florida I opened a Coke-free fridge. How is this possible? They knew I was visiting. There on a hutch I noticed a six-pack of small Coke bottles. Oh, they must have forgotten to put them in the fridge, I thought, as I grabbed one. The small bottles didn't seem quite right; they looked like some antiques the guys on the TV show *American Pickers* would love. I just figured that maybe Publix was doing some sort of throwback Coke sale. I flipped the top off and guzzled the warmest, foulest-tasting soda, which I quickly spit out into the sink. A while later my parents returned from their lunch at Mr. Dunderbak's in the Volusia Mall.

"Where my Coke? Where my Coke?!" my dad yelled.

"You mean those bottles over there? I had one and it was terrible, you may want to return it to Publix."

"It was terrible because that was original vintage-1940 Coke. I purchased them at the Coca-Cola Museum in Atlanta as an investment."

"Well, you still have five bottles."

"It's a set, a six-pack not a five-pack. You get in your car, Mister, and drive up to Atlanta to get me another six-pack."

I never drove up to Atlanta and I still find it odd that he was using a six-pack of Coke as part of his retirement portfolio.

As we got ready for bed the night before Boston, Pat said, "Drink lots of water to hydrate, it's going to be a scorcher tomorrow." Dude, we just froze to death in the rain on our tour, and on our run, and on our walk to dinner, but I still took his advice and drank cup after cup of water in our cramped Marriott Hotel room. I was up all night having to go to the bathroom. Great advice, Pat. I am sure I woke him each time I had to get up as we were squeezed into one bed with my stepmom and stepsister Mary sharing the other one.

Back in 1989 the Boston Marathon started at noon. This was due to several factors: tradition; the time needed to transport runners from Boston to the start line; and the desire to have runners pass by Fenway Park as Red Sox fans exit the stadium after their annual early game every Patriots Day. Today, with over 30,000 runners, start times are staggered.

The noon start allowed us to sleep in a bit. No 4:00 a.m. wake up like the Long Island Marathon a decade ago.

Bright sunshine drenched our room as I pulled back the curtains. That tour guide must have been right. Not only was it sunny, but the temperature must also have risen thirty degrees over the course of the night. I had packed an old sweatshirt and old sweatpants that I planned to discard at the start, but neither would be of use on this warm day. Pat and I each walked out of our hotel room in shorts and throw away T-shirts over our race singlets. A few blocks away in the center of Boston we joined hundreds of runners as we boarded the yellow school buses that would transport us to Hopkinton. As the race route was already closed to traffic, we had to take a very long ride along highways and sideroads. It took us about an hour. I kept thinking; this is far. The bus was full of the usual assortment of marathoners: the veterans who sat quietly and confidently; the nervous runners chatting on and on about extremely vapid subjects as they tried to stay calm, annoying everyone within earshot; and the "excusers." "I am just doing this as a training run," "I did a hard race last week," "My hamstring is a bit sore," "I haven't trained for this kind of heat." They were creating excuses for poor performance even before they got to the start line. I wondered why they were doing the race if they already setting themselves up to do poorly. The marathon is hard enough physically. Don't make it even harder by mentally talking yourself out of the race.

Before we knew it the bus dropped us off at Hopkinton High School, a few blocks from the race start. Those who have recently run the Boston Marathon will recognize this as the "Athlete's Village," complete large white tents set up on all the school's athletic fields. The tents were filled with nervous runners, free coffee, donuts, and fruit, all surrounded by what seems to be thousands of port-a-potties.

In 1989 Hopkinton High School was just that, a high school. A high school with no students as Patriots Day was a day off. There was no athlete's village, no free coffee, not an apple to be seen. Unlike today, the school was unlocked so Pat and I entered and found our way to the gym. The gym was empty as we lay on the wrestling mats relaxing and stretching. We made our final bathroom stop in the boys' locker room. We would be the envy of the 30,000 runners a year who now shiver, sometimes in the mud, grasping a warm cup of coffee on a high school soccer field standing in long snake-like lines awaiting the use of a port-a-potty. A warm empty gym, mats to lie on, working toilets—Oh, the good old days.

About 30 minutes before the start, we walked a few blocks to the start line. The sun was already high in the sky and the temperature seemed to be rising by the minute. Five thousand runners packed Main Street as we made our way to our designated starting location. The honor system from the 1970s had given way to race numbers affixed with designated starting zones. For Boston, these zones were based on your qualifying time. Qualifying times are based on both age and gender. The fastest time qualification being three hours for Males 18-34 and increasing by five-minute increments for every five-year age group. Females have a corresponding system beginning at three hours and 30 minutes for the youngest age group. Since Pat and I were young at the time, we were in the first start zone and lined up a few rows back from the start line. A few minutes before the start I heard "Make room, make room!" coming from my right. Eighty-one-year-old Johnny Kelley was ushered to his shamrock, taking his start position. He received a round of applause.

In no time at all the gun fired and we were on our way. Thousands of spectators held back by white metal fences on both sides of the narrow road sent us off with loud cheers. I had seen this start on ESPN many times but to be there in person it was simply awesome.

The first few miles were downhill. Very downhill. I had heard people say, be conservative, be careful of the downhills early. Those first few miles I experienced just how downhill the Boston Marathon is. I had never run so far downhill in my life. I was also very shocked at the lack of spectators. Every image I had seen on TV and in magazines was a racecourse lined with thousands of screaming spectators. I quickly learned that those spectators are located within the confines of the several towns that the race passes through along Route 135. These towns are located a few miles apart and are separated by long stretches of woods.

For the first part of the course Pat and I gently ran downhill, past ponds and barren brown trees that had not yet sprouted their spring buds. Every few miles we would enter a small town and run down beautiful Main Streets, passing Mom-and-Pop stores and restaurants. It also seemed like every resident of each town was out there screaming, screaming for us as they broke out of their cabin fever of the cold and raw New England winter. No barriers separated the runners from the crowds and little children held their hands out, begging for high-fives. As the temperature continued to rise residents created water stops to supplement the race's official stops. A few sprinklers and garden hoses also offered respite from the hot sun.

The first half of the race was an odd juxtaposition of long serene stretches of quiet nature followed by deafening crowds. Twenty minutes of silence, ten minutes of mayhem as we made our way to Boston. I had no idea of our pace as we didn't wear watches. We talked and traded barbs along the way.

At the halfway point we ran though the loudest section of the course, Wellesley College. Every single student was out screaming; with thirteen miles to go this provided a huge adrenalin boost for the runners. At this point the course also veers off route 135 onto route 16, which takes runners to Newton and the base of the Newton Hills. The crowds also increased as we closed in on the city.

As we made the right turn onto Commonwealth Avenue a few things struck me. First, it was wide, much wider than roads in the towns we had run through earlier. Secondly, toward the left side of the road was a commuter train that ran into the city. A few miles up the road hopping onto the train became a huge temptation.

To us marathoners the sun and the heat were the enemy. To the spectators along Commonwealth Avenue, it was their friend. Droves of people lined the wide street. It makes sense; who would want to be out watching runners in the rain? They turned out in full force on this first warm day of spring. They turned the grass median of Commonwealth

Avenue into a miles-long block party complete with grills heating up hot dogs and coolers full of beer.

We drudged up the seemingly never-ending Heartbreak Hill in the smoke from the grills to the smell of hamburgers and to thousands of cheers of "You can make it!" "Almost at the top!" interspersed with the occasional drunk in a Larry Bird Celtics jersey, "Want a beer?" "Run a mile for me!" Ha-ha, as we are dying here treating every water stop like an oasis in the desert.

After cresting Heartbreak Hill, the race became a blur. We inched closer to the city and the crowds became thicker and thicker as we passed Boston College then the Citgo sign and Fenway Park. The crowds in Boston literally carry you to the finish line. When I hit the wall in my first marathon there were no spectators at all along the Wantagh Parkway, just tired runners encouraging each other. In Boston there is no way you can stop in the race. The crowds wouldn't let you. I think if you tried to walk off the course after mile twenty the crowds would just push you right back onto the course. It's as if they want you to finish the race more than you do. They are proud of their city and don't take lightly to quitters in their town, no matter how wicked tired you are feeling.

On exhausted legs that had taken a beating from the early downhill miles and then grew wearier climbing Heartbreak Hill, I forged ahead. My quick and steady pace on the early downhills had slowed to a jog as I turned onto fabled Boylston Street and could see the Prudential Center up ahead, the finish line beacon (since 1989 the finish line has shifted slightly on Boylston Street).

My stepmom and stepsister were among the thousands of screaming spectators watching our accomplishment. Boylston Street is a mixture of glee and sadness. As you enter this final long stretch, you know you will be soon joining the ranks of those who have passed before you over the past century on this course. As tired as you are, you don't want it to end. You remember the long cold runs to work in the winter to Great Neck South High School, endless loops on a dark field, the bus tour of the course, the pasta dinner, and spending time with Patrick. It was all coming to an end.

And then, in an instant, it's over. After crossing the line, cheerful volunteers wrapped a big piece of tinfoil around me. I had no idea what it was as these didn't exist a decade ago. "It will help keep you warm," Keep me warm, it's sunny, it's hot, I just ran past people in shorts and no shirts grilling hot dogs! But I took it to be polite. We also received small medals. Like the 1979 Long Island Marathon medal, this medal was much smaller than that of today. My 2013 Boston Marathon medal dwarfs the 1989 version.

My stepmom found us easily at the finish area. Today with 30,000 runners, even a keen eye may not spot a family member after the finish. She was so excited as she greeted us and continued to cheer on other runners. I have seen her stand on cold Thanksgiving mornings cheering on every single runner at the Garden City Turkey Trot. To a cheerleader like her, Boston Marathon was nirvana.

We walked back to the Marriott and went straight to the indoor pool. As I pulled off my singlet, I could see that my arms, shoulders and neck were beet-red. Twenty-four hours earlier, it was winter. Today I looked as if I spent an August afternoon day at Jones Beach. If you don't like the weather, wait a minute.

I obviously skipped law school that night. The following morning Pat took a cab to the airport as the three of us boarded the Amtrak home. For some reason we hadn't purchased tickets beforehand. As the conductor came around to sell tickets, my stepmom convinced him to allow me to ride free as a Boston Marathon finisher. It had a nice ring to it.

A few weeks later I received the tiny glossy photos of my race. As I looked at my face and stride in each successive photo, they represented a visual timeline as my faltering pace along the course.

Shortly thereafter my finishers' certificate arrived. This was in the era prior to electronic chip timing with runners' times being recorded on a chip affixed to their race number. It's activated when crossing a mat at the race start line and records an official time when crossing a mat at the finish line. Prior to chip timing your time was from gun to finish line no matter how far behind the start line you were when the gun fired. My finishers' certificate read 3:01 and below it stated, based on your starting zone you may deduct two minutes from your time. For some reason Patrick's certificate allowed for a two-minute-30-second deduction even though we started together. I know I crossed the line a bit ahead of him, but technically he beat me. And he does not let me forget this. As he says, "We all have our own narratives."

Law school finished a few weeks later, as well as my teams' track season. That July I took the New York Bar exam in the Javits Center along with 6,000 aspiring lawyers. The bar exam is a two-day exam. The morning sessions each last from 9:00 a.m. to 12:30 p.m. The afternoon sessions last from 1:00 p.m.to 4:30 p.m. If you finished prior to 4:00 p.m., you were free to leave the test location. If you finished after 4:00 p.m., you couldn't leave and had to wait until 4:30 p.m. to avoid disturbing the other students during crunch time. On day one, I finished at 4:01 p.m. and sat there forever waiting for everyone else to finish. Then at 4:30 p.m., at pencils down, it took about 30 minutes for the proctor to gather every exam. I couldn't leave till almost 5:00 p.m.! As I walked to Penn Station, I vowed that no matter what I would finish before 4:00 p.m. the next day, because I didn't want to wait around, plus the next evening I had a 5K race on the Long Beach Boardwalk. Leaving the Javits Convention Center at 5:00 p.m. was not going to cut it.

Day two of the bar exam was the multi-state portion with 100 multiple choice questions in the morning and 100 additional multiple choice questions in the afternoon.

At 3:55 p.m. I was on question 90 of 100. Since it was a multiple choice test, I just quickly filled in "C" for questions 90-100 figuring C had to be the right answer for a few of them, plus you only had to pass the test. At 3:58 p.m. I raised my hand, handed in my test, and sprinted crosstown to Penn Station to catch the 4:18 train to Wantagh. As the train pulled out of the station I thought, maybe I shouldn't have done that. Oh well, I figured I would find out in October when results came out if my plan worked. I didn't return to the Javits Center until 2005 for the NYC Marathon Expo held at the same venue. The NYC Marathon was not on my mind as I sprinted away from the bar exam thinking of the childhood song, "No more pencils; no more books; no more teachers' dirty looks."

That fall I continued to teach and coach cross country. Mr. Baratta could have hired someone else, because I was not going to finish the whole school, or the entire winter track season for that matter. But he kept me on anyway. He had encouraged me to join the Army the year before and I continued to see him when I visited the Island over the years. I also made sure to travel to New York in Fall 2016 for his induction into the Nassau County Sports Hall of Fame at the Crest Hollow Country Club.

One evening as I returned home from Great Neck my brother John handed me an envelope, saying, "You passed." He had opened the envelope with the bar results. Yes, the envelope addressed to me.

"That's a federal offense."

"How did you just pass the bar? Have you read what that offense actually states and the mens rea required?"

"Shut up with the legal mumbo jumbo and give me the envelope." It simply stated that I passed. No score just said that I passed. Who knows, and who cares, if I got 200 questions correct or 130 questions correct? It's all the same. I passed.

The following summer I got a call at the end of July. "I caught the 4:11 train home from Penn Station.." Yes, John had finished the bar exam quicker than me. He passed as well. Years later, my dad was annoyed when we explained that we competed to see who could finish the bar exam faster. It was water under the bridge because we had passed. And why was he annoyed? We competed at everything- pool, ping pong, swimming, **the Presidential Fitness Test,** etc. I guarantee if he knew when he was in law school that he would have two sons taking the bar in the future, he would have been in on the contest and set the standard in 1959 for us to top thirty years later.

With my passing score in hand, I was ready to head to Fort Lee, Virginia, in early January. Those final weeks I spent as much time as I could on my old running loops. Yes, I would be coming home for visits-- but by then I would have new loops in faraway places. I would simply be a visitor on the Jones Beach bike path; and then decades later a stranger on the Jones Beach bike path. In 1979 I ran with "The Champ" in his old baggy faded sweatshirts along that path. Regulars on the path knew me as the "prodigy." We all knew each other; we all wore the same JCPenney's T-shirts and Sears catalogue shorts; and we all knew every step of that path from Cedar Creek Park to Jones Beach. Now when I return, I must dodge bikers speeding to the beach as biking seems to have surpassed running as the sport of choice there. The few runners I pass don't see the prodigy; they see an old slow grey-haired jogger. We all have our time in the sun.

On January 5, 1990 I didn't leave my house to any great fanfare. The night before I left, my dad told me to listen to all the of the enlisted soldiers' advice. He also told me to run as fast as I could on the 2-mile run of the first physical training test. "They forget who did most push-ups and who did the most sit-ups, but they remember the fastest runner and you will stand out as being motivated." As if I needed to stand out as any more motivated thanks to John's head-shaving recommendation. Just before I left, I heard one of my sisters say, "Do you think he will be OK moving away?" My stepmom said, "As long as there is ground for him to run on, he will be OK." I waved goodbye and I jumped into my seafoam metallic Buick LeSabre, with the new engine, pulled out of the driveway and headed south on Beech Street toward new ground to run on.

ALOHA

Although I had planned to pad my legal resume by serving three years in the Army as a lawyer, I enjoyed the work and the chance to move around every few years. After my initial training at Fort Lee, Virginia, I headed to Charlottesville, also in Virginia, for an introduction to military law at the Judge Advocate General's Legal Center & School, located on the north grounds of the University of Virginia. I loved it. Not only did classes end at 3:00 p.m. each day, but Charlottesville also has endless hilly running loops and great weather. A year earlier I was running loops on frigid dark nights. Now that I was free from the constraints of night law school, I took full advantage of the opportunity to run on country roads and trails in the shadows of the Shenandoah Mountains to the west. I ran for miles across many of the several golf courses in town. I had never seen such beauty and felt so good running in it.

I took my father's advice and ran as fast as I could during the PT Test on the University of Virginia track, the same track where years ago I had run my first collegiate 10,000-meter race as a first-year student. Shortly after that first PT test the personnel officer called me into his office. "Ever hear of the All-Army track team?" I sort of knew what it was as my dad had told me that if I joined the Army I could still run. The G1 (Army terminology for personnel officer) and I read Army Regulation 215-1 covering sports and recreation activities. After reading whether or not a pool was a "recreational facility" or a "water safety instructional tank," we then went through intramurals, then installation-wide sports and finally arrived at All-Army sports. The Army hosts a series of sports camps across the country for all sports: basketball, swimming, track, and even bowling. At the conclusion of each camp the respective All-Army team competes against the other services' teams.

Under track and field there was a chart with a series of qualifying times for every track and field event. The qualifying time for the 10,000-meter run was 30:00. If an athlete could certify that they met the qualifying time within the past year they could apply for acceptance to the training camp. For track and field the camp was at the Presidio, located in San Francisco, adjacent to the Golden Gate Bridge.

In late March I flew out to San Francisco and was taken by bus straight from the airport to the gym on post. There I was met by what had to have been over 100 sprinters, distance runners, and an assortment of field event athletes, both male and female. After we all took our seats in the bleachers, Mr. Garrett, the head coach, dispensed of any pleasantries and gruffly stated, "You are all here for a tryout. Just because you met the qualifying time doesn't mean you are on the team. Your units back home need you and you will be rejoining them quickly if you don't run fast every weekend."

We were then assigned to our barracks rooms, officers and enlisted alike. My roommate, Mike, was in the Infantry from Fort Benning, Georgia. He threw the shotput and discus. Not only was he extremely funny, but we also got along great. In the world of track and field, distance runners and weight throwers get along surprisingly well. After checking into my room, I quickly changed and headed out for a run. I raced across post toward the water. Now closed, at the time the Presidio was considered the crown jewel of the Army. Located within the beautiful city of San Francisco, I ran past white buildings with bright red roofs. This post didn't look like any post I had seen before. Every post I had been on previously consisted of drab yellowish-green painted wooden warehouses. As I reached the water, I saw it-- The Golden Gate Bridge. It looked so majestic compared to the Throgs Neck Bridge or Tappan Zee Bridge of my youth. The only problem was it was late afternoon. I soon realized that late afternoon in San Francisco means winds whipping off the ocean and howling under the bridge as it pushes in the daily fog and pushes back any neophytes running the bike path leading to the bridge. Undeterred, I made it and the same miserable wind guided me back towards the barracks.

Over the course of the next several weeks we ran twice a day and competed in races throughout California, races I had only dreamed of when I had seen them on TV, like the Bruce Jenner Classic and The Modesto Relays. Every Monday morning, we reported to the gym, our bags packed and sat in the bleachers as Mr. Garrett called out names. If your name was called, you had to meekly walk out of the stands, head up to Mr. Garrett as he handed you a plane ticket home and then board the bus to the airport. No goodbyes, just embarrassment. It was like junior high tryouts all over again! Fortunately, the distance runners knew where we stood each Monday heading to the gym as several seconds separated us. It was the same with the weight throwers. Sprinters, on the other hand, are separated by tenths of a second. And week after week their places may change. Sunday nights were always stressful in the barracks for the sprinters. Stress often built up to shouting matches—or more. As the senior-ranking member of the team I had to break up one too many fighters, with my shotput buddy as back up.

After a month or so the team was whittled down to two per event and the All-Army team photo was ready to be taken next the dome at the Palace of Fine Arts. Prior to reporting to the Presidio, I asked the personnel officer if I should report to the JAG (Judge Advocate General's Corps) Office to do legal work. "Nope, you are just there to run." There are only so many hours a day that you could run or throw a metal ball around, so Mike and I spent weeks touring San Francisco to the point that I started to get a bit bored going to Fisherman's Wharf, day after day. I think I knew every single attraction in the Ripley's Museum after that trip. Eventually we would travel down to Camp Pendleton Marine Corps Base near San Diego for the all- services meet. At the conclusion of that meet, we said our goodbyes and returned to home station.

My first few years in the Army I alternated track seasons in California with legal work at my assigned post-- Fort Ritchie in the Catoctin

Mountains close to Camp David. The running was fantastic in those mountains. The midpoint of the Appalachian Trail was just outside the main gate of the post, so I could run on its soft surface for hours, exploring the woods. Coming from NYC I was surprised to see foxes, bears, and coyotes on my runs. Just down the mountain was Mount St. Mary's University, home of an all-weather track and 1988 Seoul Olympics' 1500-meter gold medalist Peter Rono.

I did a handful of marathons during this time, even placing second at the Long Island Marathon. After a few years of my back-and-forth lifestyle my boss asked me "Do you want to be a runner or a lawyer?" I was falling behind my peers as far as legal work and my chances of any promotions were quickly slipping away. I decided to cease traveling to the Presidio every year, focus on the law, and run road races and marathons. Hey, Mr. Celia and Mr. Donlon did both, so could I.

I spent the next couple of years in Korea, followed by Annapolis. Annapolis is relatively close to DC, so I was able to run in the Marine Corps Marathon a few times. John had been working in a law firm and gaining weight. In July 1994 I was up at Point Lookout Beach when he asked me to go for a short run with him. On the run he declared he was leaving law firm life behind, was going to lose weight and planned to run in that fall's Marine Corps Marathon. That's a lot to take on a short run and I assumed he had cleared this with his wife.

Whether or not it was cleared with Deidre I don't know, but that fall we were both standing in the pouring rain on Route 110 in Arlington, Virginia, ready to head south in the Marine Corps Marathon. Today the race starts northward but the old course ran in the opposite direction starting with a big loop around Crystal City, Virginia.

"Make way, make way!" several Marines barked out. I was thinking does Johnny Kelley run this race as well? It wasn't Johnny Kelley, it was Oprah! She started right next to us and now the marathon was officially mainstream.

John and I ran relaxed throughout the early miles. The race route was, and still is, very spectator-friendly and Deidre was able to see us every few miles, standing on the side of the road in her leather jacket. To this day she blames me for the demise of that jacket, claiming I ruined her jacket by neither telling her about the weather forecast nor how to properly pretreat her leather coat for rain. Really? Look up at the sky; it's raining, put on a rain jacket.

We spent much of the middle part of the race discussing his new job as a lawyer for the Long Island electric company. The work was interesting, and he was not under the gun to work a certain number of billable hours like when he was at the firm. His life was much more balanced, and he was happy. Back in law school he would on occasion run in the dark with me telling me his goal of getting a yacht and working in a big NYC law firm. A rowboat with a balanced life is much more enjoyable.

We never really hit a wall, although we did slow down. Now, as in 1994, the Marine Corps Marathon ends at the Iwo Jima Memorial. Today, runners head north on Route 110, and with about 300 meters to go, make a sharp left turn and climb a short steep hill before making a right-hand turn onto the US Marine Corps Memorial Drive Access Road where they sprint. crawl, jog, or walk to the finish line right in front of the memorial. It makes for a great finisher photo.

Back in 1994 runners followed this same basic route but did not finish in front of the memorial. Rather, they continued onto the US Marine Corps Memorial Drive Access Road running behind the memorial and finished on the grass next to the Netherlands Carillon, perhaps 200 meters south of Iwo Jima Memorial. Today with fields of over 30,000 runners such a finish line is not possible. Back in 1994 as John and I had about 200 meters to the finish, he started sprinting, shouting-- "It's a race, isn't it?" I was shocked, I just paced you for 26 miles and now you sprint. I was in no mood to sprint, but I was in no mood to lose, so I picked it up. With five yards to go he started to dip like Carl Lewis finishing the 100-meter dash. We both crossed in 3:33:33. We will never know who won because chip timing did not exist in 1994.

I ran the Marine Corps Marathon the following year on a much sunnier day in order to get a qualifying time for the upcoming 100th Boston

Marathon. Each year that I returned to the start line on Route 110 the field size increased, however the registration process was still relatively simple and no one who applied of the race was turned away. The logistics of the races was changing slightly, as Gatorade was placed on the hydration stations in addition to the standard cups of water. Unsuspecting runners who didn't pay attention to volunteers shouting, "Water on your right, Gatorade on your left," would douse themselves in cups of lime-green Gatorade only to run the rest of the race feeling rather sticky.

In April 1996, I returned to Boston and was greeted by over 36,000 runners. Gone was the strict qualification system. Now, in addition to qualifying based on time, runners could obtain entry to the race through a lottery. Also gone was the ability to hang out in Hopkinton High School before the race as the new Athlete's Village sprung up overnight like the circus coming to town. And what a circus it was! Every street in Hopkinton was filled with runners. No longer did all runners start on Main Street. Runners had to wear turquoise cotton wristbands with a black letter imprinted on it. These wristbands were huge and resembled the ones Kareem Abdul-Jabbar wore in Lakers' games. Runners had to line up on various side streets according to wristband letter. After the gun fired, those on Main Street started running. As Main Street emptied out, those on side streets could join the course as their letters were called. It was complicated but it worked. To ease runners' nerves about how long it would take to snake through the streets of Hopkinton to reach the start line, chip timing was used.

This was the first time I used chip timing and it has come a long way since. Today a small microchip is embedded on each runner's number to provide an accurate time from start line to finish line. There are no more finishers' race certificates noting that you could deduct two minutes from your race time based on your approximate place at the start. In the 1990s blue mega-chips about the size of a matchbox were either affixed to race numbers or tied to runners' shoes. Runners seemed to prefer the chips tied to shoes both for physical and mental comfort because a laced-on microchip was more comfortable than a matchbox continually hitting your chest. Runners also trusted that a chip on their shoes would record a more accurate time being closer to the start and finishing mats. They feared that the mats could not activate the chip four feet higher affixed to their number on their chests. I saw many a runner with a chip affixed to a race number bending over the computer mats at the start and finish to ensure their chip was activated.

At the completion of a marathon in the late 1990s and early 2000s, runners had to either tear the microchip off their race number or bend down in excruciating pain to untie the chip from their shoe and drop it in a huge plastic bin. The chips on bibs were much more user-friendly at this stage of the event. In either case, failure to return a chip resulted in a thirty-dollar fee being assessed to you, since the chips were reusable.

A few weeks after the 100th Boston Marathon I was headed to paradise. I had orders for the 25th Infantry Division at Schofield Barracks in Oahu, Hawaii. Right before I left Sergeant First Class King told me, "25th ID, you'll be in the field a lot." Little did I know. I had seen pictures in Hawaii in surf magazines and had seen the Brady Bunch visit Hawaii in a two-part episode. The kind of two-part episodes before Netflix binge-watching. The kind of episode that ended with a cliffhanger and the dreaded "To be continued" caption scrolling across the screen, forcing you to wait an entire week to find out if Greg Brady survived the wipeout on a surfboard. Aside from that I really didn't know much about Hawaii, let alone where it was located. After a short layover in Los Angeles our pilot greeted us, "This is your Captain speaking, thank you for choosing United Airlines. It looks like we have good weather today and our flight time will be five hours and 15 minutes." What? Five hours? I honestly thought Hawaii was just off the coast of California, perhaps a 30-minute flight. I flipped open the in-flight magazine. By the time we flew over Catalina Island, the island that I had mistaken for Hawaii when I looked at maps, I knew the location of every Ruth's Chris steakhouse in the United States and knew how Paul Reiser of *Mad About You* liked to unwind when he was visiting Sedona. The next four hours I just stared and stared at the headrest in front of me. And stared.

"You run the Honolulu Marathon this morning?" Five months after my very long flight I was in line one early December Sunday evening at the

Schofield Barracks Post Exchange, the military version of Walmart. My boss two cashier stations over shouted out that question. That morning had been the 24th running of the annual Honolulu Marathon. I thought of saying, "What kind of a question is that? I arrived on this island on an early July Wednesday evening, Two days later was on a plane to Korea for a monthlong training exercise called Ulchi Focus Lens. I arrived back on Labor Day from Korea. Five nights later you called me at 3:45 a.m. waking me up for a no-notice deployment saying, 'You need to be ready to go, wheels up at 07:30, have your ruck with you. I can't say where you are going or when you will be back.' Then when I returned from that deployment in early November you said, 'I hate to do this to you but tomorrow you have to go to Fort Lewis Washington for the Corps Warfighter Exercise.' Now knowing all that, how in the world do you think it would be possible for me to have prepared for a marathon?"

Discretion is the better part of valor.

"No Sir, I didn't have enough time to train, maybe next year."

Over the course of the next year, once again I didn't have enough time to prepare, but ran the race anyway, along the way learning the valuable lesson: never underestimate the marathon.

Not only is the weather in Hawaii perfect for year-round running along beautiful beaches, on mountain trails, or through famous Waikiki Beach, but the race scene is extremely varied. Unlike large metropolitan areas in which one can find a handful of races each weekend, often several local 5K competing against each other for participants, it does take some digging to find smaller races on Oahu. On the other hand. there are grand affairs such as the annual Great Aloha Run and the Honolulu Marathon with thousands of finishers.

The smaller races tend to be tightknit events with locals gleefully greeting each other upon arrival, seemingly knowing every detail of each other's lives and health status.

"How's the ankle, Bob?"

"Did you get in your long run last week, Shirley?"

"Are the keikis starting kindergarten this year?"

Queen Kapi'olani Regional Park on the Pacific Ocean, bordered by the Honolulu Zoo to the west and Diamond Head to the east, is a welcome oasis of green grass amongst the thin stretch of white sand surrounded by Waikiki's 118 hotels boasting 30,000 rooms for Oahu's biggest import: tourists. Although one of the most famous beaches in the world, only one block from the shoreline, Kalakaua Avenue cuts a path through high-end stores such as Burberry's, touristy restaurants, hotels, and countless ABC convenience stores, seemingly one ABC store on every block. Kapi'olani Park offers a quiet respite from Waikiki's hustle and bustle.

On the western edge of the park sits the Waikiki Bandshell, which in addition to hosting various concerts, also serves as the finisher T-shirt distribution center the day after the Honolulu Marathon. To the east lies Diamond Head towering over the park. The two-mile path that borders the park is a favorite running spot for both locals and tourists. More than one runner has taken a spill or twisted an ankle on this path, tripping over the gnarly banyan tree roots that have grown through the asphalt. It's also a starting point for longer runs through the surrounding neighborhoods. An early morning run around the park offers the highlight of hearing the lions roar as the sun rises over the ocean.

It was at Kapi'olani Park that my friend, and great running partner, Nicole learned just how tight the running community is. Prior to my arrival in Hawaii, while I was stationed at Fort Meade in Maryland, one of my duties was to recruit law students from both the University of Maryland Law School and University of Baltimore School of Law into the Army JAGC.

"Aren't you the guy who interviews law students for the Army?" queried a colonel standing in my office doorway.

"Yes Sir."

"Great. I work over at the dentist's office here on post and my son just graduated from law school and wants to join the JAG Corps. He'll stop in next Tuesday for an interview."

As glanced down at my calendar I noticed "Day Off" written in red for that day. "Sir, I have off next Tuesday."

"Like I said, my son Fred will be here next Tuesday."

Fred's interview went very well. About a year later at 6:00 a.m. PT formation in Hawaii I looked to my right and said to the office newbie, "Aren't you the guy who cost me a day off?" Fred's wife Nicole is an avid runner who I ran with often in Hawaii. Years later I ran the NYC Marathon with both Fred and Nicole.

As Nicole and I arrived at Kapi'olani Park on Saturday for a short local race, we were not greeted by "How are the keikis?" We both felt like Owen Wilson and Vince Vaughn of *Wedding Crashers*. Over time we learned that the residents are extremely friendly and welcoming.

On the other end of the spectrum lie the big annual races such as the Great Aloha Run (GAR), held every February on President's Day. Twenty-five thousand runners congregate in the early morning hours in the parking lot of Aloha Stadium. Bus after bus shuttles runners to the start line at the Aloha Tower eight miles away in Honolulu. Amongst these thousands of runners are approximately 5,000 service members in the accompanying "Sounds of Freedom" division. The race is awesome in that it raises hundreds of thousands of dollars for local community charities. The race is also a terrific event for those who don't feel capable of running a marathon but wish to challenge themselves.

As a runner I loved the race with its finish at the 50-yard line of Aloha Stadium. As an Army lawyer the race was an annual nightmare. Every year the race director presented a huge trophy to the commander of the service that had the highest number of runners. The Navy, Air Force, and Army all coveted this award. Commanders offered all types of incentives. Since the race was on a federal holiday, if you ran you could have the following Friday off. If more than fifty percent of the unit ran, the entire unit could have that Friday off. I suspect lots of individuals paid the thirty-five-dollar entry fee, slept in on race day and took Friday off. The dilemma I had was that the Army is limited in what support and endorsement it can offer to a private organization and the GAR is put on by a private organization. Our legal office had an entire five-inch-thick binder, labeled GAR, stuffed with legal opinions on the left and right limits of support that could be offered. That binder is handed to every new lawyer in the office accompanied by, "Good luck." I don't know how many times I heard "Well, that's the way we always did it." Starting in the fall of each year until each February I carefully walked a tightrope crafting out ways to legally continue the "Sounds of Freedom" division.

One now defunct race was the Mid-Pacific Road Runners Club Oahu Perimeter Relay. Year ago, Mr. Celia said you could see Long Island on foot by running various road races. I saw all of Oahu by foot over one night. One very long night. As the name indicates the relay circled the island of Oahu, starting and finishing at Kapi'olani Park. It was a logistical nightmare, but the organizers did a masterful job every February. Teams of seven runners ran thirty-five legs covering a grand total of 134 miles. Each leg ranged from approximately three miles to seven miles. Teams were free to choose how to divide their legs, with most teams simply having runner one run a leg, then have the next six runners run a leg in succession, and then repeat the process with runner one starting again. This process repeated itself five times. Due to the difference in the length of each leg, runners one and two ran the most miles, close to thirty miles each, whereas runner seven topped out at about 18 miles.

The race was capped at 140 teams. Start times were staggered, to avoid congestion at relay handoff locations, with the first twenty teams leaving Kapi'olani Park about 2:00 p.m. on whatever Saturday in February had the fullest moon to provide light throughout the night. Every hour until 8:00 p.m., twenty teams stepped off, the fastest of which left at 8:00 p.m. I ran with six infantry soldiers who were members of the 25th Infantry Division's war planning staff. It's not as if I was thrown onto a random team, as I had daily interaction with this group, providing legal advice to ensure that all their plans complied with the Geneva Conventions and other international laws.

At 8:00 p.m. sharp our lead runner took off with nineteen others. As soon as the gun fired, 20 vans raced out of the park and drove to the first handoff spot over six miles away. We arrived at the changeover spot with nineteen other vans and joined other vans still there from the previous stagger. The changeover spot was a huge strip mall parking lot. This was no four runners by 800 meters relay that I had run in high school, and I wasn't too certain the warm up protocol so I just jogged a bit as I saw our runner come into view. I took the baton and headed off on the most scenic road on Oahu; it is the road seen during the opening of each episode of *Magnum P.I.* with Thomas driving on a winding road next to waves crashing against rocks. That was my leg, except it was dark and I was not driving red Ferrari while wearing a Detroit Tigers baseball cap with cool music playing in the background and TC's helicopter flying overhead. My leg had an odd amount of mileage and ended in a beach parking lot. I entered the van and quickly read the race instruction sheet that laid out every leg distance, starting location, finishing location plus warnings for each leg, i.e., watch out for speeding cars on the winding road seen in the *Magnum P.I.* TV series. I wish I had read that before my leg. No roads were closed for the relay and vans drove up ahead to the next changeover spot, leaving runners on their own in the dark. A review of the instructions also shed light on the fact that relay leg distances were based on parking lot size around the island. Every leg was basically from whatever parking lot could hold several vans to the next parking lot that could hold several vans, hence the odd lengths of each leg, i.e., 4.3 miles from the Zippy parking lot to the next beach parking lot.

As we drove through the night I had about three hours until my next leg. Running a hard six miles, then sitting in a van for three hours, then running again followed by sitting in a cramped van in an endless cycle wreaks havoc on your legs. My second leg was run along the windward coast of the island. At times, the road was only feet from the ocean, which was lit up beautifully by the full moon. My only concern was the race instruction sheet stating, "Be careful, we had problems with wild dogs on this leg last year." As I ran alone at midnight I looked to the beautiful ocean on my right and continued to look to my left for Dobermans ready to pounce from behind the next bush. Leg three took me on a 3:30 a.m. jaunt from Sunset Beach to Waimea Bay on Oahu's North Shore, famous for its thirty-foot waves in the winter ridden by the best surfers in the world. I could hear these huge waves crashing to my right.

As we continued to circle the island not only did the running take a toll, but the lack of sleep did as well. Pretty much no one sleeps at all during the perimeter relay. Every thirty minutes or so the vans stop, and runners shout encouragement as baton handoffs are made-- not the best sleeping conditions. By the start of my fourth leg the sun was high in the sky as I ran on the hottest part of the island, the Leeward side. Not often seen in tourism magazines this part of the island is rather dry with cactus dotting the sides of the road. By the time I ran my final leg on a bike path that went right past the Arizona Memorial my legs were shot. But I didn't care as I gazed at the stark white memorial across the harbor. My legs may have been tired, but it didn't compare in the least to what those sailors experienced December 7, 1941.

I have no idea what our team's place or time was. All I remember is our anchor leg, Dave Ross, who was built much more like a football player than a runner, sprinting down the sidewalk in Waikiki towards Kapi'olani Park ready to knock over any tourists who got in his way. After 134 miles and 16 hours in a van runners get cranky.

Not only did I have a great experience seeing part of the island I never saw before, but I was also now fully immersed in the Hawaii running scene and was ready to take on the Honolulu Marathon ten months away.

Movies, TV, and magazines always feature the beaches of Hawaii with their crystal- clear blue water, white sand, and palm trees. Yes, those exist but make up only a fraction of the islands. Each island in the Hawaiian Island chain is shaped like tall green cones thousands of feet high. The lush green peaks of each island slowly descend downward to the beautiful beaches that form a white sandy half-mile wide ring around each island. These exterior rings are where most hotels are located. Head inland a bit and the islands are filled with tropical rain forests complete with towering waterfalls. Due to this unique geography one day you can run flat loops around beautiful sunny Kapi'olani Park and the next day be two miles inland running for 30 minutes uphill in the rain along Round Top Road feeling as if you are on the set of *Jurassic Park* running past leaves as big as cars, followed a thirty-minute dash downhill through groves of guava trees.

The relatively small size of each island offers ample opportunity for extremely varied training. Long forgotten were my endless nighttime loops around Wantagh Elementary School's fields or runs along the Jones Beach bike path. One evening I could leave work and drive 20 minutes to the North Shore, park at Shark's Cove (I never actually saw or heard of a shark ever being there) and run along the flat Ke Ala Pupukea bike path to Sunset Beach and back. The path, which is surrounded by thick tropical vegetation, offers views of the famous Bonzai Pipeline. Along the way I shared the path with hundreds of free-range chickens, roosters and surfers balancing their boards on their bikes.

If I wanted to stay closer to home, I could run from my office on Schofields Barracks heading west on Trimble Avenue and begin a long, steady ascent for six miles up to the top of the Kolekole Pass, to reach the 2,000-feet high summit in the Waianae Mountain range. The first mile of the run passes through the post's golf course, a few homes, and a gas station. For the next four miles the road weaves through some valleys as well as Army training sites, a red flag at each signifying live firing as a warning to be careful. The final mile is the steepest as the road switches back and forth to the peak. At the top runners are rewarded with a spectacular view of the entire western coast of Oahu followed by a nice six-mile run, all downhill. A military guard post sits on the border of the Army post and the Navy base that lies on the other side of the pass. Once a year the pass is open to the public for a half-marathon that starts on the Army post and finishes on the Navy base.

On weekends I could drive down toward the city and run along the roads surrounding Diamond Head to Ala Moana Park and Magic Island. Every Sunday night I would do my long runs in town along these routes with Nicole since she and Fred had an apartment in Waikiki. And every Sunday night as we ran along the Ala Wai Canal that forms the northern border of Waikiki we used to see a man walking his large pet pig. As

President Biden would say "C'mon Man." C'mon man, you're living in the city, not on a farm. Where is that pig housed, in the living room of your apartment? Maybe that's not too odd, as years ago a man in Harlem had a full-grown tiger living with him in a tiny apartment. That is until, you guessed it, the tiger attacked him. To this day Nicole reminds me of seeing Pig Man walking into the sunset along the canal.

My training was coming along beautifully. I was somewhat busy at work so made sure I kept everything flexible, and my week-to-week plans were moving along great. There is an old Army adage that every plan is great until the first shot is fired. That shot came in the form of our division's warfighter exercise. In late October, the dates were announced, with the start date being the Sunday two weeks prior the marathon race day and the exercise ending the night before the race. Two weeks straight, both day and night in the field didn't seem like the best marathon taper to me. I suddenly remembered Sergeant First Class King's farewell remarks from Fort Meade "25th ID, you will be in the field a lot."

I didn't have to assess the situation long as a friend of mine from Annapolis called a few days later proclaiming, "I'm running Honolulu, can you pace me?" TJ had never run a marathon before, and we had done several longish run together on the Baltimore and Annapolis Trail in Annapolis.

"How fast you looking to run?"

"About four and a half hours."

"Done deal."

I figured how hard could four and a half hours be? No running for two weeks leading up to the race, no problem for this pace. How wrong I was. My mom used to say, "Pride cometh before a fall." Boy, did I fall hard.

The registration process for Honolulu was easy and with a new thing called the Internet you could even register online. Back in the 1990s the Honolulu Marathon even allowed runners to sign up the day before the race at the Expo. Marathoners of today, imagine that, registering the day before a marathon. Today many marathons' race capacity is reached often up to six months in advance, requiring runners to invest several hundred dollars in entry fees for a race they have no idea they will run depending on injuries, work schedule, etc. over the course of those next six months. To put icing on the cake, in 1997 the fee for military members was two dollars. Over the years I have overheard several soldiers say after finishing a PT run on Friday morning, "I felt pretty good today, I am going to sign up for Sunday's marathon."

TJ and I both registered over the Internet and for an additional fee were able to purchase of our race-timing microchip complete with race logo stamped on the small plastic white circle.

With about six weeks until race day my motivation went down a bit. Based on the warfighter I knew I would not run too fast, plus I was now a pacer. I continued to run but my runs progressively got shorter. I rationalized my lighter running routine, thinking to myself, "How hard can it be? I've done dozens of these races." Never underestimate the marathon. No matter what pace you intend to run, you must be physically and mentally ready to be on your feet for 26 miles.

On Sunday, November 30, I hopped into a HUMVEE and rolled out to the field. My rucksack was devoid of any running apparel or sneakers. From now until Saturday December 13, I was strictly in heavy boots and BDU (Battle Dress Uniform). Notionally our Division's Headquarter was in some foreign country, but in reality, we were in an open field at the base of the Kolekole Pass. For the next two weeks we would be engaged with battle against our dreaded foe that on paper seemed eerily like an actual country. We seemed to constantly be at war with this foe as they were our adversaries in every field exercise. Couldn't we just negotiate a peace treaty, call this off and all go home? Everything our adversary threw at us was computer-generated. We had to either respond defensively or make some offensive maneuvers ourselves.

Our compound consisted of a series of green canvas tents cobbled together to form one large headquarters. Inside was a buzz of activity as my division planning staff perimeter relay partners constantly monitored the computers, calling out for assistance, "JAG, can we target such and such?" "Personnel, when are we getting those replacements?" as they acted and reacted to the battle.

Just outside of the main tent was the mess tent; a small structure in which our one hot meal per day was prepared and served to us. Scattered throughout the area were several sleeping tents. I volunteered to do the night shift: 7:00 p.m. to 7:00 a.m. The night shift can be extremely busy as often we fight at night to take advantage of the cover that darkness provides.

For the next two weeks I embarked on the worst pre-race marathon prep ever. My nights were filled with answering questions about the Geneva Conventions, explaining the rules regarding EPWs (Enemy Prisoners-of-War) and assorted other legal questions. The first night is always the hardest as you must flip-flop your sleep schedule, but by night three your internal clock has flipped the switch. After getting relieved of duty at 7:00 a.m., I would head to the mess tent for some sort of eggs, sausage, and a muffin. Soldiers eat extremely fast for a variety of reasons, including the desire to get back to work and the desire not to congregate in a mess tent that could serve as a large, crowded target.

With breakfast consumed by 7:10 a.m., I headed over to my sleep tent; an eight-foot-wide by eight-foot-long by eight-foot-tall green canvas sweat lodge. Inside was a small green cot and my rucksack, all planted on tall wet grass. As the sun continued to rise each day the canvas captured it, acting like a radiator to heat the tent to well over 100 degrees. Under the base of each thin metal leg of my cot I placed a lid from a large jar of jelly that I filled each day with rubbing alcohol. The lid and alcohol formed a moat that the eight-inch-long centipedes and other insects could not traverse, thus allowing me lie alone in that hard cot without the company of roaches. Hawaii is beautiful, but within those beautiful rainforests live some of the nastiest looking bugs in the world.

For the next several hours I would toss and turn, alternating sleeping and sweating. At about 6:00 p.m., I would put on my uniform and "battle rattle," consisting of helmet, flak vest, and an awkward fitting belt from which hung an endless variety of pouches for items such as first aid kits and bullets. Just a few months prior those ammo pouches caught the eye of my commander.

My boss had called me at 3:45 a.m. telling me to be ready for "wheels up" at 7:30 a.m. for a no-notice deployment. I packed as best as I could. I had returned home from Korea just five days earlier so I had tossed all my military equipment in the attic thinking, "I won't be needing this stuff for a while." I reassembled my gear as best I could in the hot dark attic then raced to the office. Once I learned where we were headed, I quickly researched everything I could of the laws of that country. I then reported to the Infantry Brigade Commander whose unit I would be providing legal advice to. Wheels up at 7:30 a.m. turned into wheels down at 7:30 a.m., then 8:30 a.m., then 9:30 a.m. There is an old Army saying, "Hurry up and wait." And we waited and waited. I got a bit bored, so I snuck out of the pre-staging area and walked over to the Inn at Schofield Barracks Shoppette to grab an ice cream cone. The vanilla ice cream was dripping down the sides of the cone onto my hands, and I am sure the chocolate was smeared on my face, as I arrived back at the pre-staging area only to hear the Commander shout "OK, now that you have your ammo, let's load the buses and head to Hickham!" (Hickham Air Force Base is adjacent to Pearl Harbor Naval Base.) I tossed what remained of the cone in the trash, wiped any incriminating chocolate off my face, and got in line. I stood there in a long line of infantry soldiers, all of whom had full ammo pouches, as bullets had been distributed while I was sneaking out to get an ice cream cone. I tore a few pages from my chest-pocket notebook, crumpled them up, and shoved them in my ammo pouches. As the lengthy line of soldiers walked across the tarmac toward the plane, our commander walked back and forth along the line, ensuring that we were all dress right, dress.

"Those are the weirdest looking ammo pouches I have ever seen, Captain."

"Well Sir, you never know what you will get at CIF." (CIF being Central Issue Facility, the Army has an acronym everything.)

As I sat on the plane wondering if tossing paper at any foes would be a good strategy, I said the guy on my left, "If anything goes down, dude, you gotta lend me some bullets."

Dangling from my ill-fitting belt out in the field during our warfighter sat two 1940s-era plastic canteens full of water smashing into my hips on each step. In 26 years, I don't think I ever drank out one those canteens but we sure were required to keep them filled because "It's in the regulation." Commanders cite "It's in the regulation." constantly without ever producing a copy of said regulation. I wish I had the guts just once to say, "OK, show me the regulation."

Prior to heading to answer tough legal questions about fictitious farmers wanting to know if they can file fictitious claims against the US Army for fictitious cows injured by fictitious landmines, I would chow down on the military calorie bomb: the MRE, Meal Ready to Eat. MREs did, and still do, come in a thick tan plastic pouch, plastic so thick that it is almost impossible to tear open. Stamped on the outside is the name of the "entrée" such as beef stew, or spaghetti. Anything else inside is random. It's just an odd assortment of candy like Skittles, tiny bottles the size of a thimble filled with red Tabasco sauce, crackers, and cheese-spread stuffed into an equally hard to open plastic pouch, coffee creamer, and some sort of pound cake. Also, inside is some sort of heating element into which you place water in a pouch that contains magnesium, iron, and salt. The chemical reaction instantly heats up the water, which you use to heat up your beef stew. The chemical reaction smells horrible. When I would wear my uniform into Cam's elementary school Career Day each Spring, the eight-year-olds are at first fascinated by the chemical reaction. That fascination quickly turns to pleas of "Open a window, it smells horrible in here!" Some old timers love the MREs, creating bartering circles to procure the items needed for their secret recipes. "If you mix the coffee creamer with the cocoa powder, add in some Tabasco sauce then heat it up you have yourself a nice spicy candy bar." No, you don't, you have Tabasco sauce, coffee creamer, and cocoa powder congealing in the bottom of a white Styrofoam cup. All too often when the traders approached me, I would just say take the whole thing, handing over my MRE knowing that I was not interested in consuming any of its contents.

Such was my carbo-loading leading to the Honolulu Marathon. I ate eggs each morning then headed straight to bed. I then ate portions of an MRE before sitting in a chair for hours answering questions about fictitious farmers. I could feel my awkward belt getting tighter and tighter as the Honolulu Marathon finish line seemed further and further away.

Around the third night of the exercise, I realized that there was a lull each night from around 2:00 a.m. to 3:00 a.m. Decks of playing cards were pulled out from secret compartments and Solitaire filled computer screens. I can only assume that the nightshift individuals running the computers for our foe were either asleep or also playing poker. I figured I could use this time to get in some exercise. Every night at 2:00 a.m. I would say to my paralegal "Cover for me." as I put on my full-battle rattle, left the compound, and took long walks in the dark up to the top of Kolekole Pass and back. It reminded me my Wantagh night loops. Had I known beforehand about our headquarters turning into a poker game each night, I would have pre-stashed sneakers in the bushes along the Kolekole Pass and changed into them. Each night as I returned, I could see the small light on in the mess tent and smell the bacon and eggs being prepared. Although I knew those two weeks were not the best pre-race preparation, I still look back fondly on those 2:00 a.m. walks.

Except for one night. Large mean wild boars frequented the area. One night as I was heading down from the summit, I heard some rustling in the bushes, but not the rustling you hear when a squirrel scampers through the woods. At 2:30 a.m. on a pitch-dark road in the rainforest your mind plays tricks on you. However, the bright eyes I saw from the bushes when I shined my flashlight were no David Copperfield trick. Apparently shining a flashlight straight into a wild boar's eyes pisses them off and it let out a shriek that in no way sounded cute like Wilbur the pig in *Charlotte's Web*. As that beast dashed toward me I ran down that hill as fast as I could, those canteens smashing into my hips every step of the way. I don't know how long the boar followed me, but if there is a world record for running in Army boots with full battle rattle on for 400 meters I hold it. I got back to our headquarters, sweaty and out of breath, slumping into a chair, muttering, "Don't ask." to my paralegal.

Nights turned into weeks. I had no idea how the battle was going. I have a challenging time concentrating on made-up events, be it a war against a fictitious foe, or a moot court session in preparation for trial. Finally, Saturday December 13 arrived. As I left the headquarters tent a little after 7:00 a.m., I called back to the day shift crew "Wake me when it's over!" I assumed the battle would rage on until around noon, a winner would be declared, and we could break down the tents with the sun still overhead and head home. So, when my alarm rang at 6:00 p.m., I was a little bit more than surprised, and I was angry. I dressed and headed into the headquarters. "Is this almost over?" Apparently, our foe was more formidable than usual and refused to roll over and die. As the battled raged on I counted down the hours until the 5:00 a.m. marathon start time.

Finally, at 9:00 p.m. victory was declared. Still undefeated against this particular foe! Right after calling EXDEX (end of exercise) the commanding general shouted out, "All those stupid enough to be running the Honolulu Marathon tomorrow morning are free to leave!" I grabbed a ride back to the main post in a HUMVEE, jumped in my car, and drove to my house to shower for the first time in two weeks. After I cleaned a couple weeks' worth of sweat and dirt off, I scarfed down an extremely hot microwave personal pizza and chased it down with a Coke as I drove down to Waikiki.

That first Coke in two weeks was the sweetest nectar ever. Years later I attempted to give up Coke for Lent. I read that caffeine withdrawal was a serious issue, so Monday morning at work I downed a five-hour energy drink and chewed a pack of Jolt chewing gum to avoid the jitters. Wow! I could barely talk, I couldn't type a word on my computer as my fingers flew over the keyboard, and I continually paced back and forth in my executive administrative assistant's office, climbing up and down off the furniture while uncontrollably laughing. She quickly told me to give up something else for Lent.

Back in high school my cross country team met every Friday night at Mike's Firehouse Pizza on Merrick Road right near the entrance to Cedar Creek Park to carbo-load before our Saturday invitationals. If it was good enough for Mr. Brynes, it was good enough for me, plus it had to be better than an MRE the night before a race. I drove down the H2 to the H1, the Totino's pizza burning the roof of my mouth the entire way.

I arrived at Fred and Nicole's apartment shortly after 10:00 p.m. and TJ was already there. Fred and Nicole lived in one of Waikiki's many high-rise apartments. They liked to proclaim they had an ocean view. They had at best a "partial" ocean view. From their 15th floor unit if you looked carefully, you could catch slivers of the Pacific Ocean between the Red Lobster and Illiki Hotel across the street. Their patio also was the roosting spot for many of Waikiki's pigeons. Nicole was constantly racing onto the patio swinging newspapers to shoo them away. "Coo coo coo coo" was the melody of their apartment.

With about six hours till race time, catching glimpses of the ocean and chasing pigeons were not my main concerns. I needed sleep. I volunteered to sleep on the sofa. However, as my sleep cycle for the past two weeks was to sleep during the day and work at night, I was wide-awake. As I lay there, in lieu of sheep I tried counting the lights in the hotel rooms across the street. I wound up spending most of the night standing and walking around on the patio. Fortunately, the pigeons were scavenging the day's leftovers on the beach and never bothered me. Their apartment was only a few blocks from the start line, and I spent the night watching the herculean effort of hundreds of race volunteers transforming Ala Moana Boulevard from a six-lane thoroughfare for vehicles into the start line for 30,000 runners. It was incredible; once the road closed to traffic around 1:00 a.m., they quickly dove into action setting up endless tables of water and Gatorade, putting up the metal starting arch, and doing a million other things to welcome us in the morning. If you have ever run a marathon and not witnessed this in action, you have no idea how much effort is put into the event.

At around 3:00 a.m. runners started to descend from hotels and walk west on Ala Moana Boulevard toward the start. From overhead I could see more runners make their way from side streets and converge onto Ala Moana. They looked like silver dots as many were draped in the tinfoil blankets distributed at the race expo.

TJ and I joined the procession at about 3:30 a.m. with Nicole promising us she would be right outside of her apartment as we would run by at about the 7.5-mile mark. Fred made no such promises. I don't even think he was awake. TJ and I walked down Ala Moana sans tinfoil blankets as I could not attend the expo and TJ, the marathon novice who picked up our race packets, had no idea what the blankets were when he was offered a few. Not that it really mattered. It was already warm, and bit humid, as we lined up in the middle of the pack, Ala Moana shopping center to our right and Ala Moana Beach Park to our left. Dri-Fit clothing was still not in vogue so I had cut off the sleeves of a white cotton second infantry division T-shirt to craft my own singlet. I hoped that the famous unit crest of a yellow lighting bolt on a large red taro leaf would draw more cheers than my Bethpage GO shirt.

Although it was extremely early everyone seemed wide-awake, except me. It was getting close to the time that I had been going to sleep for the past few weeks. Although the field size was comparable to the number of participants at the 100th Boston Marathon, it did not feel as crowded as the runners were spread across six lanes of traffic, more the triple the size of Main Street in Hopkinton.

TJ and I discussed the fact that we would stick strictly to ten minutes per mile. Starting mid-back was not a problem, first because based on our projected pace we were at the right spot and second, with chip timing it really didn't matter any more where runners lined up.

At 5:00 a.m., the boom of the huge Howitzer, which both startled runners and set them in motion at the same time, signaled the race start. A howitzer is a large long-range artillery weapon designed to fire mortars, or blanks, in the case of the marathon start. Every summer I had to draft the legal opinion that it was OK for the 25th Infantry Division to use one of these big guns for the ceremonial marathon start.

Within seconds of the Howitzer blast the sky to our left was instantly lit up by spectacular fireworks that would rival Macy's Fourth of July show; the red and white rockets lit up the sky and illuminated the Pacific Ocean into a sea of red with their reflections. There is no marathon start in the world as grand as Honolulu's. With the smoke of the Howitzer and the sight of the red rockets as our guide, 30,000 marathoners headed westward on Ala Moana Boulevard to invade the ghost town that was downtown Honolulu on a early Sunday morning.

Within a mile, runners passed the Aloha Tower. TJ and I hit the mile exactly in 10:00, right on pace. Although it was warm it certainly was not unbearable and the early 5:00 a.m. start kept runners under the cover of darkness for almost the first two hours of the race. We continued to click off ten-minute miles as we made a large loop around the center of Honolulu. The town was eerily quiet as we passed restaurants and bars decked out in Christmas decorations, which to a northerner like me felt out of place. I was used to snow and cold air and hot chocolate around the holidays. A huge blow-up Santa in a Hawaiian Shirt open to the belly giving the shaka sign at mile three didn't sit right with me. Like I said, it was a ghost town devoid of spectators except for a few bar employees here and there closing after cashing out the till.

At mile six we turned back onto Ala Moana and headed east towards Waikiki and Diamond Head. I was surprised at how easy and consistent our pace was. Ask any marathoner and they will say the same. "The first six miles flew by." It's the final six miles that make or break the race. We were still fourteen miles away from the make-or-break point. At mile 7.5 Nicole gleefully cheered us on. Fred was nowhere to be found, claiming he feared I would throw cups of water on him if he appeared.

As a race in a tropical location, there was an ample supply of water along the course, as well as Gatorade. I did also notice something new being handed out: gels. These tiny packets about the size of a McDonald's ketchup packet were new on the running scene. I had never seen one before and certainly didn't want to try one out for the first time on race day. Early gel packets were filled with a peanut-butter-like substance designed to provide electrolytes and carbohydrates to runners. Taken with water they were fuel on the go. Over the years more companies have entered the market, offering a variety of flavors, both with and without caffeine. For many marathoners today. choosing the right gel is a science experiment as they try new varieties on their weekly long runs.

As we entered the mile-long stretch of Kalakaua Avenue that cut through Waikiki, passing water, Gatorade, and gel stations, I thought back to my dad handing me a Coke at mile twenty shouting, "Kick it in!" Even if gels existed in 1979 I doubt my Dad and I would have put them on our training table. He was not just old-school for sports; he was oldest school for sports. "Why do you need to be spending money on some toothpaste in plastic packet-- Coke has everything you need."

As we passed hotels and the old Waikiki Theatre marquee beckoning us to see *Good Will Hunting*, we were cheered on by many tourists doing the "first day in town early morning walk." The time difference between the mainland and Hawaii varies from a six hour difference from the East Coast to a three hour difference from the West Coast. For tourists arriving from the East Coast, 5:00 a.m. on day one of their trip feels like 11:00 a.m. and they are all up bright and early excited to see their first Hawaii sunrise as they aimlessly wander Kalakaua Boulevard before the sun comes up and the ABC stores open.

At the easternmost point of Waikiki we did a big loop around Kapi'olani Park, catching our first glimpse of the finish line we would be crossing in a few hours. We were still hitting ten minutes a mile exactly as we continued our conversational pace. We were catching up, with me continually asking about Annapolis, a town I had previously lived. "Are the Peppertones still playing at Ego Alley on Thursday nights?" Along the way we bumped into a few runners I had served with over the years at various locations.

Rounding Kapi'olani Park in the dark the runners had thinned out considerably and we no longer had to dodge runners along the course. I thought to myself, why was I so worried the past two weeks, this is a piece a cake. I should write the new training book *Run Your Best Marathon With No Training*. It would be a bestseller, the new *The Complete Book of Running* for the masses. Pride cometh before a fall.

In the movie *Something About Mary*, Matt Dillon, playing the role of Private Investigator Pat Healy, says to Ben Stiller, "First crack in the armor, Ted." As we left Kapi'olani Park and headed east on a long gradual uphill along Diamond Head Road under the dark silhouette of Diamond Head volcano to our north, I had the first crack in the armor. Maybe because this was the first time that we were running uphill, maybe it was because it was getting close to my bedtime of the past two weeks, maybe it was the MRE carbo-loading, or maybe it was a combination of all three. I was getting concerned as we passed gated mansion after gated mansion, plus the house from MTV's *The Real World*. MTV tried to keep the house's location a secret, but my buddy Andy and I figured out within two minutes what house it was so we spent weeks jogging on the seawall path behind the house hoping to get a glimpse of the first reality TV show's celebrities. Months later when we watched the show, we noticed ourselves jogging in several background scenes.

The tales of seven strangers put together . . . will have to wait. I was faltering already but didn't let on to TJ. There was a clearing at the top of the long climb and to our right we saw the sunrise over the Pacific. If you ever want to see the perfect Hawaiian sunrise, enter the Honolulu Marathon, and run at exactly ten minute per mile pace; you will be in for the treat of a lifetime. We gradually ran down the other side of Diamond Head Road and I felt reinvigorated. Maybe it was the downhill, maybe it was the sunrise, but I was feeling my second wind. Eventually I would need my third, fourth, fifth and sixth winds that morning.

We loped through some nice neighborhoods before embarking on a long out-and-back flat stretch on Kalaniana'ole Highway, miles 11 to 22 of the course. The sun, now high in the sky, not only raised the temperature but also reflected off the white roadway, a sharp contrast to the dark roads we had earlier trotted over.

TJ and I passed the halfway point in a little less than two hours and fifteen minutes. In addition to focusing on preserving my limited reserves, I subtly monitored TJ's progress. Pacing a friend in a marathon is a wonderful experience, but it does double the mental stress, as you not only have to monitor yourself, but you must also continually monitor those you pace.

As we headed back to Kapi'olani Park and the finish line, not only was I hot and tired, I began to wonder if I was pacing TJ or if TJ was now pacing me. Somehow, we maintained a ten-minute pace that felt harder and harder by the mile. At 22 miles we exited Kalaniana'ole Highway turning left onto Kealaolu Avenue, a huge green hedge serving as a border between the road and the Kahala Hotel's golf course. It was along that hedge that I had a brilliant idea-- perhaps the only idea that could be the difference between finishing the race or dropping out of the race. There were no crowds next this tall hedge to push me back onto the course if I dropped out like those in Boston. It was just TJ and me.

"TJ, at mile 22 let's stop and walk for two minutes, then start jogging again so our trip to the next mile marker will not seem as long, seeing how we would've walked the first part of it."

"Awesome idea. I'm dying." I had no idea that TJ was feeling equally as bad as I, plus it was TJ's first marathon, so we had to finish. For the next two miles we alternated walking with jogging. During those two miles residents offered us oranges, bananas, and pretzels. And even beer. I just stuck with water, drinking one cup as two doused my head. My homemade cotton T-shirt singlet was drenched and must have held five pounds of water in its fibers. At Mile 24.5 we reached the base of Diamond Head Road and had to summit the hill in reverse from the morning. The sun was now overhead; there would be no glorious sunrise at the summit. Not only were we about to embark on the final hill of the race, but I was also dead on my feet. "TJ, go ahead and I will catch up to you at that gas station at the top of the hill."

"What gas station?"

"The Texaco station right up there on the left with the big red sign."

There was no gas station up there on the left. I was hallucinating. Every time I drive that road when visiting the Island, I always say, "Heather did I ever tell you about the time I thought there was a gas station right here?"

"Yes, a million times, now pay attention to the road." Driving in Hawaii with Heather is like Magnum driving with Higgins or *Hawaii 5-0*'s Steve McGarrett driving with Dano.

To this day I have absolutely no idea why I saw a gas station. TJ insisted that we slowly walk-jog up the hill. We crested the hill at mile 25 as I verified that there was, in fact, no gas station at the top. From here it was all downhill. No matter how you feel in a marathon the final mile is always uplifting, as you know after the first step you take in that final mile you now have less than a mile to go. We hung a slight left into Kapi'olani Park and the finish line was in sight. Crowds cheered wildly from both sides of the road. We crossed the finish line in four hours and 29 minutes; yes, somehow, we had reached our goal despite the hardships and hallucinations in the final miles. Seconds later a race volunteer placed a shell lei around our necks, the finisher's medal from the 1990s. I am not sure if they still award these today, a small lei adorned with at least 30 small tan shells.

A few seconds later we stepped under the mist of several showers, set up at the finish area, reveling in our accomplishment. However, the revelry was short lived. My warfighter was technically not over as I had to report to Schofield Barracks for the post-exercise After Action Review (AAR).

I gingerly walked through Waikiki back to Fred and Nicole's apartment, past the tourists who had now been up for hours high-fiving anyone wearing a shell lei. As I drove up to Schofield Barracks, I did my own internal race AAR. It was pretty short: don't underestimate the marathon ever! There are no shortcuts and there is no magic wand that you can purchase at an expo. The secret ingredient is simple. Run every day and always remember pride cometh before a fall.

The exercise AAR went well. Apparently I gave the right legal advice to fictitious farmers. As I headed home to finally sleep in my own bed I felt as if I had completed two races. The fireworks-adorned journey through the holiday village that is Honolulu in December and the slow slog chasing gas stations feeling like Don Quixote chasing windmills.

The following day was Marathon Monday in Hawaii. All race finishers headed to the band shell at Kapi'olani Park to pick up their certificate and T-shirt. In Hawaii only finishers receive T-shirts. Which makes sense. There are three unwritten rules of race shirts: never wear the shirt before the race; never wear the shirt in the race; and never wear the shirt of a race you didn't finish. A few days later several sample race photos arrived in my yahoo inbox. Gone were the days of receiving one-inch glossy photos in the mail weeks after the race. I deleted my race proofs without even looking at them. But I shouldn't have felt too badly. My buddy Andy ran the race as well. The following day the Honolulu newspaper had a photo of the oldest race finisher, someone in their eighties. Right next to the oldest race finisher, crossing the finish line, was Andy. He caught a lot of heat for that for weeks at PT.

I closed out the 1990s by running the Honolulu Marathon the following year, properly-trained and rested, not chasing any gas stations. On my last day in Hawaii in July 1999 my administrative assistant, Betty, said, "I am running Honolulu Marathon this December. Can you sponsor me?"

"Sponsor you? Do you mean give you a training plan??

"No, sponsor me. I am running for a charity."

In eighth grade, I had done the 20-mile March of Dimes walkathon on the rain-soaked paths of Eisenhower Park. I had no idea that this had shifted over to the marathon. As I spoke to Betty, I didn't know that big changes for the marathon were on the horizon; changes that unfortunately would pit one group of runners against another.

On December 31, 1999, I ran the World's final 1900s marathon in Daytona Beach, Florida. The race started on the hardpacked sand famous for allowing cars to drive along its shores. We ran north to Ormond Beach, then traversed the intercoastal waterway, followed by a long loop through wetlands before heading back to the sand of Daytona Beach. My younger sister Karen biked the entire racecourse with me, keeping me company, as there were only a few hundred runners in the race. Running alone with her past alligator filled swamps felt a million miles and a million years away from the crowds of Boston and Honolulu. But one constant remained. I heard a shout of "Kick it in!" as the finish line came into view. My parents and I quickly left the race, stopping for lunch at Hops Restaurant and Brewery, and remembering to each take 50 dollars out of the ATM next to the restaurant just in case Y2K caused the world to crash in a few hours.

For me, my world did crash, as sadly that was the last race my dad saw me run.

*Wantagh Park Swim team with my brothers and sisters in 1972, the year I
(on far left) first questioned my Dad about the marathon*

My Mother, on left in foreground, cheered at every meet, but never placed any pressure on us

Little League baseball team on which my non-stop bunting on 3rd strikes lead me (center, 2nd from left) to realize baseball was not my sport

Mike Byrnes, 1968 USA Olympic Track Coach, my junior high school home room teacher, social teacher and first track coach. Imagine having the Olympic coach as your first track coach! Even today I still use many of the same training workouts Mr. Byrnes had us doing back in the 1970s. A true visionary, Mr. Brynes created the first high school national track championship meet. (photo courtesy of National Scholastic Athletics Foundation)

Dad and I at a high school cross-country meet; his trusted stopwatch dangling from his neck

May 6, 1979, Long Island Marathon prerace photo, 6 am on my front lawn

Mile 13 of the Long Island Marathon with Mr. Ed Donlon

Medal from 1979 Long Island Marathon, about the size of a quarter

My college coach, two time Olympian and American Record holder in the 5,000 meters, Matt Centrowitz. Matt instilled in us the philosophy to take ownership of our running careers and to be flexible in our training adjusting for weather, school load and other factors

Heading up Cemetery Hill at Van Cortlandt Park with my college roommate Mike Regan.   Mike raced past me heading down this hill, and pretty much raced past me in every event as he went on to run a 4-minute mile and anchor our school's distance medley relay in the NCAA Championships.

Coaching at Great Neck South High School during law school. This awesome group of individuals won back-to-back county championships. Mr. Bob Baratta, a member of the Section VIII Hall of Fame is second to the left. Mr. B. was the most supportive and kindest boss I ever had, and never ever got angry, even when I messed up a photo like this (I am on far right)

My Step Brother Patrick and I in Central Park near the finish of the 1984 NYC Marathon, held on a brutally hot day. Pat had only started running 6 months prior to this race and eventually qualified for the Boston Marathon

1991 All Army Track team. I think my self (second row from bottom, far right) and the entire team were told not to smile for the picture

Halfway point of 1988 Marine Corps Marathon, back when there were far fewer runners and the roads were less crowded

Happily heading out to the 25th Infantry Division Warfighter in December 1997

Unhappily running the 1997 Honolulu Marathon the morning after the 25th Infantry Division Warfighter

Honolulu Perimeter Relay

My Dad and Stepmom visiting Hawaii when I was stationed there

Fred Schoenbrodt and I excited to start the Appalachian Trail with our enormous backpacks

Day 2 of our Appalachian Trail hike having second thoughts

Seoul Marathon, Sungnyemun Gate, mile marker 1, one of the most spectacular sites in all marathon races and certainly one of the most historic, as this gate was built in the 1300s.

Finishing one of Korea's wonderful races along the Han River

Yoido Island, the start and finishing point for weekly Half/Full Marathons along the Han River in Seoul

Brigadier General John Miller leading 500 Soldiers on an early morning run at Panorama Farm, the home cross-country course for the University of Virginia

25 - Finishing the 2013 Boston Marathon

Conducting the promotion ceremony for Lieutenant Colonel Jeremy Steward, the Assistant to the Run Group Leader in Army Physical Fitness training. Jeremy played football for Virginia Tech and took up running while in the Army and has performed marvelously

Cam and I with Kizhan Clarke, All American wrestler, and my first student at American University

Heather and I at the 2016 Sandbridge Turkey Trot, the site of the world record for most candles blown out at one time. Each runner was handed a candle on the start line and we all blew then out at the same time.

Heather and I at the Surf n Santa 5 Miler in Virginia Beach. This race was the site of my second world record, most Santa's running in one location. J & A Racing in Virginia Beach hosts a series of fantastic races every year. This particular year every runner received a Santa suit in their pre-race packet in order to set us up for the record. It does get very hot running in a Santa suit.

Heather and Cam at Carderock Elementary School's fun run

Cam and I at a virtual race, the caption of this photo could be either "false start"
or "slow reaction time" depending on your point of view

Lunch at The Shamrock Restaurant in Thurmont Maryland after our 2016 Cross Country team season opener against Mount St Marys. Standing in the back is Edmund Burke, qualifier for the US Olympic Trials in the marathon, and Matt. Seated next to me is Kerri Gallagher, world championship qualifier in the 1500 meters and the current Director of the Manhattan College Track and Cross Country programs

Matthew Centrowitz, bottom center, at practice at American University a few days after his 1500 meters victory at the 2016 Rio Olympics

Finish of 2021 Baltimore Marathon

Twiggy still going strong at age 19

HEART AND SEOUL

Y2K didn't cause the world to come crumbling down, but the new century did bring with it significant changes to the marathon. However, these changes did not come in a vacuum. The entire world was changing, in large part due to rapid advances in technology, especially the Internet. Not just Internet speed, but perhaps more importantly Internet content.

The Internet made the marathon more accessible to the masses, not in terms of the ease of registering for races online, but the Internet brought the marathon into people's homes. No longer was the marathon an event televised about once or twice a year in which the cameras were focused on swift individuals racing through the streets of New York City or up Heartbreak Hill in Boston. No longer was the marathon the event that some odd individual in the office on the day after the marathon stood on tight and wobbly legs chatting about the previous day's achievement at the water cooler.

The marathon was now the event your friends posted photos of on Facebook, MySpace and Instachat. Due to the Internet, the marathon now began attainable, even for those without a running background. And right there at your fingertips were marathon-training plans geared to all levels of runners. No longer did you have to reply on a small index card handed to you by your dad to get the plan that would get you across the finish line. You could just "Ask Jeeves" and hundreds of links to various plans would appear before your eyes. Jeeves, and eventually Google, could even find an online personal coach for you.

Thus began the second running boom. And all these new marathoners had a new wave of gadgets and nutritional supplements to help them on their journeys. No longer did runners have to rely on their dad's car odometer and elementary school clock hands to calculate distance and pace. Data from satellites miles up in the sky could now beam down to runner's wrists providing pace, distance, heart rate, and a variety of other data points. One of the first of these watches on the market was about the size of a can of sardines. They were huge and once affixed onto the wrist runners would patiently hold their wrist skyward for what seemed like hours until the watch synced with the overhead satellites. But the size and wait were worth it! Not only did these watches provide great feedback while training, but they also ensured runners did not start out too quickly in the actual marathon.

For those not fully confident that their GPS would guide them along the way, race directors offered special "pacers" to usher runners to the finish line. Gaggles of individuals would run behind "pacers" with balloons tied to their shorts and holding signs with goal race times: 3:10; 4:20 etc. Not only did they guide runners along at the needed pace, but they also provide encouragement along the way. Although once at an Expo I met the Pacer who pepped me up by saying "It's going to be hot, it's going to be hilly, we'll see what happens." It was as if I was talking to SNL's Debbie Downer. I decided to go on my own. I never saw that pacer on the course, not even for a minute.

To take runners' minds off the road ahead, music now filled their ears. First in line was the iPod, which was slightly smaller than a deck of cards and was affixed to runners' arms with wires dangling from earbuds to the device. This was replaced by the Shuffle, slightly larger than a postage stamp, but like the iPod, required the dangling wires for use. Eventually earbuds replaced both. And for those without an iPod or a Shuffle, race organizers offered live music at every mile of the race in the fantastic Rock and Roll Marathon series.

Although I did use a Walkman during law school to keep me awake on my endless nighttime loops, and years earlier in junior high school carried a small white transistor radio to listen to Yankees - Royals playoff games during cross country practice (yes, in the old days playoff games were played during the day so that children could watch their favorite teams), I have eschewed music while running. I prefer to hear the bullfrogs' voices echoing off the banks of the C/O Canal during the summer and the knocking of woodpeckers on the bare trees in winter.

No longer did marathoners have to gulp Coke during a race to hydrate and get some sugar. Entire aisles of sporting goods stores now offered gels of every flavor and texture and sports drinks complete with every variety of bottle and hydration backpacks to store these liquids.

Many runners also saw the marathon as an avenue to not only reach their personal fitness goals but also as an opportunity to help others. Charity organizations sprung up to fill the void. While raising money for a variety of great causes, runners, in turn, could receive both support prior to the race in the form of coaching and group training runs (complete with fluids and gels) as well as support on the course.

Online training plans, online coaches, GPS watches, Shuffles, gels, sports drinks: "If You Build It, They Will Come." Everything a potential marathoner would need was built, and boy, did they come out. Race fields swelled. And swelled. And swelled to the point that logistically racecourses could not meet the desire. Long gone were the days of mailing in a registration form confident that as long as the US Postal Service delivered your entry form, you were in the race. Signing up at the race expo was a luxury of the past.

The larger races started to require runners to register months in advance at a predetermined date and time. Many even instituted lotteries with random names selected to receive the coveted race starting number. Runners would flock to their computers at 7:00 a.m. on xx day and try to register as quickly as possible. Races of over 20,000 would sell out in a matter of hours. On occasion websites crashed as thousands of runners logged on simultaneously. It was harder to get a marathon entry slot than it was to get a ticket to a rock concert. I vividly remember standing in a humid convenience store in Krong Siem Reap, Cambodia, trying to log onto the Marine Corps Marathon website in the middle of the night for registration. I handed over Cambodian riel after riel to the storeowner to keep the Internet connection alive until I secured my spot in the race to be held seven months later.

Race organizers also held a certain number of slots for those individuals who were running as part of a charity organization, who met a certain qualifying time, who attempted and failed to gain entry into the race for set number of years, and a variety of other criteria.

The thousands upon thousands of runners influenced the starting process for races. Race organizers now separated runners into starting waves sending off groups of runners every thirty minutes or so. Chip timing providing an accurate finishing time and place for all runners no matter what wave they began in.

All these changes came at a cost. Runners now had to decide months in advance if they wished to run a marathon, hoping that they maintained fitness and did not get injured over those upcoming months. The costs of races skyrocketed due to the associated costs of hosting an event of over 30,000 people. Race entry fees commonly rose into the hundreds of dollars. Due to race-entry caps many individuals could not secure a race number for what may be their favorite event. And finally, the sheer number of runners at the start area increased the stress and anxiety exponentially. Long lines for port–a-potties, crammed starting lines, and difficulty finding parking were among the chief complaints.

The changing dynamics of the marathon created and continues to create an alarming ugliness to the sport   When I first started running marathons in the 1970s every runner I bumped into was friendly, freely offered advice and everyone wished the best for each other at the start line. The honor system was used to line up in the proper area, even though no timing chips were in existence. And every runner seemed to be out there to run the event as fast as they could, be it three hours, four hours or five hours.

As the marathon moved into the 2000s people began to run the marathon for a variety of reasons including general fitness, charity, or to set a personal best. All of these are great reasons. Unfortunately, starting in the 2000s, at times, "faster" runners took on the belief that unless you are on the starting line to set personal record and run as fast as you can, you don't belong there and are not a "real runner". You are labeled a "hobby jogger."

This reasoning is flawed on many levels. Recall when I spoke about coaching, I said never assume everyone runs for the same reasons as you. Every person on the starting line has a right to be there and has a valid personal reason for being there. Secondly, there is a good chance that there would not even be a race without these thousands of runners. City officials would not close 26 miles of roads, often on a weekend morning, for 150 marathoners out to chase their personal records. It just wouldn't happen. The marathon is a big business. A race brings in millions of dollars for a city. Runners need hotel rooms, runners need food, runners buy souvenirs, etc. City officials would be reluctant to host an event for 150 people.

Yes, race day logistics are more complicated, but so are so many things in life and you learn to adjust. Before the Internet I might have had to answer ten phone call inquiries a day. After the Internet I would receive over 300 emails a day. And I certainly was not the only person. Workers adjusted. They either answered emails as they came in or answered emails in batches. Simply arriving at the starting area, a little over an hour or so before the start ensures that runners can take care of all pre-race tasks, even with the large fields.

Race directors will also provide a race number for faster runners, so these new marathoners are not taking away a place from a "faster" runner.

Finally, the disparaging term "hobby jogger" makes no sense to me. Aside from the top marathoners in the world, no one gets paid to run a marathon. For everyone else it is a hobby-- a hobby that some may take more seriously than others, but the bottom line is it is a hobby, it is not a livelihood for most. I seriously doubt that NCAA college basketball players walk by a pick-up basketball game and disparagingly call those individuals "hobby basketball players."

I once asked a person who was complaining, "How exactly do these individuals affect your race" (aside from getting you upset over nothing and distracting you from what you should be focusing on)?

"Uhh, uhh . . ."

I have run at the front of the pack, the middle of the pack, and the back of the pack. Every person I have come across, no matter where they are in the pack, is trying equally hard. They all add to the tapestry of that race, and they should all be welcomed with open arms. You must admire any runner who can hold down a job, raise a family, and train for a marathon, all at the same time.

Throughout the early 2000s I dove headfirst these huge events. In 2005 I walked into the Javits Center in NYC for the first time since I raced out of that building in 1989 at the completion, or almost completion, of my bar exam, to pick up my NYC Marathon race packet.

For most of the first decade of the new century I was stationed overseas and had the opportunity to see Berlin, Paris, Seoul, Nagano, and Dublin on foot. In 2003, right before I packed up to head to Korea, I ran a wonderful race in Kansas City called the Trolley Run. This almost all downhill four-mile run started four miles outside of the city and finished at Country Club Plaza. Thousands of people enjoyed both the downhill course and the huge post-race party.

Moving overseas is difficult enough with a family. The equation only becomes more difficult when cats are involved, one of whom escaped in the San Francisco airport when TSA had to put the cat container through the X-ray machine. As Twiggy darted one way, I darted the other, and eventually captured her in front of the Cinnabon. If you ever want to see a cat at its angriest, peer into a cat's travel cart in the baggage claim area after a 14-hour flight. You would think the cargo crew played a weird trick on you and replaced your cat with a Tasmanian devil. And for the next week that Tasmanian Devil will not give you a second glance. I've got a new job and a new home on the other side of the world, yet I inconvenienced you Twiggy because you had to take the exact same flight as the rest of us. Twiggy is still around today, and just as mean at age 19 as she was as a spryer cat coming off the plane in Korea or Frankfurt after one of her many transpacific or transatlantic flights. No matter what I do, that cat will not run away. I have left doors open and even installed cat doors in the hopes she may find a new home. And there she still is every morning at 6:00 a.m., demanding food.

That cat has outlived her nine lives plus some. Once she fell out a fifth-story window and acted like nothing happened. We were living on the top floor of a small apartment complex in Seoul. "Where's Twiggy?" It's 6:00 a.m. and Twiggy is not demanding food. I look out an open kitchen window and Twiggy is in the garden

five stories down. And when I say garden, I mean the private fenced garden of the Korean lady who lived on the first floor. I had been in this building for all of two days and I went down to the first floor and knocked on her door. One of the oldest, and nicest ladies I ever met, opened the door. I am sure wondering, who is this American at my door at 6:00 a.m.? I spoke no Korean and she spoke no English, so I started meowing and pointing towards the area where her garden was. "Meow, meow," pointing and she had no idea what was going on and just kept smiling. So, I got on all fours, kept meowing, and started walking towards her garden. I guess a light bulb went off and she let me into her garden. I grabbed Twiggy who looked at me like, "What's for breakfast, dude?"

I am surprised the pet store in Kansas City even sold me Twiggy because I was once turned away from a pet store when I wanted to purchase a turtle. It was Christmas Eve and I had no present for Heather. I knew she loves turtles so figured I would get her a turtle for Christmas. Problem solved. I raced to the pet store and saw a lonely wood turtle standing in a small glass container. I told the "pet expert" that I wanted to purchase said turtle. Maybe because I seemed to be in a rush, maybe because it was clear I knew nothing about turtles, maybe because it's part of his job, I don't know-- but the guy started interrogating me and he easily called my bluff.

"Have you ever owned a turtle before?"

"Yes."

"And what type of turtle was that?"

"One with a shell on it is back."

"Where did you keep this turtle?"

"In a box."

"What did you feed this turtle?"

"Stuff turtles generally eat."

"Sir, I am sorry. I can't sell you this turtle in good conscience, obviously you are not a good fit for this pet."

"Not a good fit? Dude, if it wasn't freezing outside, I could go in the woods and find a turtle. Every person coming in here on Christmas Eve is looking for a puppy. Not one person who has entered this store seems interested in that turtle. You need business, I need a turtle, let's work this out."

I drove to every pet store between DC and Baltimore that Christmas Eve hoping that the pet expert was not one step ahead of me calling stores warning them of me. I finally was able to purchase a wood turtle and placed a big red bow on its shell. I guess technically I could have stopped in a Kay Jewelry Store at the Mall and been all set. However, once I get my mind fixated on something, be it striking out my Dad blindfolded, running a marathon, or buying a turtle, I stick to it. That turtle is still alive and lives with Twiggy, two additional cats, two dogs, one tortoise, three red-eared slider turtles, 20 fish, and 13 guinea pigs. I want to invite that pet expert over to my house and ask him why I am not a "good fit."

I had been stationed in Korea previously back in 1993. During that tour I was stationed in Seoul on Yongsan Army base, a huge sprawling installation nestled on the banks of the Han River and in the shadow of Namsan Mountain with the Seoul Tower at its summit. For most of my initial tour in Korea I ran mostly on the installation, which was large, seeing how it did host weekly 5k and 10K road races all within the confines of its huge red brick walls. I did venture off on occasion to run.

My third night in Korea I headed out the main gate, took a left, and ran along the sidewalk, avoiding the motorcycle drivers who had a penchant for driving on sidewalks. As I looked up at the red and green lights of the Seoul Tower and ran past storefront after storefront with shop names in bright red lights in a language I could not read, I thought of my law school classmates. Due to the time difference, they would be waking up in NYC ready to head to law firms. I knew I had made the right decision in joining the Army.

The time difference was something my dad could never fully get a handle on. Prior to going to Korea, I had made a chart with "Time in Korea," "Time in Florida," and red highlights of the Florida times not to call as I would be asleep in Korea during those highlighted hours. Almost every other morning I would be woken by "Time to get up for the daily dozen?" The daily dozen were twelve exercises developed in the 1920s that comprised the fitness routine of my dad's Army era. I can only imagine what these exercises were; I could envision sets of jumping jacks, some sort of exercise lying on your back and pretending to ride a bicycle in the air, people tossing large, heavy, tan medicine balls back and forth, etc., the things you would see photos of in a gym museum. And almost every other morning was the same reply, "I have no idea of what the daily dozen are and take a look at that chart right next to the phone you are holding, what time does it say it is in Korea right now?"

"0400, don't you get up at this time, back during the Korean War we would be lucky to sleep in this late."

"Yes, I am in Korea, Dad, but I am not in the Korean War, talk to you later."

Over the course of that year, I did grow weary of running the same loops on base as well as doing the same racecourses each week against the same runners. The only change was that the annual Law Day run had an ambulance as the pace car, simulating lawyers as ambulance chasers. I wonder how many pats on the back the gym manager got when he came up with that one. I also grew weary of military police pulling me over during my runs. Running on the installation required the wearing of an orange safety vest. These were available for checkout at the gym and were about the size of the vests you see construction workers wearing on the highway. Anyone running on the installation, *anywhere* on the installation, had to wear a safety vest. This included running on grass fields, running on sidewalks, and even running in races on closed roads. A friend of mine was once yelled at by a commander for not wearing a safety vest on an indoor treadmill. The commander yelled, "Get with the program!"

I can understand safety concerns as a result of cars hitting runners. Over the years I have personally known too many individuals killed by cars while running. Ever since I started running on the Jones Beach bike path I have avoided running on roads. I prefer to run freely and not worry about cars at all; hence, I always drive to parks or trails to run. Three blocks from my house is the 184-mile long C/O Canal towpath. This dirt path was used 100 years ago by mules pulling canal boats filled with wheat and coal, from the farms and mountains of Maryland down to Washington, DC. Walkers, bikers, and runners use the path-- a real gem that starts in the heart of DC and travels up to Cumberland in western Maryland. Every morning as I drive to the canal I cannot for the life of me understand people in my neighborhood running on roads, including on one long winding road with blind spots and no sidewalks. These same individuals constantly fill the neighborhood chat with complaints about teenagers driving too fast on the roads, yet they blissfully run on these same roads with earbuds on. I always want to shout out, "You know there is a 184-mile dirt path less than a quarter mile away?!"

My distain for running on the installation reached its peak when I was running on a grass field near the post gym. At the time I was wearing a bright orange long-sleeved shirt with several reflectors sewn into the sleeves, across the chest, and across the back. The second my foot hit the sidewalk I heard, "new naw, nee naw" coming from behind me. I glanced over as a patrol car pulled up alongside of me.

"You need a safety vest to run on post."

"Officer my entire shirt is a safety vest."

"I understand, but the regulation says you need a safety vest, not a safety shirt."

Ugh, show me the regulation! One Sunday evening in July 1993 I was jogging, with required vest, on a large grass field near the post gym. From above I heard the rotor of an incoming helicopter. I jogged far enough away to get out of the rotor wash and watched as the copter landed and President Clinton headed down the stairway. In my mind I can only think as he gazed out, he wondered, "Why is that Soldier wearing a safety vest on grass?"

As my tour ended, I vowed that if I ever returned to Korea, there would be no more on post running for me. I got that chance about a decade later. With Twiggy now destroying my office every night (we had not yet found a house to live in and Twiggy could not stay in the hotel with us, so each night Twiggy took out her anger from the flight on anything she could get her claws on in my office) and me fresh off the Trolley Run in Kansas City, I asked my fabulous administrative assistant, translator, and Korean tour guide Ms. Yi if she could look on the Internet and find any races for me near the Army post. She sent me a link to a race just two weeks away on Yeouido Island, just a ten-minute drive away from the post. The only problem was the entire link was in Hangul. The only words I could make out were 5k, 10k, 21.095K, and 42.195K.

"Ms. Yi, can you please enter me in the 5K race?"

"Why are you doing the children's race?"

"Ms. Yi, no adults run the 5k?"

"Adults run either the full course or half-course."

Seeing how I had just run several adult-filled 5Ks and the 4-mile Trolley Run in Kansas City, I could honestly say to myself, "We're not in Kansas anymore."

Marathon running is extremely popular in Korea and every person you meet on the street can tell you all about the history of the marathon in Korea. If you say the name Hwang Young-cho immediately the response will be, 1992 Olympic Marathon Champion. Lee Bong-ju will quickly be recognized as Boston Marathon Champion. You could not garner the same reaction in America if you said the name Galen Rupp.

In addition to being the nicest and friendliest people I have ever met in the world; the Korean people are very knowledgeable and very passionate about the marathon. And man, do they put on great races! Since I did not want to be a man among children in the upcoming 5K race at Yeouido Island, I decided to get in shape so that I could do the full course. In Korea, the marathon is referred to as "the full course." If you run into an individual running along the Han River bike path they will ask, "Are you training for the full course." Rarely will they ask, "Are you training for the marathon?"

Since I didn't want to explain to the Military Police that my shirts were, in fact, reflective and could serve as a vest, I decided to explore the parks and paths of Korea. Fortunately, the April 2003 edition of *Runner's World* had a feature on the places to run in Seoul, Korea. This was a marvelous starting point. I immediately set out to explore both World Cup Park and Olympic Park both on the banks of the Han River, albeit each park on different ends of the city. Built around the stadium used for the 2002 World Cup soccer tournament, World Cup Park consists of several paths meandering around small human-made ponds, every tree carefully placed and manicured. To the west of these ponds and paths lies the best feature of the park, two huge old landfills that had been covered in dirt, grass, and trees. Atop one was a golf course and atop the other was a series of paths crisscrossing well-kept gardens. The view from the top of these mountains was spectacular. In the Winter one could easily run for an hour on all of these paths, all the while looking north towards the snow-covered mountains that make up the border between North and South Korea. You would think you were looking at the Rocky Mountains; it was breathtaking, even though you were in the heart of one of the most bustling cities in the world.

Olympic Park, built for the 1988 Olympic Games, was a park that surrounded several of the games' venues, such as the building used for gymnastics. Like World Cup Park this park had a human-made lake and several paths as well as Pagodas that were surrounded by vibrant Cherry Blossoms each Spring. The highlight of this park was the birch trees each fall. The yellowest leaves I have ever seen adorned the white-stemmed birch trees, a remarkable contrast against the blue sky.

Weekends were spent running in these parks, whereas runs during the week were along the banks of the Han River. Twenty-seven bridges traverse The Han River, and each seems to be more decoratively lit up than the next each night. On the south side of the river lies a bike path like no other. This path, over 50 miles in length, has directional arrows, separate lanes for runners and bicyclists (no need to hear "On your left," as you run), and even has portions made of the rubber material found on tracks. Small parks dot the landscape alongside the path, often filled with individuals doing group calisthenics as the sun rises. The path is used by hundreds of friendly runners. Almost every day as I ran along the path a friendly runner would join me and the first question would be "Are you training for a full course?" When I would reply "Yes," the next question would always be "Have you ever run the Boston Marathon?" When I would reply "Yes," the person would always say, "Boston is my dream. I want to go there one day." I spoke no Korean. Often these runners spoke limited English, yet we had great conversations along the banks of the Han.

An additional benefit of running along the Han was the numerous small snack stores that lined the path. I always ran with a few thousand Won in my shorts pocket so I could purchase a Coke, Gatorade, or water bottle along the way. One hot afternoon my limited Korean language skills got the best of me. I was thirsty and stopped at a snack store pointing at a small green bottle that I thought was water. The proprietor handed it to me and said 10,000 Won (about ten dollars). I was like, that's sort of high for water, but the guy has to make a living. I grabbed the bottle, twisted off the lid, and gulped it down; my throat was instantly on fire. I had inadvertently purchased and chugged Soju, a clear, colorless Korean drink that is about 50% alcohol. The next day I asked Ms. Yi the Korean word for water.

The path was at its peak at dark as one runs along the lighted route, looking across the river as the green and red lights of the Seoul Tower atop Namsan Mountain glistened down. The thousands of lights in apartment towers and buildings created a light tapestry that surpassed even NYC, and each bridge displayed a luminous neon light show complete with waterworks. Not only was this path a fantastic place to train, it also served as a place to unwind after a day at work. At the time I was a defense lawyer and had several murder cases. Attorneys pay an emotional toll when representing clients charged with murder and facing the ultimate punishment. I ran along the Han late at night looking at the lights, and not for my physical health, but for my mental health. The individual who lived next door to me in our apartment complex was the chief South Korean negotiator with North Korea. We spent many late nights on the elevator as he went to the banks of the Han River to whack golf balls as I headed out for a run. A simple "Rough day?" from either of us was all that was needed to convey the message that it was time to blow off some steam along the Han. Not only did I have a buddy to blow off steam with, but my landlord's son attended UCLA on a track scholarship, held the Korean record for the pole vault, and was headed to the Olympics in a few years. Whenever Mr. Kim stopped over to fix a light bulb or something, we would spend hours talking track.

Although the parks and the Han River were great running venues, I did all my long runs in preparation for marathons at Seoul Grand Park. Seoul Grand Park is not one park but rather a compound that contains an amusement park, a zoo and a large hilly wooded area with hiking trails. A long, winding, carless road through the woods connects all three parks. Every Thursday morning, I would arrive at the park at about 7:00 a.m. for my two to three hour long run (my work schedule was very flexible since I was the boss). Long runs in Korea in the winter are absolutely freezing. If you have ever seen the TV Show *M*A*S*H*, there is an episode where everyone is bundled up. That episode is representative of every day from about December First to March First. I would get to the park on Thursday mornings and start my run with a brain freeze like you get from drinking a Slurpee too quickly.

Every long run started with an hour running up and down the twisting trails of the hiking section of the park. I suffered the only running-related injury of my life on those trails. Once I glanced off the trail to see icicles forming on a waterfall, tripped on a rock, smashing my shin into a boulder. I continued my run. A few hours later, I noticed my leg was still bleeding a lot and I figured that's not right, so I went to the ER. The doctor grabbed what appeared to be a stapler that you would find on your desk and said, "Let me staple that up."

"Staple that up? Doc, what about stitches?"

"Stitches are for cosmetic purposes, like a cut on your face. No one is going to see your shin, and this works just as good," he said as he shot staple after staple into my shin, which he did not numb in any way. I thought those things were going straight into my shinbones. He treated my leg as if it were the pages of a school report that he had fashioned together.

"In about a week just take a staple remover from your desk and yank those out," was his final doctor's order as I limped out of the ER.

Aside from this fall I have been fortunate with injuries. That is because as soon as I feel the slightest ache, I immediately back off. Even when I was young, I realized that running is a lifelong sport. Taking a few days off to walk or swim and let an injury heal may slightly hurt my fitness in the short term, but in the long term I would not have to deal with long-lasting injuries. Running through an injury is not going to solve anything. The injury will just keep getting worse and worse. Taking a few days off is the best course of action.

After I completed an hour-long loop through the woods, I would head over to the Seoul Zoo, pay the 2000-Won entry fee, and have the entire zoo to myself on those cold early morning runs. I would run along the winding paths past elephants, giraffes, and howling wolves as zookeepers stared at me wondering, what's with this guy? Lily the white tiger would pace back and forth in her enclosure as I approached her area each Thursday morning. I would run back and forth in front of her area and she would run back and forth at my side, only separated by some small bushes and metal bars. It was an absolute joy to see the animals; I would run there for hours. I would jog in place to read each and every sign along the way. The only place that scared me was the lions' den. The moat between the lions and I only was ten feet wide, certainly within jumping range for a fit hungry lion. Heck, I think I have seen Twiggy jump ten feet.

In addition to great running venues, Seoul offered a stellar menu of races. Every Sunday morning various organizations hosted half-marathons and full marathons at Yeouido Island. Located on the south side of the Han River, Yeouido Island is home of the 63 Tower, also known as the Golden Tower, that at one time was the tallest building in Korea. Every race was an out-and-back event along the Han River bike path. For the 30,000 Won entry fee runners got a race number, a high-tech T-shirt and a runner's gift that varied from week to week. Gifts ran the gamut from runners' watches, rain jackets, and hats to bags of dried fish. Unlike races in America where it is considered bad luck to wear the race shirt prior to or on race day, almost every single runner ran in the race shirt on race day in Seoul. Overhead photos of races would show a sea of powder blue shirts along the Han River. A feast of drinks, stews, soups, bread, and cakes greeted finishers. Large running groups such as The Joy Running Club or the Sub Three Running club would congregate after races and chow down as they socialized. On occasion Hwang Young-cho would attend races to hand out awards to the winners. I never got to meet Frank Shorter, my first marathon inspiration, but I did get to meet the runner who crossed the Olympic Marathon finish line first twenty years later.

Every Sunday morning thousands of runners would line up for either the full-course or half-course race. And every Sunday I was treated like a celebrity. It seemed like I was the only foreigner who went to the races. Every single person I bumped into to would smile and say "Fight on!" to me. Ms. Yi signed me up for races almost every weekend. I treated the half marathons as long tempo runs. Even twenty years later I can close my eyes and visualize every step on the Han River bike path and hear "Fight on!"

With great places to train, and experience with the Korean running and racing scene, I asked Ms. Yi to sign me up for the big race in Korea, The Seoul International Marathon, which is held every March. In the cold winter leading up to the marathon I continued to run along the Han River, in the parks and with Lily, the white tiger.

Even though it was 2005 and expos were in full force in the US as well as in other countries, the Seoul International Marathon had no expo. On the Thursday night before the race I looked out my window and down at the road to see a motorcycle approaching my apartment. Stacked about ten feet high on the back of the motorcycle were marathon race packets. In Korea, your race packet was delivered right to your door! This delivery service was included in the 30,000-Won race entry fee (about thirty dollars).

The packet included a race-timing chip (the kind that one had to tie to their shoe), a number with a large capital letter "A" printed next to my number to indicate my starting zone, and the coolest race T-shirt ever. The entire front of the shirt was a photo of marathon runners passing the Sungnyemun Gate in the previous year's marathon. Even today when I wear this shirt at the C/O Canal and pass any Korean American runners they get excited when spotting my shirt.

It was about twenty degrees when I jumped into a cab and headed to the race start area at Gwanghwamun Plaza in the center of the city, a few blocks up from City Hall. When I arrived, the plaza was packed with thousands of runners, but it was extremely orderly. On the right-hand side of the road was a huge theater in which runners could stay warm and use the restrooms.

About 15 minutes before the 8:00 a.m. start time runners lined up according to the letter printed on their race bib. All foreigners were given the letter A no matter what their previous time was and were allowed to start in the first zone. I had done the NYC Marathon with the strict entry into each starting corral and was shocked that there were no fences, no race marshals-- just runners using the honor system heading to their proper start zone. The start zone was like a horseshoe with letters A and

B at the tip, C and D at the base of the horseshoe, and E and F on the other side. Each letter went off at five-minute intervals, and each was sent off with the shot of a cannon and the release of thousands of balloons. As a group headed out the other groups would slowly walk up to the start line. It was amazing how well this system worked.

Before we headed out I experienced something that would never happen at a marathon in the US. About two minutes before race start, music started blasting and a man over a microphone shouted out something in Korean. All of a sudden, every runner started massaging the back of the person in front of him or her. Not just pats on the back with a "Good luck, buddy." This was like a full-on deep-tissue massage by a total stranger. Once the initial shock wore off, I gently tapped the back of the runner in front of me. As I was patting this runner's back the man on the mic screamed out even louder. Everyone turned around and started massaging the back of the person who had just massaged them. As the awkward massages continued, everyone was smiles and encouraging each other. I can think of a million things that could go wrong if this were done at the NYC Marathon.

At exactly 8:00 a.m. we were off, racing down a flat eight-lane road towards City Hall. At about the two-kilometer mark (approximately 1.2 miles-- during my time in Asia and Europe I became very familiar with the metric system, the system teachers told us in 1970 would be the system the US would be using by the year 1980. I guess the metric system went the same way as the flying cars they told us we would be driving by the year 2000), we passed the Sungnyemun Gate, the same gate on the race shirt. The Sungnyemun Gate is one of several gates built in the 1300s when a wall surrounded the city of Seoul. The Sungnyemun Gate served as the south entrance into the city. In all the marathons I have ever run there is no finer landmark to run past.

The next several kilometers were a series of long stretches on the flat boulevards of Seoul. I spent a lot of time on the outskirts of Seoul in the parks and along the river yet had never really seen the city itself. I used this morning as an opportunity to sightsee. Once thing I liked about kilometers in a marathon was that they come so quickly as compared to miles; although there were 42 of them as compered to 26 miles. The math also seemed a lot easier as far as far as pacing: five minutes, ten minutes, 15 minutes, etc.

As I toured my favorite city in the world, clicking along at five-minutes-per-kilometer pace, I was struck by the absence of spectators. Here and there at big neighborhoods, such as Dongdaemun Market, there would be pockets of spectators, but for the most part we ran the streets in silence. Of course, for me the silence was continually interrupted by shouts of "Fight on!" Korean police along the route substituted as spectators. They stood silently, dressed in big, light-grey, puffy jackets holding thick, wooden, black batons and were spaced out about fifty feet apart on the sidewalk along the course. Interestingly their faces were turned away from us as they vigilantly patrolled the sidewalks for any race intruders. I must have run by the backs of one thousand police officers during the first half of the race, thinking the entire time, where were you last year in NYC when a lady dashed out from a bakery holding a marble rye and tried to cross Fourth Avenue in Brooklyn amid thousands of runners knocking me down?

After quietly touring the heart of Seoul we headed over one of the long flat bridges that traverse the Han River for the second half of the race. Aside from the wind howling from the river below, the trek across the bridge was absolutely silent. To our right was the Olympic Stadium, our finishing point. Although the stadium seemed so close that an outstretched arm could touch it, we still had 13 miles to go, winding through the southern portion of Seoul before reaching the same finish line used in the 1988 Olympic Games.

The silence of the last hour and a half was quickly and mercifully ended by the beating of several janggu drums as we exited the bridge and entered the southern part of the city that included the Gangnam district, made famous by the song of the same name. Not only were there drums, but there were also bands, there were cheerleaders, and there were thousands of spectators. It was like walking out of a dark movie theater into the bright sunlight. The entire race instantly came alive. The empty sidewalks governed by solemn police officers with their backs turned to us were replaced by hordes of spectators three to four deep, often crowding onto the racecourse.

The energy and cheering at the halfway point of the race made Boston Marathon halfway point at Wellesley College seem like a quiet gathering. If any runner was drained as they crossed the bridge they no longer were after the lift provided by the spectators. Chills ran down my spine as I passed the drummers and headed towards Lotte World, the Walt Disney World of Korea.

Every step of the way on the second half of the course was fantastic. Cheering crowds willed the runners along. Not only were these fans exuberant, but they were also knowledgeable. As runners passed, they shouted out paces and predicted finishing times to runners. The marathon is a big sport in Korea and the Seoul Marathon is like the Super Bowl of marathons.

As I continued to click off a five-minute per kilometer pace, I was happy with the math being so easy, but I didn't know what five-minutes per kilometer would yield for 42 kilometers. I didn't care. I loved running past the sights and sounds of the southern part of the city, like Lotty, the mascot of Lotte World. I was never quite sure what Lotty was. I think a chipmunk, which would make sense as I saw chipmunks in cages in markets sold as pets.

Around 30 kilometers into the race I found out what five-minutes-per-kilometer pace was as a pacer with a big sign reading 3:30 passed by. I quickly jumped in with that group and joined the moving party. I had never run with a pace group before this and didn't realize what I was missing. The entire remainder of the course runners passed drinks and gels to each other; at the same time, they shared encouraging words. Not that I understood any of these words. Occasionally, a member of our group would shout out, "Fight on!" I greatly appreciated the efforts to make me part of the team. Although I didn't understand a word that was being said, I did understand that the numbers and the math on my watch was suddenly becoming more complicated. No longer was my watch displaying multiples of five. I had no idea if we were now going faster or slower than five minutes per kilometer but didn't worry. I figured that's what the pacer gets paid for. Actually, I doubt the pacer gets paid. I did notice a few runners struggling to stay with the group, but I figured that was normal now that we were into the final stages of the race.

Unfortunately, the view of the stadium came all too soon. The race was ending too quickly, and I was feeling great. No wall pushed me back like in so many previous marathons, and there was no visions of gas stations that didn't exist. As we turned off the main road in front of the stadium we wove our way through a throng of spectators ten deep shouting wildly, no fencing separating us from their outstretched arms patting our backs.

After running through a delirious crowd for about 300 meters we took a short dip as we entered the dark tunnel leading into the stadium. The tunnel was only about 50 meters long and a slight rise brought us into the bright sunlight of the stadium as we stepped onto the track for our final victory lap. The soft surface of the orange track at first felt uncomfortable after spending 26 miles on concrete. Within a few strides I had my sea legs and looked up at the jumbotron. There on the screen I saw a fifty-foot version of myself running on the Olympic track! I quickly picked up the pace and shot passed our pacer and began sprinting around the bend towards the home stretch. And in that instant my question from 1972 was answered "How is he running so fast after 26 miles?" I was running fast because of sheer joy, the joy one gets from accomplishing the goal they set out to achieve. The joy of sharing a morning with the people in the city I had come to love.

As soon as I crossed the finish line, a race volunteer placed a thick maroon blanket with a gold Seoul Marathon logo around me, even though the temperature had risen into the fifties after a chilly morning start. Every single finisher received the same thick, cozy blanket, which was about the size of a blanket for a twin bed. Seoul Marathon treated us like royalty. There was no thin tinfoil blanket tearing and flapping in the breeze. As we were ushered out of the stadium, I walked over to our pacer to thank him. I gave a short bow as I said "Gamsahamnida." He bowed in return saying, "Fight on!" I then showed him my watch that had a time considerably faster than the 3:30 sign he was holding . . . like more than ten minutes faster. He smiled the biggest smile I have ever seen and said, "We were all feeling good today."

We exited the stadium. We were led to the track right behind the Olympic Stadium, which is the warm-up track. What you don't see on TV as you watch track and field during the Olympics is the warm-up track. Runners cannot warm up for their events on the main track because other races are in progress, therefore there is a 400-meter track right outside of Olympic Stadiums for pre-race warm-ups. As soon as we entered that track there were hundreds of chairs with hunched over runners occupying the seats. Right in front of each chair was a wooden angled box, like you see at the shoeshine booths in the NYC subway. This was odd. My curiosity got the best of me as I took a seat. Instantly a race volunteer said, "Would you like me to remove your chip?" and motioned for me to place my foot on the box. As she untied my shoe to dislodge the race-timing chip, I looked to my left and right and saw a line in each direction with runners seated with one shoe on a box. It looked like a massive Payless ShoeSource. No bending over on aching legs to remove a chip here. Blankets, and now chip removal, the Seoul Marathon took care of every need. And then the medal handed to us was the icing on the cake. It was a huge medal shaped like the Sungnyemun Gate.

As we made a circuit of the track various snacks and drinks were handed to us. The one drink I declined, which I declined at each race, was the small blue aluminum can with the word SWEAT written in white lettering. I am sure if I read the entire can, there would be smaller words about sweat replacement, etc. But I could never see myself drinking from a can that said "sweat" in large bold letters. By the time I had completed the 400-meter circuit I had consumed about four marshmallow-filled chocolate moon pies and a bottle of water to wash them down. Unfortunately, there was not a can of Coke to be found. After we completed a circuit, we exited into a large parking lot with a few grass islands dotting the asphalt. Small groups of runners laid claim to these islands, sitting on their race blankets, and slurping down warm bowls of a thin broth with cubes of white tofu mixed in. As I walked toward a road where I could catch a cab home, I was hailed over to each island, where I was offered tasty soup. I must have stopped at 15 post-race parties and my trip to find a cab kept being interrupted. I just couldn't say no as I was hailed over by group after group; they were all so kind and friendly as we celebrated our marathon finishes.

I slowly made my way out of the Olympic Stadium area and slumped into the back seat of a cab. The drive home was an adventure, seeing how I never knew my apartment's address in Korea. All of my mail was sent to my Army Post Office box on the Army post. I didn't even know the name of the street on which I lived. I just knew how to drive to my apartment; I was in no condition to take the wheel from the cab driver. All I knew was that I lived near the Hannam Bridge that crossed the Han River from Gangnam to Hannam-dong. I also knew how to say oenjjog (left) and oleunjjog (right). As we slowly drove on the Olympic Expressway towards the bridge and my home, I was the ultimate backseat driver shouting "oenjjog yeogi!" (Left here) or "oleunjjog yeogi!" (Right here) whenever I spotted a familiar landmark.

As was now the custom with marathons around the world in the new era of the Internet, a few days after the race several sample race photos appeared in my inbox. No longer did I have to use a large magnifying lens to at peer at small glossy race sample photos.

The day after the Seoul Marathon my legs felt fine and I spent my remaining three months in Seoul running in the parks, at the zoo with Lily, and along the river. I was scheduled to fly to my next duty station in DC in mid-June and noticed that there was a Han River Sunrise Marathon on the day of my departure. After I asked Ms. Yi to register me for the race, I came up with a plan that I thought was brilliant. My flight departed Incheon International Airport in the early afternoon on Sunday and arrived at Dulles airport outside of DC early Sunday afternoon. The 14-hour flight and the 14-hour time zone change were pretty much a wash, allowing me to depart and land at pretty much the same time. I could run the sunrise half-marathon, make it to the airport with enough time to check-in, and assuming Twiggy didn't escape again in the airport, make it to my flight in plenty of time. Then when I arrived in DC, I could run an evening race. Two races, on the same day, on opposite sides of the earth.

The first half of the plan went off without a hitch. As I ran along the Han River for what I thought was my final time I soaked in all the sights: the Seoul Tower, the bridges, and the buildings, as the most brilliant orange sun I have ever seen in my life rose through the humid haze engulfing the river. I heard "Fight on!" more than I have ever heard in my life, or maybe I was just more aware, as I wanted to fully sense every second of this final run in Seoul. I made it to the airport with plenty of time to spare.

As Pat Healy would say in the movie *Something About Mary*: "First crack in the armor." When I created my brilliant plan, I neglected to consider that I never sleep on airplanes. I just can't get comfortable no matter what I do. I just sit and sit, looking forward to the next meal to give me something to do. Once I arrived in DC, I was not only tired because I had been awake for hours, but my legs were as stiff as a board. Running a half-marathon, then sitting for 14 hours in a crammed seat in economy class, does wonders for your leg muscles. I was feeling a bit cranky, but certainly not as cranky as Twiggy, based on the glare followed by hisses when I peered in her cage to check on her at baggage claim. The poor cat had made two transpacific flights in the cargo hold of an airplane with a fall from five stories in between-- who can blame her for being a bit feisty?

I grabbed a Coke from Hudson News as I exited the airport. Later that evening I found myself on the start line of some long forgotten 5k during one of DC's numerous summer heat advisories. I had never lived in DC previously, so I had no idea that a city could get so humid. The heat, humidity, jet lag, tiredness, and stiff legs made for a tough outing. But after 3.1 miles, I was able to say to myself that, that morning I had woken up on the other side of the world, had run a half-marathon there, and here I was in DC, finishing a race on the evening of that same very long day. I hope I never again have the opportunity to try that stunt.

Years later, when I was stationed up at the Second Infantry Division on the border between North and South Korea, I returned to the Seoul Marathon. Life in an infantry division that is on constant alert is a lot different than life in an Army garrison in Yongsan, Korea. Although I was registered for the race, I had not asked my boss if I could actually have the weekend off in order to travel to Seoul to participate. Grudgingly, our chief of staff gave me a weekend pass but not before reminding me "Make sure you run with your phone." Sure enough as I passed Lotte World the phone rang, "Hey, can we legally use a helicopter to . . .?"

Not that it really mattered but a few months before that race I had a detached retina. As the doctor peered into my eye, I heard him say, "Wow, it's not just torn, it's also twisted." That night as I lay in the pre-op room at Yonsei University's hospital in Seoul I kept thinking, the one time I authorize basketball for PT instead of our usual run I wind up here, with a patch on one eye and no vision in the other. Dr. Hwang did a wonderful job. The next morning as he took the bandages off my eyes and asked how many fingers he was holding up, I could say "du" (two). I returned to see, yes, I could now see, Dr. Hwang each week. As I healed, he gave me strict instructions: no boxing; no taekwondo; no hitting soccer balls with my head; and no running, but jogging was OK. I really had no interest in boxing, soccer, or taekwondo so I was good with that. The jogging versus running thing intrigued me. Dr. Hwang and I had lengthy discussions debating how fast I could run and still be jogging. He could never really give me an accurate answer. I think he just wished I would leave his office. Jogging, running-- who cares about the difference, I just wanted to be able to see out of my eye, so I slowly jogged in the mountains of Camp Casey as I prepared for my second running of the Seoul Marathon.

I closed out the 2000s on a high, running the Berlin Marathon. The course and crowds are absolutely spectacular, and I can understand why the marathon world record is set and reset on that course year after year. As I ran under the Brandenburg gate toward the finish line, I strained as I realized I could finish in the same time I had run thirty years earlier. I was excited that now in my late forties I could match the times of my youth. Later that day I called John and all he said is, "Thirty years later and you are at the same place you were thirty years ago, zero improvement." I guess you could look at it that way. But I though nothing was going to get me off my marathon high; not knowing of the events waiting in the shadows in the next decade.

ROLLER COASTER

On August 10, 1976, my backyard was strewn with green leaves. It was as if every leaf on our trees was ripped off by the winds of Hurricane Belle. I dutifully picked up the leaves and placed them in a big pile for my dad to burn. I am not exactly sure how my dad could get live green leaves to burn but I know that he always had a large supply of lighter fluid on hand in our garage, along with a variety of other chemicals. Turpentine, red spider spray, spray paints, brake fluid, Clorox and ammonia all sat side by side on a wooden table coated in painting dripping, all waiting for the ash of a Pall Mall cigarette to blow up our house. I didn't dare ask any questions about Hurricane Belle, or even hurricanes in general, to avoid the mandatory, how-dare-you-ask-me-a-stupid-question Sunday dinner report. I just picked up leaf after leaf.

Growing up, I was always fascinated by weather. Every August I watched Neil Frank, director of the National Hurricane Center, track the latest hurricane off the East Coast. Very few of these storms reached Long Island. Although every car ride with lifeguard Hank Daly involved a discussion of three things; seagull rookeries; an offer to purchase me cheesecake in Oceanside, a town about ten miles off the route home; and a recap of The Great Hurricane of 1938. The 1938 hurricane was so powerful that it changed the landscape of eastern Long Island. Each evening by the time I arrived at Hank's house, after dodging his nightly question, "Tell me, young Boyle, do you like cheesecake?" I had heard once again how the 1938 storm created the Shinnecock Inlet and that another big storm would strike one day so we needed to be prepared. And each night as he got out of my car, he would remind me to "Keep an eye on that storm off of Florida," or wherever Neil Frank's eagle-eye was fixated. I would wonder exactly how I was supposed to, "Keep an eye" on a storm 600 miles away. I watched him walk across his lawn, which had a rowboat sitting on it. This was no quaint rowboat that had been filled with soil to make a flowerbed. This was a full-size ocean-rescue rowboat complete with oars that I am sure Hank practiced in at night to the bewilderment of shoppers across the street at Otto's Deli.

One storm that Neil Frank and I did keep an eye on was Hurricane Gloria that raced across Long Island during the beginning of my law school career in 1989, knocking out power for a few days, making my night runs even darker without the aid of streetlights.

Aside from these two minor hurricanes, my life had not been affected much by the weather. I did live in Kansas during the tornado outbreak of May 2003, the week that saw more tornadoes (338), than any week in recorded history. But aside from a few windows being blown out I was spared the wrath of these storms. Twiggy spent the week under a bed, I guess to avoid being swept up in a twister like Dorothy's dog Toto.

So, as I watched runners fight wind and rain at the Marine Corps Marathon, the week before I was scheduled to run in the 2012 NYC, I didn't think much of the hurricane named Sandy off the East Coast. For years I had heard warnings of incoming storms that would strike NYC or Long Island, only to have the storm head out to sea.

That Sunday and Monday I watched the news as the storm got closer and closer to NYC but figured that at the last minute the storm would head out to sea or if it did make landfall, it would knock some leaves off trees or knock out power for a few days like Belle and Gloria. I could not have been more wrong.

On Tuesday morning I woke to the news that Superstorm Sandy had devastated the NYC metropolitan area. The subways were flooded, entire neighborhoods like Breezy Point were in flames, and houses were swept out to sea. As I drove to work my initial thought was there is no way there will be a marathon this weekend.

Over the next few days both Mayor Bloomberg and NY Road Runners Club President Mary Wittenberg continually reiterated that the marathon would still be held that weekend. I was well into my taper for the marathon and had been running well. I was now close to age 50 and had a bit of a renaissance with running, curious to see how fast I could run once I passed the half-century mark. However, as physically fit I was, mentally I was on a roller coaster twisting and turning like the mouse cars of Rye Playland.

One minute I read from the NYRRC website that the marathon was still on; the next my brother-in-law Healy would call and say, "You have no idea what it's like up here. Cops and firefighters lost their homes. They have been working 24-hour shifts, and there is no way they will be able to work on Sunday to cover the marathon route." My emotional side wanted to believe the NYRRC that everything would be all right. My intellectual side agreed with Healy.

As the city slowly pumped water from the subways and put out the fires on Breezy Point, new flames were fanned in a debate over whether the race should go on. On one side were the runners. They were filling website message boards with comments about how hard they trained, how far they traveled to get to the race, and how the 26 miles of the race route were clear of water and debris. On the other side were those who believed that not only was it not appropriate to hold a marathon so close to the devastation of the storm (although the NY football team had a game during race weekend in the Meadowlands), but also that race supplies such as thousands of water bottles and blankets could be put to better use helping those whose lives had been uprooted. The debate reached a climax Friday afternoon during Mike Francesa's WFAN sports radio show with Mike arguing with callers about the realities of holding a marathon two days from then.

In the midst of this debate, I boarded the Bolt bus to head up from DC to NYC on Friday morning. This was my first trip on bus. Amtrak was still not operating, and no cars could drive into the city. I was torn the entire bus ride. The marathon requires both physical and mental energy, possibly more mental energy. My mental energy gas tank was on empty. However, I forged ahead, as I planned to meet a few friends in the city for the marathon.

As soon as I got off the bus near Penn Station and Madison Square Garden, I glanced at the front cover of the *New York Post*. In bold letters it read "ABUSE OF POWER" above a photo of the generator that sat at the NYC Marathon finish line getting ready to power of the finish line tents and timing mats. That headline said it all. Intellectually, I knew that race was off, but the NYRRC website proclaimed the race was still on. I quickly checked in my hotel and took a cab over to the site of my NY Bar Exam, the Javits Center. The Expo was filled will all the same booths, all the same pomp and circumstance, perhaps even more so than the last time I had been at the NYC Marathon back in 2005. But the mood was different. As I walked around looking at shirts, gels, and other gadgets, there was a palpable buzz of "Is it still on?" As I picked up my race number, the volunteer said "It's still on," behind a smile that appeared to be painted on like the smile of the little drummer boy in the TV holiday classic.

In 1989 I raced out of the Javits Center clicking my heels, thinking no more school or test ever. In 2012 I walked out thinking "Am I doing the right thing?" The answer to that question came quickly, because as soon as I entered my hotel room, I got a call from Nicole screaming "It's off, check the news!" Nicole, my running buddy from back in Hawaii, was now living in New Jersey with Fred and their growing family. She had entered the marathon and was headed to the Expo right as the race cancellation was announced. I quickly tried to figure out the Hyatt's TV remote, which first offered my discounts at the Hyatt Spa, then an offer for a Hyatt Credit Card, followed by room service options. I finally got to real TV where saw Mayor Bloomberg and Mary Wittenberg standing somberly at a podium explaining that the race was off. I was a little relieved. My dilemma had been solved for me.

As I entered Central Park the next morning on the southeast entrance near the Plaza Hotel, Kevin McAllister's retreat in *Home Alone 2*, for an early morning jog, I was met by a sea of runners in long-sleeved orange NYC Marathon shirts. I have been in Central Park for firework shows, for races, for Diana Ross' concert and many other joyful events. The mood on November 3, 2012, was the most somber I have even felt in the park. As I ran past the zoo and then toward the bramble and ultimately to the reservoir I heard rumors swirl about NYRRC offering automatic entry to the 2013 race; I overheard complaints about Mayor Bloomberg and Mary Wittenberg; I overheard groups plan to meet at the Verrazano Bridge and run the entire course on their own; I overheard lawsuits being planned to sue NYC and the NYRRC for travel expenses, entry fees, and lodging costs.

I wanted to scream, "You know there are other marathons!" or "You know the mayor has a hard job and had to make tough decisions!" but I didn't. I know that people needed a time and space to vent.

As I jogged on the same roads I had run on with Matt over twenty years ago, I thought to myself that I had been running lots of years, had seen lots of good and bad things in the world, and if a canceled marathon is the worst thing that happens to me in my marathon career, how bad can things really be? Until, five months later.

I was lying on my hotel bed drinking a Pepsi (the Hyatt in Boston didn't sell Coke), relaxing shortly after running the 2013 Boston Marathon when my phone rang. My nephew Pat's name popped up on the screen. After debating whether I really wanted to talk to him, I hit the "on" button after four rings to hear a scream "Are you OK!?"

"Yeah, I am lying here drinking a Pepsi."

"You survived? You're OK?"

"Pat, I have run lots of marathons. I am tired plus I am old now, so maybe more tired, but I survived."

"Turn on your TV."

I couldn't believe what I was seeing as the bombing was replayed. The finish line area that I had been in minutes before was under siege. The finish line that I had been watching on TV for over thirty years was filled with smoke. My first thought was not that I could have been there. I instantly thought of my stepmom and how worried she must be. When she came to watch Patrick and I in 1989 she was standing in the exact spot of the second explosion. I quickly called her and left a message "Hi, I am in my hotel room, and my run went OK." Then, following military protocol, I called Delphine, my awesome administrative assistant at the Army law school, at the time my duty station. I told her I was fine and to let the boss know. A few minutes later my very confused stepmom called me, "Why are you telling me you're in a hotel room and why are you telling me your run was OK?" "Oh, I guess I forgot to tell you I ran the Boston Marathon today."

I didn't sleep at all that night as I looked out my hotel window overlooking the Boston Harbor, watching hundreds of blue lights on police boats drift in the calm waters. I constantly checked the news and was heartbroken reading about people, even children, dying and people losing limbs. The next morning as my cab passed the finish line area on the way to the Amtrak, I saw the devastation first hand. Thin strips of yellow police tape cordoned off the entire area. To this day I am emotionally conflicted. As a defense lawyer I have represented and written the appeals for individuals on death row and have my beliefs of the death penalty, yet I was on the site of so much death and destruction caused by two young men. I have never worn my 2013 Boston Marathon shirt; it sits in a drawer with the tags still attached.

As I peered out the cab window past the police tape, I could see the finish line painted on the sidewalk. I thought, would it ever be the same? The small-town charm Pat and I encountered as we laughed and stretched in Hopkinton High School gym, watching Bill Rodgers cross that finish line in first place year after year, or joking with the young captain who served as aide for the commanding general of the Massachusetts National Guard just 24 hours ago in the gazebo on Hopkinton Town Common. I yearned for the simpler marathon carefree times, the times of just two years ago that now seemed like a century ago.

I spent most of the 2000s overseas. While briefly stationed stateside I was able to run both the Marine Corps Marathon and the NYC Marathon. In the early years of the new century my dad was ill so I flew from Germany to Florida once a month to visit. It was Thursday 3:00 p.m. flight from Frankfurt to Dulles; watch "Friends" in a bar at Dulles; flight from Dulles to Orlando; arrive around midnight; go to Alamo rental car; sleep in rental car; 6:00 a.m. sunlight beams into the rental car waking me; drive to Ormond Beach; three days running on beach; watching *Who Wants to be a Millionaire* (original Regis edition); getting yelled at for drinking 1940s Coke; Monday drive to Orlando; fly to Dulles; fly to Frankfurt; arrive Tuesday at 5:00 a.m. and drive directly to work in Mannheim.

And every month he would say, "Are you coming again next month?" I would point to my running shoes that I always left by the front door and say, "I have to, my shoes are here."

In July 2010 I arrived in Charlottesville. So much had changed in the US, and I was dying to be back near family, friends, and familiar running routes. One thing that didn't change was Twiggy; she was just as mean, if not meaner, after yet another long flight. My duty station was at the Army's law school, the same school I had attended twenty years ago on the north grounds of the University of Virginia.

My first order of business was getting a cell phone, as it appeared to me email was out of date and texting was the main line of communication. My problem was I had no idea what texting was. Back in Korea when my eye was out of whack and I was in the hospital, people kept texting me well wishes and all I could think was, how are these words getting on my phone? I found a Sprint store and told the sales rep all I needed was a basic phone that could make phone calls and text. "Well, here you go, $79 a month unlimited calls and texts."

Since household goods take about a month to ship from Germany to Virginia and my TV was on some container ship in the North Atlantic I proceeded to watch "The Jersey Shore" every night on my phone.

My first phone bill was $300! I paid the bill right away, knowing the failure to pay just debts is an offense in the military. I then called Sprint. "Your agent said $79, and my bill is $400."

"Well, Sir, you had a lot of Internet data usage."

"All I did was some texts, calls and watch *The Jersey Shore*."

"I think *The Jersey Shore* is all that data usage."

"Why did you sell me a phone that had Internet when I told the rep I only wanted text and calls?"

"Every phone comes with Internet. You didn't have to use the Internet though."

"How do I cancel my account?"

"What we can do is add data to your account. This brings it up to $100 and I will backdate this for you and make it retroactive to when you purchased the phone."

"Great."

I had no idea what that all meant but it seemed good. Next month my bill was ($200). If I had read the bill I would have seen July bill $100 (the new rate); July payment $400; credit ($300); August bill $100; credit $200. I am like, what? But I paid $200. Next month bill is ($400). If I had read the bill, it would have said August Bill $100; credit ($300) new credit added ($200) total credit ($400).

And each month the bill kept getting higher and higher and I thought, wow those roaming fees when I go to New York are a lot. I had no idea I had credit and every month I was paying the credit amount thus doubling the credit total.

After a few months, my bill was in the thousands of dollars. I called Sprint and the agent said, "Let's see, last month you had $1200 credit and you paid $1200 bringing your credit to $2400."

"Credit? How do I know I have credit?"

"Sir, numbers in a parentheses are credit."

"No one told me that."

"Sir, did you ever read your bill?"

"No, I just saw the numbers and paid it. What do we do now?"

"You have $2400 of credit towards your bill."

I didn't have to pay a phone bill for two years after that, but I do check my bill each month. Every month Heather says, "Why aren't we on a family plan?" I just think, do you really want to be on a family plan with a guy who can't read a phone bill?

Aside from my phone bill issues, it was great to be back in Charlottesville. My boss was absolutely wonderful. Brigadier General John Miller was not only a brilliant lawyer and fantastic leader, but his son was on the track and cross country teams at Furman University, at the time one of the top-ten Division 1 cross country programs in the country. Not only was he very flexible in allowing time off to get races or take a bit more time at lunch to run past the Darden Business School and run a loop around the beautiful University of Virginia campus, but he was also very encouraging and knowledgeable about the sport. Although he was more of a basketball player himself, he organized two spectacular runs at Panorama Farms, UVA's extremely hilly home cross country course. Over 500 runners in formation singing cadence on the thick, green, grassy course as the sun rose on the Blue Ridge Mountains was simply stunning.

One of the many benefits of being in the Army is the sheer number of running partners available. Running is a big part of Army life. Every morning's physical fitness session includes a run and the bi-annual fitness test includes a two-mile timed run.

On occasion I heard individuals complain, "Why do we do so much running?"

I always answered, "Didn't you read the brochure before you joined? Every single Army movie, every single Army TV show, every single recruiting brochure has scenes or photos of soldiers running. Did you actually think that was just Hollywood? How did you possibly think you wouldn't be doing any running in the Army? Its like booking a cruise and not realizing you will be on the water."

Since running is such a big part of the Army, running partners are never in short supply, whether it was my old Perimeter Relay teammates in Hawaii, Brian Andes waiting for me at 6:00 a.m. every day at Fort Hunt Park in Virginia to run along the Mount Vernon Trail as the sun rose over the Potomac, or Brendan Mayer when I arrived in Charlottesville.

I met Brendan years earlier when we were both stationed at the Second Infantry Division on the border between South and North Korea. I had only been in Korea for a few days before I learned of both his running ability and competitive drive. One Saturday morning our installation was hosting the Korea-wide Triathlon Championships. I am not certain if Brendan had ever done a triathlon, but if he hadn't, he sure had a big mouth for a newbie. I had done a few triathlons and enjoyed the swim and run portions, but never got into the bike leg. To me it was just too boring. Plus, biking just reminded me of my youth and having to bike to jobs, newspaper routes, baseball games, school, etc. To me, biking was transportation, not a sport.

The triathlon began with a swim leg in the Camp Casey Pool (water safety training facility). Since the pool was only eight lanes wide the race was divided into several waves of eight participants. After one wave exited the pool, another wave would enter, and so on. Each separate wave was timed and at the event's conclusion the times were merged to sort out the winners. Brendan and I were in different waves. After the times were collated I was ahead of Brendan in the results, however, in his mind he would have beaten me if the race were head-to-head.

The following week he got his chance, or at least hoped he got his chance. At the exact same pool were the Korea-wide triathlon relay championships. Brendan and I would be the anchors for our respective teams. He could not shut his mouth as he went on and on about his team had the Korea-wide bike champion and his team would be so far ahead by the run that I could never catch him. That Korea-wide bike champion rode on the same rubber tires as everyone else in the race and he got a flat tire. It was pure joy as I began my run leg as Brendan waited and waited for Mr. Flat Tire to come down the road.

Aside from the triathlon issues I actually like Brendan. Originally from Yonkers, he ran the same Van Cortlandt Park cross country course as me in high school (he edited this book pointing out that I had a portion of the VCP course incorrect) and loves the Yankees. Yet he did turn his back on New York's Team, St. John's, and cheers for the rival Georgetown Hoyas in basketball. Additionally, Brendan is the quintessential New Yorker straight out of central casting. If any agents ever need a 40-year-old with the accent and attitude, call Brendan.

Charlottesville had grown since I had last lived there. The UVA cross country course that I could run on only a few blocks for the Army law school back in 1990 had moved six miles away to beautiful Panorama Farm. Taco Bell and Exxon Gas Station now broke up a twenty-mile single-track dirt Rivanna Trail that circled the city. Still runnable; hikers, walkers and runners now had to carry a printout to figure their way on the course. "Exit at Fifth street, cross the road, cut through Taco Bell parking lot and rejoin the trail." But these were minor inconveniences. Charlottesville may be the best city in America as far as running options. Brendan and I would run in the shadows of Shenandoah Park along the hilly gravel Free Union Road or on the Saunders Trail Boardwalk toward Thomas Jefferson's Monticello before breaking off the trail and making a sharp right turn heading up and up to the apple orchards of Carter Mountain, the highest point in Charlottesville. The best part of long uphills is the return trip down. Other days we would run at Farmington Country Club, a course that has big, clean, warm bathroom huts at each hole that are larger than my house's bathrooms. To say the course is well-maintained is an understatement. I assume they try to maintain the beauty by keeping runners off the course with signs that state, "No Jogging." Brendan would justify our trots across the fairways saying we were running, not jogging, so all was good. We were both lawyers and we interpret words all day.

The sheer beauty of our runs is not what separates Brendan from other runners. It's his personality and our conversations. In addition to talking about the latest Yankee score, the latest WWE results, what The Situation was up to on *The Jersey Shore*, or the latest *New York Post* headline, out of nowhere Brendan would say the absolute craziest things on a run.

"That was right after Son of Sam stole my Mom's Volkswagen." Son of Sam terrorized NYC in the late 1970s and he lived on Pine Street in Yonkers near Brendan. He would say these things not bragging or as an exaggeration. He is a typical New Yorker, and things like Son of Sam stealing your car is no big deal. He was also a caddy and even went to college on a caddy scholarship, which I thought only existed in the movie "Caddyshack." He knew everything about golf and golf courses. When we ran by Farmington Country Club he would say "This area is the back nine, based on starting tee times golfers will not be here for another hour so we're good".

But what fascinated me the most was that Brendan smoked! I would pull into the Saunders Trail parking lot at 8:00 a.m. on a Saturday for a 1500-feet run to the top of Carter Mountain, and he would be smoking! As soon as I got out of my car he would take one final drag, toss the cigarette, and say, "Let's go. Got to be back home soon, Yankees have an early start today." And he would run up that hill without taking one deep breath, then sprint all the way down. Often on weekend afternoons he would want me to go with to the local VFW, Veterans of Foreign Wars, not to trade war stories but rather as Brendan would say, "It's the only bar in town that lets you smoke." Fortunately, seven years ago Brendan kicked the habit. I think getting married and becoming a father helped in that regard.

So, it should come as no surprise that in April 2011 we found ourselves standing in the dark at the Charlottesville Downtown Mall at the start line for Charlottesville Marathon/Half-Marathon. I am almost certain Brendan smoked a cigarette before the start. The race was a low-key affair with only a few hundred runners, easy entry process, and a small race expo held the day before in the freezing cold Charlottesville Ice Rink. It was the perfect simple carefree marathon that I was yearning for two years in the future after Boston.

The first half of the course was along the roads Brendan and I ran on every day; 6.5 miles out and back along 21 Curves Road and next to Farmington Country Club. Aside from being endlessly twisting, 21 Curves Road was the home of the meanest dog I have ever seen in my life. Every time we ran past a large house with a vast front yard, Stephen King's *Cujo* would come tearing across the lawn howling, only to suddenly shriek when foiled by the electric fence surrounding the property. I knew every tree in the area just in case Cujo broke through that electronic force field. Along the way we mingled with many coworkers and students from the Army law school who were in the companion half-marathon.

Just prior to the halfway point sprinting runners engulfed us, half-marathoners kicking it toward their finish while at the same time annoying Brendan to no end.

"Half-marathoners to the left, full marathoners to the right!" shouted volunteers as Brendan and I veered right. Only 400 hundred runners veered right for the 6.5-mile loop that we would need to complete twice (the course has now changed). This course went up and downhill along winding roads save for a short flat stretch on a bike path alongside the Rivanna River. At times we saw no one in front of us and no one behind us. It was just like a regular run, and we talked the whole way.

For a first marathoner, a small low-key race was perfect for Brendan. I think small low-key marathons are an option that first-time marathoners should consider. The energy and excitement of a large city marathon is great. However, standing on your feet for hours at an expo, being exposed to new gadgets, exploring a new city, finding a place to eat and sleeping in an unfamiliar hotel bed causes sensory overload. Then on race morning the logistics of getting to the start line in a field of 25,000 or more runners is daunting, especially for a first-time marathoner. In some cases these are first-time racers, as for many individuals the marathon is the first footrace they have ever entered. An unfamiliar city and hotel, two hours to negotiate getting to the start line and many runners are mentally wiped out before the gun goes off. Sleeping in your own bed and simply walking straight from your car to the start line reduces pre-race stress.

Brendan and I kept a steady pace for both 6.5-mile loops. The old Charlottesville Marathon was considered one of the hilliest races in the country, and for good reason. There is a road on the course simply called Steep Hill Road. The hills did not deter Brendan, who was cheered along the course by new Army lawyers who had recently begun classes at the Army Law School and were now staffing all the water tables. Brendan was their physical fitness trainer each morning at 6:00 a.m. They cheered wildly for him. In addition to instructing them at PT, Brendan helped them integrate into the Army. However, I doubt he mentioned anything about the Army offering smoking-cessation classes to anyone who wanted to kick the habit. After Brendan left Charlottesville, I took over the physical fitness running program with my assistant to the run group leader, Major Jeremy Steward.

We crossed the finish line to the applause of one person, Brendan's fiancée, now wife. Actually, crossing the finish line is still a disputed matter. There was a huge balloon arch hanging over the finish area on the Charlottesville Downtown Mall. With about 100 yards to go Brendan said, "Let's sprint it in! and he turned on the heat. He turned on the jets right up to that balloon arch and stopped. I stayed with him the best I could however did not stop at the arch and continued a few steps to the finish mat signifying the actual finish line. After his Usain Bolt finish, Brendan caught his breath, walked over to me, and at that point officially crossed the finish line. Just like the old triathlon days he claimed victory. However, the next morning's edition of the Daily Progress newspaper told a different story listing my time several seconds faster than his. He spent a week claiming he was misled by the arch and he studied race photos to see who got to the arch first. If the race distance was from the start line to the balloon arch, then yes, Brendan won. Did this marathon resolve any issues with previous races between us? No, as recently when we discussed the results over text he simply wrote back "Disputed."

Nevertheless Brendan ran awesome in his first marathon. His first and second half splits were identical and that was impressive considering how hilly the second half was. The finish line area was somewhat anticlimactic as all the half-marathoners who made up the bulk of the race field were long gone. It was like, what do we do now? So, we quickly headed out, Brendan to catch an early Yankees' game and me to drive to Sunoco to grab a bottle of Coke.

The great runs that spring over hill and dale and the evenly paced Charlottesville Marathon gave me the itch to return to the NYC Marathon that fall. Fortunately, I had run a fast half-marathon the previous January in Miami, securing a guaranteed entry based on time. I figured that all the hills I had run in Charlottesville would set me up perfectly for the bridges on NYC as well as the hills of Central Park. The guaranteed entry did make registration easy as far as entering the race; however, I did get sticker shock at the price of $270 dollars! Wow-- had marathon entry fees skyrocketed. Some quick math told me that this was about ten dollars per mile or about $1.50 per minute in the race. A few decades earlier I had paid $4 for the Long Inland Marathon and $2 for the Honolulu Marathon; pennies per mile. As Bill Murray replied in "Meatball" when asked about Camp Mohawk and if the high cost was worth it, "Yes, sure is, it's the best darned camp around." The same holds true for the NYC marathon, "It's the best darned marathon around."

Train as you fight is an old Army expression and I always recommend training over the type of terrain you will be racing on. Believe it or not this even include races on flat surfaces. It takes practice to run a long time on a flat surface. Mile after mile on a flat road can cause your legs to tire as you are continually using the exact same muscles. If your race is all on flat roads you need to train on flat roads. If that is not possible, during a race that is on a flat roads make sure you change your stride for a few hundred yards every few miles to break up the monotony in your leg muscles. Races with a few hills force your legs to do this naturally.

Over the next several months I ran on roads, on trails, and on tracks to prepare for what would be my final carefree marathon before I purchased my ticket for the Space Mountain rollercoaster ride of hurricanes and bombings.

Training for the NYC marathon brings its own unique set of challenges. Not only does the course contain several deceptively long bridges, a long gradual uphill stretch along Fifth Avenue, followed by the hills of Central Park, all requiring training on hills; most importantly the logistics of the NYC Marathon, require mental preparation and patience.

Like the Boston Marathon, the NYC Marathon is a point-to-point course requiring race organizers to shuttle runners from the finish area to the start line. However, this process is perhaps tenfold more difficult in NYC compared to Boston, both because of the geography of the course and the sheer number of runners needing transportation to the start. In Boston, 30,000 runners board yellow school buses at the Boston Commons and are driven on a highway out to Hopkinton. Shuttling 30,000 runners is an extraordinary effort yet runs pretty smoothly as runners only need to board one bus for the journey to the start. In comparison, NYC Marathon race organizers must get close to 55,000 runners to Staten Island for the start at Fort Wadsworth. To do so a series of buses and ferries are utilized.

From wake-up in a midtown NYC hotel until the gun fires on the Verrazano Bridge could be six to seven hours, many of those hours spent on buses and ferries followed by sitting in corrals on Fort Wadsworth waiting for the walk out to the bridge. It takes mental preparation to be ready for this. All too often I have seen runners walk out toward that bridge and their mental energy tank is on empty, having spent the previous four hours fidgeting on the wet grass fields of Fort Wadsworth. I overheard grumbles of, "Can we finally start and get his over with?" Big city marathons, especially the NYC Marathon, require a pre-race plan. Every detail should be accounted for so that runners can focus on the task at hand and relax. What clothes will I wear to the start that can easily be discarded? What will I do with my time as I sit idly in my start corral for 45 minutes? Should I bring a book or newspaper to read? What time should I eat an energy bar? Do I need gloves? Should I run with my phone? All of these issues should be sorted out the night before, allowing runners to remain calm, focused, and relaxed at the start area.

All energy should be directed inward, ignoring outside stimulus. Yes, the energy of the crowd is great and provides adrenaline, but runners should save that adrenaline for the start, not waste it three hours in advance. The other trap I see at the start of big city marathons is "copycat syndrome." One runner will see a runner stretching in a certain way and think, "Hey, should I do that stretch?" or overhear a runner say that "Having two cups of Dunkin Donuts coffee is the key to a great race" as a non- coffee drinker grabs a cup, thinking this is the secret. Runners are a bundle of nerves in the start area, all reaching for that brass ring that will get them to the finish line. I always say, "Dance with the person you brought to the dance." Stick to your normal routine and don't do something last-minute thinking that person you just saw or overheard holds the only key to the success.

And this holds true in the weeks leading up to a marathon. The Internet is a wonderful tool to acquire training knowledge. However, too much reading of various running message boards can be both confusing and counterproductive. All too often runners will read that such and such runner did this pace or distance in practice and begin to doubt their own training without thinking deeper. Maybe that person whose workout you read has more time to train or maybe they did that run in better weather than what is in your area. As you prepare for the marathon, focus on yourself, and don't worry about how others are training, it a futile distraction. It's hard enough preparing for and running your own marathon, let alone worrying about someone else's. Confidence and relaxation in preparation and on race morning are just as critical as all the miles run in training.

Fortunately, my military background helped me reduce a lot of the pre-race NYC Marathon tension. TV viewers may see the NYC Marathon start at the base of the Verrazano Bridge and figure that runners just staged on the road leading up to the bridge. At least that's what I thought for years. Little did I know that runners stage at Fort Wadsworth, a Coast

Guard Base on the west side of the Hudson River. For years I drove past the signs reading "Fort Wadsworth, last exit before toll and bridge," without thinking for a second what Fort Wadsworth was, as my focus was on getting across the bridge and then dealing with every aggressive driver in the tri-state area converging on the Belt Parkway as I drove out to Long Island.

Prior to the 2004 NYC Marathon I trained with my buddy Ray Jackson. Ray is the earliest riser I have ever met. We would meet each morning at the Key Bridge that traverses the Potomac River from Rosslyn, Virginia, to Georgetown in DC. My only caveat to our runs was that I would not meet him unless the meet up point started with a five. I was ok with running at 5:00 a.m. or 5:15 a.m. but I could not tolerate Ray's 4:00 a.m. runs through DC. One morning Ray mentioned that there was a Navy lodge (military hotel) on Fort Wadsworth and we should stay there the night before the marathon. We both quickly made reservations. A few weeks later we stayed in the best-kept secret when it comes to the NYC Marathon. The hotel is 300 yards from the start line! Ever year thereafter I made reservations one year in advance of the marathon.

With my hill training in my back pocket and my Navy lodge reservation locked in, I boarded the Amtrak in Charlottesville, Virginia, and headed north to meet Fred and Nicole for the 2011 NYC Marathon. Although Nicole had trained for the Honolulu Marathon years earlier, injury prevented her from racing, thus this was to be her first marathon and she was determined not only to finish but to also soak up every moment of the atmosphere that makes the NYC Marathon special.

To minimize all pre-race jitters, I had booked a room in midtown from Friday evening through Monday morning through Hotwire plus had two rooms set for the Navy lodge on Saturday evening. I loved the old Hotwire where it was a guessing game as you waited for your hotel name and location to appear after making payments.

On Saturday, Fred and Nicole drove over from Jersey and we all headed over to the Javits Center. Not only was this Nicole's first NYC marathon it was her first marathon expo. She was like a kid in a candy store wandering from booth to booth and taking obligatory photos holding her race number. I try to stay inside the Javits Center for as little time as possible, be it for the bar exam or a race expo. Eventually we made it back to my hotel, packed our overnight bags and race equipment, and began our journey to Staten Island. First stop was the Staten Island Ferry, which shuttles passengers from lower Manhattan past the Statue of Liberty over to NYC's forgotten borough, the suburbs of Staten Island. This ferry, in which Madonna's video for "Papa Don't Preach" was filmed, is NYC's best tourist attraction considering the price-- free.

We arrived just as the previous ferry took off so we had one hour to kill until the next ferry, idly sitting in the vast ferry terminal waiting room. Normally such a wait the night before a race could cause anxiety, however in Fall 2011 NYC's Occupy Wall Street protest movement was still going strong. The epicenter of the movement was Zuccotti Park, in lower Manhattan, less than a half mile away from the ferry terminal. Since the early November night air was cold, I assume that several protesters decided to spend the night in the warm ferry terminal as opposed to a tent on a cold cement slab. For one hour we sat on hard plastic chairs as individuals in plastic "V for Vendetta" masks took over the joint shouting "Banks Got Bailed Out, We Got Sold Out!" or "O-C-C-U-P-Y! What does that spell? OCCUPY!" I could understand their rights to protest but I am not sure they were reading the audience. Aside from Fred, Nicole, and I dressed in old sweats with small backpacks slung over our shoulders, there were three other individuals waiting for the ferry, slumped in chairs, half-falling asleep after a hard day working in one of NYC's service industries heading back to their homes on Staten Island. The few of us not exactly fat cats of Wall Street. The shouts of "All day! All week! Occupy Wall Street! All day! All week! Occupy Wall Street!" helped take our minds off the race.

Eventually we boarded the ferry and headed west, the tall buildings of NYC growing smaller by the minute. As we crossed the dark, cold waters of the Hudson River I could make out some of the buildings near the finish line in Central Park. As we continued heading west, I kept thinking that's a far way to run to get to the finish line. Many marathons are a loop, so it is hard to get perspective of how far a marathon actually is. You get that perspective in a point-to-point race like Boston or NYC as you are shuttled to the start on a yellow school bus or ferry, all the while thinking that's a far distance to get back to where this trip started.

Fred and I had gotten that perspective fivefold just a few years earlier. One January as we sat in his Greenwich Village apartment, one of us mumbled the words that we would rue four months later. "You read that new Bill Bryson book, *A Walk in The Woods*? We could do that." Instantly our plan was set in motion. Bill Bryson and his buddy Katz were expert hikers compared to us as we sat in that cramped apartment discussing how we could hike the Shenandoah Park portion of the Appalachian Trail (AT) that snaked through Virginia. The AT travels south from Georgia to Maine, covering over 2,000 miles. Years earlier when I was at Fort Ritchie, Maryland, my first duty location, the AT passed right by post, and I ran on it often. Those runs didn't seem too difficult. The trail was mostly flat as it crossed the border from Maryland into Pennsylvania. How hard could a hike be?

"Look here the Internet says that portion is 140 miles, we can knock that out in five to six days."

"Yeah, in the Army we used to hike 12 miles in three hours. So, we wake up at 7:00 a.m., then hike 12 miles until 10:00 a.m. We can fish, hang out in hammocks, eat, then knock out eight to ten more miles from like 3:00 p.m. to 5:00 p.m. and then have a cookout each night."

That May Fred met me in Charlottesville. As our friend Dave Crawford helped load our backpacks into his car he said, "These are really heavy, what do you have in here?" We had tents, we had tarps, we had seven pairs of clothes, we had bags and bags of food, we had twenty cans of Coke, we had fishing rods, we had hammocks, and an assortment of magazines to read. And to be really outdoorsy we had the official AT guide with each tenth of a mile described in detail.

As Dave drove us north along route 29 through Green, Madison and then Culpepper counties towards our starting point in Front Royal, Virginia, we could see the Blue Ridge Mountains to our left and quickly realized that each mile he covered speeding north at 60 MPH was a mile we had to walk back south, with extremely heavy backpacks.

As we unloaded our packs, Dave had to hoist mine onto my back as I could barely lift it. "Good luck, see you in Waynesboro on Saturday."

The section of the AT Fred and I chose travelled through Shenandoah National Park from Front Royal, Virginia, in the north to Waynesboro, Virginia at the southern end of the park. Skyline Drive weaves through the park along the ridge line about 3,000 feet above sea level. In the fall that road can be bumper to bumper with DC residents heading west to catch a glimpse of the glorious fall colors, and a glimpse of the rear of the car in front of them traveling at 5 MPH coated with "My Child Is A Superstar" stickers.

Our first crack in the armor was the fact that Front Royal is pretty much at sea level and the first nine miles of hike was all uphill to get to the 3000-feet level of the AT as it wove through Shenandoah Park. As we climbed and climbed our 20-mile a day goal slowly slipped away. As soon as we reached level ground, we pitched our tents right next to the AT and quickly fell asleep. In the middle of the night the beam of a strobe light headed towards our tents and awakened us. To this day we have no idea what that light was-- all we knew is that neither of us said a word and didn't move a muscle in our tents as that strobe light continued to flash for 15 minutes in front of us. It seemed like an eternity.

The next morning, we assessed our situation. It was already hot, and our legs were stiff from our nine-mile uphill hike weighted down by about at least 60 pounds of needless equipment. "Saddle up," Fred barked as we headed down this long, brown, endless ribbon of a dirt trail. After less than ten minutes, I heard the crash of something running into a bush.

"That's a big deer, Fred."

"That wasn't a deer, that's a bear."

We never considered this possibility back in our NYC apartment. Sure, the guidebooks mentioned bears but we thought we would have zero chance of encountering one. At least this bear seemed afraid of us and ran the other direction.

We forged ahead in the heat, our silence on the trail only to be suddenly broken by popping coming from behind me. Not only did we hear popping, my backpack shook, and my back was now coated in warm liquid. Did strobe light man follow us and shoot me in the back? I tossed my back off as quickly as I could only to realize that my soda cans were exploding in the heat. My liquid gold was slowing draining out into the dry dirt below our feet. I continued with a very wet, sticky, albeit lighter backpack.

I have been on Skyline Drive many times and the road seems rather flat. On the other hand, whoever mapped out the AT in the exact same park decided to have the trail go up and down each of the tall peaks in the park. We walked up and down getting thirstier by the minute and our Coke was down the drain. Fortunately, we had empty canteens, water purification tablets, and a guidebook telling us exactly where we could find water right near the AT. "At mile marker 110.5 turn left at the oak tree, walk 100 feet and there is a small stream." Unfortunately, neither of us knew what an oak tree was, compared to a maple tree, compared to the million other trees we kept passing in the park. We would guess and eventually find streams, gulping down water, not even taking the time to purify the water, so thirsty we just figured we'd deal with the dysentery later.

And so, one day turned to the next, trudging along that awful, endless, brown ribbon of a trail. Our second night, in the misery that is the AT, was spent in one of the trail's many huts scattered along the route. These three-sided wooden sheds have several wide, flat boards inside, in which hikers can throw down a sleeping mat and spend the night undercover protected from any rain. However, the open fourth side of the hut is the wide entrance for any animal that is interested in what you packed for dinner. Fred and I followed proper protocols and hung our backs outside on a tall pole supposedly out of the reach, sight, and smell of any bears. The three individuals we shared our accommodations with didn't see the need to properly store their packs. I spent the entire night lying on my wooden plank of a bed watching a million mice go to town on those guys' packs under the moonlight, all the while hoping I would not catch a hantavirus.

We left our companions and their rodent-filled packs and continued heading south. We had no idea how far we had traveled and no idea what lay ahead. After another long trek up and down the tallest, steepest hills in the park I rounded a bend and there, slightly downhill from us, 50-feet away, was the hugest black bear in the park, if not the entire state of Virginia. I quickly signaled for Fred to backtrack as we slowly walked backward up the hill we had just ambled down. My mind raced: run from a black bear; fight a grizzly bear, grizzlies climb trees? I was confused. I had learned these lessons on various shows like "When Animals Attack" but wasn't sure what to do with either species of bear. Fred and I sat on a rock looking down at the bear that seemed more interested in digging for grubs than in us. It may have been the biggest bear in the park but must have also been the dumbest bear in the park because it searched for grubs-- only 50 feet away from him were our backpacks full of nuts, oats, and other things I assume bears eat.

"Let's just wait here for another hiker to come through and let them deal with the bear." Our moral compasses were so askew at that point that we threw out that idea not because it would be wrong to fail to warn the next hiker about the bear, but because Fred said, "We haven't really seen any hikers today. We could be here all night waiting for someone else to come." Our next plan was for me to approach the bear and whack it in the head with my fishing rod. That was a good throwaway plan; we didn't fully flesh it out. Throwing rocks at the bear was tossed out, too, because we thought angering it wouldn't work out well. My suggestion that we try to walk through the woods to work our way around the bear was met by, "I have walked twenty miles today. I am not walking one step more than I have to, and I am staying on this trail." Eventually we made a pact. We would forge ahead and make noises hoping the bear would flee. If one person was attacked the other person would promise to jump on the bear's back and hit it in the head with our small shovels. We shook on it and made our move. As we got closer and closer, the bear just kept looking for grubs to eat. The bear didn't even look up as we walked by so close that we could have pet it. It was as if Gentle Ben had wandered up here from the Everglades.

About one minute after we passed the bear we came into a clearing, and we were on the Skyline Drive. What? We had been traipsing through those woods for days and here 50 feet away from us the whole time is the Skyline Drive? The beautiful flat, bear-free, Skyline Drive! And there right across the road is a restaurant and general store? Our plans changed quickly. By the trash area we ditched clothes, we ditched tarps, we ditched fishing rods, and we ditched food. From there on out we did the AT Light. We walked in the grass alongside Skyline Drive, we ate at the rest stops along the way, we hitched rides when we were tired, and even spent a night in the park's Skyland Resort eating steak and watching TV, while lounging on comfortable beds. A few days later we rolled out of the park in the back of a dump truck, our AT adventure completed.

Our AT misadventure was a long-forgotten memory, as Fred, Nicole and I exited the ferry and caught a cab to the entrance to Fort Wadsworth. As we entered the post on foot to our right under the cover of darkness, the extraordinary effort to create the Athlete's Village, staging corrals and start area were under way. A few minutes later Nicole looked up, eyes as wide as saucers, "Wait a minute, we have to run up that?!!!" Nicole was looking up at the beautifully lit-up Verrazano Bridge that towered above the dark water below, the cars traversing the bridge seemingly 500 feet above us. The perspective Nicole had was totally out of whack as we were on the waters edge almost directly under the bridge. In reality, although high above the water, the Verrazano Bridge is almost flat with very little rise or descent as each side of the bridge sits on high land. "Relax, tomorrow morning we start on the road way up there and the first mile is only slightly uphill."

That night I fell asleep to the sounds of metal banging into metal as the staging area continued to come to life. I was awakened to the knocking on my door, "Check it out, the race is on TV!" I clicked on the TV to the image of a cheerful reporter in a thick blue puffy jacket, "We're here at chilly Fort Wadsworth as marathoners start to arrive for the NYC Marathon!" Huddled behind her were shivering runners sitting on the ground awaiting the start three hours away. As I lay in my warm bed watching the reporter gleefully interview Betty from Iowa who was running her first NYC Marathon as hundreds of runners photobombed the camera shouting, "Woah, go NY!" I felt guilty being so warm and comfortable as runners shivered in the cold 300 yards away.

About an hour before race time Nicole handed our bags to Fred, who headed off the post to catch a cab, and then the ferry, toward Central Park to see us at the finish. The area near the Navy lodge on post was roped off and completely empty save for a few elite runners allowed onto this half of post to warm up in solitude. We walked in silence across the empty fields toward the bridge. Right under the bridge stood a ten-foot-high temporary chain link fence, the border between the serene south part of post and bedlam to the north. With one step across that border the mood changed, and the adrenaline started to flow. "Catch you at the park," I said, as Nicole and I parted ways, headed to our separate corrals and different wave start areas. I slowly made my way toward my corral, passing thousands of runners in Dunkin Donuts' caps, one of the race sponsors that hands out free wool caps on chilly race mornings.

With over 50,000 runners crowding onto a small bridge the NYYRC has instituted a strict staging area complete with corrals sorted by past or predicted marathon race times. About 45 minutes prior to wave start times runners are instructed to enter their designated corrals. Each corral holds about 200 runners and entry is only gained by showing your race bib to an eagle-eyed race marshal, who can spot a forged or doctored number from a mile away. Once in the confined area of the white metal gates the waiting begins. Some runners jog in circles, others sit on the curb in silent contemplation, while others nervously chat to anyone who will lend an ear.

Suddenly the parade to the start line begins and corral after corral files onto the Staten Island Expressway. At this point any semblance of order is tossed out the window as runners from all corrals merge; each runner pushing and fighting to get as close to the start line as possible. Why, I have no idea, as the chip timing records accurate finishing times no matter where a runner begins the journey.

Once on the bridge runners must head to designated color-coded areas on the bridge-- orange on the eastbound lanes, blue on the westbound lanes and green on the lower level of the bridge. The NYRRC does a remarkable job getting 55,000 runners safely across that bridge. With four waves divided into three color codes, runners are only running with 5,000 runners or so for the first several miles of the race. Although the start on TV makes it appear that 55,000 runners are all descending into Brooklyn at one time in one place, the racecourse is actually three separate racecourses for the first several miles. I never knew this until I ran the race. The bridge is designed for vehicle traffic, not runners. And those vehicles enter and exit the bridge from different roads depending on if they are eastbound or westbound and if they are upper level or lower level. David Katz, the fantastic course designer, and official course measurer, took the different exits and entrances into account when he designed three separate courses that eventually merge in Brooklyn several miles into the race.

In the past I have started on the upper level, which is like a party for the first two miles, with runners stopping dead in their tracks as you almost crash into them as they take selfies with the NYC skyline in the background, boats below shooting plumes of colored water into the air, and runners disrobing, tossing sweatshirts onto the road as they begin to warm up.

In 2011 I started in the green zone, the lower level, and loved it. First, when I drive the bridge I prefer the lower level, as trucks are not permitted and there is less chance of traffic. Secondly, it seemed it like many folks didn't want to run on the lower level, so they moved back to lower-seeded corrals which is permissible. As Adam Levine belted out "Moves Like Jagger," I found myself ten rows back from the start line. Running on the lower level was extremely quiet with each runner's footsteps echoing off the low, dark ceiling. It was the perfect place to get into a rhythm and settle into a steady pace. When driving over the bridge the ascent and descent are barely noticeable, and the same holds true while running. Yes, the first mile is slightly uphill, but certainly manageable.

Once off the bridge the race is surprisingly quiet as the runners trot over the various on and off ramps of the bridge not a spectator in sight. That all changes once runners hit the very long stretch of Fourth Avenue in Brooklyn. I was feeling great as I passed thousands of spectators, as well as firehouse after firehouse with their sirens blaring, adding to the excitement. I made it through Fourth Avenue without incident unlike the year the lady with a marble rye knocked me over as she attempted to get home from her weekly Sunday morning bakery trip.

The crowds in Brooklyn were most dense at around mile eight as we veered right and ran up a short uphill in a quiet tree-lined neighborhood. It was as if we ran under a canopy of golden and red leaves for a few blocks. The next few miles in Brooklyn weave through residential areas, the crowds not as thick as those on Fourth Avenue. I approached the long, steady climb of the Pulaski Bridge where to my left could see the NYC skyline. It was like the Emerald City, my Oz, halfway home. On the crest of this bridge is the halfway point of the race. The halfway point comes with remarkably little fanfare, as most spectators don't venture out onto the bridge.

As I crossed the halfway point and gradually descended into Queens, I was under the pace needed to qualify for Boston. I hadn't entered the race with that goal, however, as I passed the industrial areas of Queens, I realized I hadn't been to Boston in almost 20 years and it would be nice to return.

For many runners in the NYC Marathon, as well as myself, the Queensboro Bridge from miles 15 to 16 is the make-or-break point in the race. The grade of the bridge is not very steep; the length of the ascent combined with the location of the bridge can be a killer. By the time runners reach the bridge they have been on their feet for 15 miles, the adrenalin of the start has worn off and the realization has sunk in that there are still double digits remaining in miles until the finish. Plus, the bridge is both silent and dark. Runners cross the East River on the lower level in the dark, with no spectators. In that dark silent stretch the mind can start playing tricks on a runner. Why am I doing this? Runners are mostly alone at this time, with only their thoughts as a guide, and during this long mile the decision must be made-- continue to glory or call it quits. Unfortunately, some are tempted to cave into the screaming pain in their legs and minds. Once off the bridge at mile 16 runners are only blocks from Central Park. Stop now and it's a short walk to family and friends; turn right off the bridge and head up First Avenue, there's no turning back. Once runners head north up First Avenue, the only way to Central Park it to complete the race.

The spectators help make that decision for the runners. As tired and lonely as a runner is on that quiet, dark bridge the switch is flipped as soon as they come off the bridge and make the hairpin turn onto First Avenue, which is the single loudest, wildest block in any marathon in the world. It's Wellesley College and coming off the bridge in Seoul combined, then multiplied by a factor of four. Any runner who had thoughts of throwing in the towel two minutes ago has a quick change of heart. Plus, I didn't ever want to dare stopping the marathon at that point with 20,000 NYC fans in a one-block radius. "You thinking of quitting, Fuggedaboutit!"

The run north on First Avenue was the highlight for me, as it is for most runners. Although that stretch of the road has the most spectators and it the loudest, it oddly felt simultaneously like the most crowded and least crowded portion of the race. Certainly, the crowds were out in droves on this sunny Sunday morning, however First Avenue is so wide that the crowds don't feel as close to you compared to Brooklyn, and later on in Central Park.

My personal highlight along this broad avenue was the fact that the crew from Elvis Duran and the Morning Show were manning the water station at around mile 20. Certainly, Danielle, Froggy, and Skeery Jones, who I listened to every morning on my drive to work, could help me break through any wall.

Crossing the Willis Avenue Bridge into the Bronx I was struck by how vocal the crowds were. Although runners only pass through the Bronx for about one mile, it seems like every resident in the borough comes out, loud and proud, ensuring that the home of the Yankees is not forgotten in the runners' memories. After crossing the Madison Avenue Bridge back into Manhattan, I began a long slow wet run down Fifth Avenue. Even though the marathon has moved to an early November date over the years to avoid the heat that struck several October versions in the 1980s, Fifth Avenue generally feels hot, with runners alternating gulping down one cup of Poland Springs water, while tossing one cup of water over their heads; both small green Dixie cups then tossed onto the ground, leaving the dark wet pavement dotted in green.

Sunny 2011 was no different than previous years. As I ran down Fifth Avenue the entire road seemed wet for miles, green, slippery, crushed cups strewn all along the route. As usual the crowds were five to six people six deep on both sides of the road forming a thin human tunnel for us to pass through.

The crowds only increased, and got louder, as we entered Central Park for a few miles of up and down rolling hills on East Drive. The park reached its zenith of beauty as we ran past and under golden leaves, many of which slowly drifted down in the slight wind, and I reached out to grab them like a child on the schoolyard. My runners high was interrupted by a high-five incident, just before we exited the park near mile 25. I had been running the entire race with a small rock in my hand right hand, about the size of a marble. The week prior to the race I had run to the top of Carter Mountain and picked up a small stone intending to carry it during the race so if I ever felt tired or felt like giving up I would squeeze down on the rock to remind myself of the hard miles running up and down Carter Mountain. Running with a small trinket goes back to my high school days. Before a race Mr. Brynes would have us place a blade of grass from Cedar Creek Park, the park in which we did all our hill workouts, in our racing shoes, thus making sure we took a piece of our training to the race. As I was about to exit the park, a young person reached out to give me a high-five and I instinctively responded. However, my instincts forgot that I was holding a rock. As my slightly-opened hand made contact with a 12-year-old, the force of the high-five set in motion a series of events. The rock was dislodged and was suddenly airborne heading into the crowd of onlookers. I glanced back as I saw the rock angle towards the chest of a gentleman in a NY Yankees cap. The rock gently bounced off his chest and slowly fell to the ground. "Who the

F$%^ threw a rock at me!?" That shout was worth more than a million vapid cheers of "Let's go, you can make it, you're all winners!" as I high-tailed it onto 59th Street to avoid a confrontation with the Derek Jeter fan.

The horses and carriages that line the outside of the park were replaced by thousands of spectators standing near the most welcome sight in the race: the one-mile-to-go sign. Re-entering the park at Columbus Circle, I ran towards the finish line, gleefully counting off the 400-meters, then 300-meters, then 200-meters to-go signs.

As I was handed my medal and tinfoil blanket, I did mathematical gymnastics starting with the baseline Boston Marathon qualifying time of three hours, then adding five minutes in five-year age increments until I reached my age and verified to myself that I qualified to return to Boston. I also completed a quick self-assessment, checking off the block that running hills in Charlottesville made bridges and hills of the NYC course seem minor; train as you fight. The second block checked was that I stayed focused and relaxed throughout the entire staging process of the race. A big city race can be overwhelming and maintaining an inward focus was critical to my success. I also think the relaxed atmosphere of the lower-level start was great kick-start to the day.

As I walked onto Central Park West, I quickly found a hot dog cart and handed the proprietor a twenty-dollar bill soaked in sweat and Poland Springs water in exchange for two dirty water dogs and an ice cold can of Coke. I then sought out Fred on the mile-long block party that the closed road had become. Vendors, family members, and friends greeted weary finishers hobbling out of the park. After linking up with Fred, I quickly walked back to my hotel, showered and retuned as we both joked and waited for Nicole to appear from the now darkening park.

The NYC Marathon is held on the first day of daylight savings time, that miserable day each year when dusk arrives at about 3:30 p.m. on the East Coast and you know winter is getting ready to take a hold. Due to the nature of the NYC Marathon course and the number of runners in the race, four separate wave starts are needed to facilitate 55,000 runners running across the Verrazano Bridge. However, those 55,000 runners must be transported to the start area. Thus, the waves cannot begin to step off until 9:30 a.m. Certainly, waves could start earlier but that would mean runners would have to be transported to Fort Wadsworth at 4:00 a.m. and arrive in the dark. Basically 9:30 a.m. is the earliest waves could logically commence. With wave one heading out at 9:30 a.m., and each successive wave spaced out by approximately 30 minutes, the final wave does not hear their starting gun until 11:00 a.m. Any runner in that final wave who runs over four hours and forty-five minutes enters the finish line area at dusk or even into the early night.

Nicole came out of the park just north of the Tavern on the Green restaurant wrapped in a tinfoil blanket, beaming and shouting, "That was awesome!" For the rest of that day as dusk turned into darkness, she wore that tinfoil blanket like it was Superman's cape. The next morning, I made sure to mail her a copy of the *New York Times* that listed every race finisher by name.

Two years later I returned to the NYC Marathon, a few months after the Boston bombing. This time it was Fred's turn to run as Nicole flip-flopped as support crew. The Navy lodge was the same, the course was the same, and the jokes with Fred on the ferry the night before the race were the same. But that was all window-dressing covering up the fact that the race was different. Security was beefed up substantially, as it had to be. Central Park was surrounded by fences. Spectators could no longer watch a loved one run on Fifth Avenue, then cut across the park to the finish line. The finish line festival on Central Park West was gone, replaced by whatever large trucks the city could find to block all roads within a three-block radius of the park. I exited Central Park to an empty road, devoid of any vendors, friends, and family. We were quickly ushered away from the area. Nicole and I wound up sitting in the lobby of the NoLo Hotel at Broadway and 77th Street waiting for Fred to appear in his Superman cape. He came hobbling in as we greeted the first-time marathon finisher. But he deserved better, and he deserved more. All the finishers deserved a warm welcome reception. But the bombing in Boston took that all away. We all knew it had to be this way and we wondered if it would ever be the same. It was so simple in 1979, my dad dropping me off at Eisenhower Park, me finishing the race and sitting on a picnic table, and my dad just walking up to me.

I returned to NYC the following year, this time battling 50 MPH winds the entire way. A point-to-point marathon is great if the wind is at your back. It is horrible if the wind is in your face. And 2014 was horrible. The wind howled the entire night prior to the race, creeping into every open vent at the Navy lodge. On race day the 59 MPH wind gusts forced race organizers to move the start of the wheelchair division to the other side of the Verrazano Bridge. That year I was on the upper level and the crosswinds tossed me sideways on every step. Generally, the run across the Verrazano is a highlight. That morning I just wanted to get off that bridge.

Shortly after the race I decided, that's it. Yes, the marathon was so different than when I first started. But so was I. I was no longer at 15-year-old boy. I was no longer a young Army Captain racing off to the Presidio each spring to run along the water, watching the fog roll in under the Golden Gate Bridge. I was satisfied; I had run a marathon at two hours and fifty minutes or faster for three straight decades, a marathon under three hours and ten minutes for four straight decades, and a marathon under three hours and twenty minutes in each of the past five decades. I had seen the world on my feet. I had my fun. Plus, I was getting ready to retire from the Army. It was time to move on. As Roberto Duran said, "No Mas."

Until I took a long walk with Cam.

PLAN A, PLAN B, PLAN C...

"Don't forget Cam needs a haircut at 3:00 p.m. today."

At 11 a.m. on July 29, 2015, I had officially signed out of the Army after 26 years to begin my retirement of relaxing and fishing. It lasted four hours. As Cam sat in a little red fire truck at the barbershop watching Barney, I wondered, what's next?

The following morning, I went for a jog along the C/O Canal and returned home to watch reruns of *Quincy MD* on TV Land. After watching two episodes of Jack Klugman arguing with his assistant, Sam, I was officially bored. We were living near Washington, DC, and Matt was coaching at American University about 20 minutes from my house.

American University is in a quiet neighborhood in the Northwest area of the city. However, just a few miles away is the heart of the nation's capital and its famous monuments. The school offers the best of both worlds; a beautiful, quiet campus with students relaxing and socializing on the large grass quad, yet within minutes those same students can get firsthand experience seeing how our government operates. Academically, the school is one of the top universities in the country.

Years earlier, I had been to that quad for a five-mile road race along the tree-lined streets of Tenleytown. I also followed Matt and the AU cross-country team as Matt developed a national powerhouse cross-country team, ranking in the top twenty in Division 1. As my retirement approached, I spoke with Matt often about my desire to return to teaching and coaching, and we talked often on the phone in the few years leading up to July 2015. Actually, when your phone says "Matt," you never know what you are going to get. But you know that Matt will have a hilarious story and you always feel better after speaking to him.

I received one such call late at night when I had about one year left in the Army. Every six months, soldiers are required to take a physical fitness test that includes pull-ups, sit-ups, and a two-mile run. In July 2014, I was over 50 years old and needed a time of 13 minutes and ten seconds on the two-mile run to score the maximum points for that portion of the test. I was woken up to the following conversation.

"You been training?"

"Yes, I've been running a bit every morning."

"A bit every morning? That's not going to cut it, you got to be out there running at least ten miles a day."

"Ten miles? All I have to run is a two-mile."

"Two miles? This isn't high school anymore, we run ten kilometers. You know what it's like to run hard for 30 minutes, baby."

"Ten kilometers? Matt, all I have to run is 13:10." (Matt's American record for the 5,000 meters was 13:12.)

"13:10?! Are you trying to make fun of me?"

"Matt, what are you talking about?"

"Oh, Kevin, sorry, wrong number."

Click. If I knew who Matt was trying to call, I would have quickly called them and warned them that they were about to get a call from Coach, and that they better have been training.

With Matt's understanding that I was not goofing on his American record, I called him, and within four days of my retirement, I was up in Rhode Island at American Running Camp along Narragansett Bay. The camp hosts adults, college runners, and high school runners. Pat Tyson, one of the camp co-directors, a teammate of Matt's years ago at the University of Oregon, and Steven Prefontaine's roommate, placed me in charge of a group of fifteen boys from Guilford High School, the same high school my college roommate, Mike Regan, had attended. I spent the week running intervals, running hills, and doing fartlek's on the hilly cross-country course of Portsmouth Abbey. I felt like I was back at Great Neck South High School, and it was 1985 all over again. Yes, the marathon had changed a lot over the years, but the simple sport of running on grass fields up and down hills hadn't changed a bit. A week earlier I had been reviewing a brief in a death penalty case to be filed at the US Supreme Court, and now here I was getting a second chance to coach.

Evenings were even better as I sat at dinner with Matt, Pat Tyson, and Bill Dellinger. I heard story after story about workouts from the 1970s. I felt like I was living in a 1975 edition of *Runner's World* magazine. Matt is at his best when telling stories, but he is not always up on the latest trends in America. Back in 2015, every Coke bottle had a person's name written on it. Once, at camp, Matt put a dollar into the Coke machine and out popped a bottle with the name Matthew on it. "Who's in there, who's f$%^ing with me?" Matt believed a camper was somehow lodged inside the Coke machine, waiting for the opportunity to hand out a special bottle to him.

Over the next several weeks I got to know the other coaches: Kerri Gallagher, now program director at Manhattan College and a member of the USA World Championships team for the 1500 meters, Chris Kwiatkowski, now at the University of Washington and an Olympic Trials Marathon qualifier, and Edmund Burke, a NIH employee and an Olympic Trials Marathon qualifier. My first night on campus after we returned from camp, we all headed out to Chipotle, and from that evening on they helped me transition into civilian life. I am forever grateful for their kindness and mentorship.

That first season we had a talented group of runners, including several first-year students who went on to win league titles, participate in NCAA championships, who all now are embarking on fabulous careers in a variety of fields. Like the coaches, Matt Rainey, Liam Purdy, Brendan Johnson, Adriana Hooks, Alaeldin Tirba, and Brianna Belo welcomed me with open arms and helped me make the transition back into coaching.

Matt used a similar system to what I was used to back at St. John's: Tuesday and Thursday practices; Saturday meets; and other days on your own. His recruiting was certainly finer-tuned compared to my initial meeting with him 35 years earlier at Bethpage cross-country course. I did find out that, that October morning at Bethpage was Matt's first recruiting trip ever. Looking back, I can cut him a break.

Matt also was better-rounded compared to his initial coaching job at St. John's. Back in 1981, Matt was running at a world-class level while coaching at the same time. He had a laser-sharp focus on the track. Now, as an older coach, and as a father, he was looking beyond the track not just for himself, but also for his athletes. He continually emphasized, "What is the plan for the day after graduation?" He once told me that he had me and Edmund as coaches because he wanted the team to be around people who had careers outside of running so they could have exposure to life after college track.

Another aspect of Matt's coaching that was wonderful was that he had children who competed in college and, therefore, he understood the needs of student-athletes. All our meets, except for league championship meets, were in the local area. We seldom had overnight meets. Why? Because Matt did not want students-- yes, the runners are students-- to miss classes. I have seen coaches take their teams out of classes on Thursday and travel hundreds of miles to meets held on a Friday when there is a local meet one hour away on a Saturday. To me, this is insane. By missing Thursday and Friday classes, students are missing 40% of their class time and are constantly playing catch up. Plus, the six-hour van rides exacerbate the problem, as that time could be spent in the library. Matt understood this and kept our meets local, and the teams always appreciated this.

Finally, Matt understood the concept of powering down to his assistants. All too often assistant coaches are labeled "stopwatch holders," meaning the head coach creates all the workouts and all the assistants do is time workouts or drive vans to meets. Matt once said to me, "I need your advice. I need you to tell me how the runners are feeling, and I need your input on practices. I need an assistant coach. If I wanted someone to just stand around with a stopwatch and drive vans, I would get a team manager."

Although I had said *no mas* to the marathon, I continued to run and enjoyed competing against other "grey-haired" runners in the 50-and-older division. I did sort of have a renaissance with my running. Now that I was in my second half of life I loved the challenge of trying to run under 18 minutes for a 5K or 38 minutes for a 10K-- times that I was running back when I was 15 years old.

However, the best part of early retirement was that I got to spend more time with Cam and Heather. Eight a.m. was *Octonauts* and *Paw Patrol*, followed by the drive to kindergarten with one of many cats sitting next to Cam in the car. No longer the solo evil queen, Twiggy now shares the house with three cats, two dogs, three turtles, one tortoise, twelve guinea pigs, and twenty fish. With Cam dropped off at school, I was free to run, followed by standing on the infield of the American University track, hearing Matt and his hilarious stories. "You'll never guess who called me last night, can you believe xxx is now . . ." Running and coaching was just like law school all over except for the boring night law classes.

And just like 30 years ago, Plan B became Plan A. Back in 2005, I worked with Frank Ranguossis, an Army Reserve officer who was active for one year in my office. Frank was a brilliant attorney working for the Department of Justice. He also worked as an adjunct professor at American University, teaching the latest block class possible-- 8:20 p.m. to 10:50 p.m.

"Hey, I hear you are coaching at AU now. I have to travel a bit in my new DOJ job, can you ever sub for me in American Constitution?" Even though I was not the best law student, over the years I had picked up a few things about Constitutional Rights, especially regarding those accused of crimes. I had even worked on some First Amendment religion issues in the military, one of which still causes angst at Thanksgiving dinner.

When I first arrived at Schofield Barracks in Hawaii, a large white cross sat atop the Kolekole pass, the same pass I walked up to in the dark prior to the Honolulu Marathon. The cross, which sat on the mountaintop for over forty years, was visible for miles. If a person at Sunset Beach over fifteen miles away on the North Shore looked up toward the mountains, they could see the cross. Eventually, an organization challenged the cross's position on federal land under the First Amendment's Establishment Clause. When deciding cases regarding government support of a religious organization, the Supreme Court uses—actually, sometimes uses-- a test called the Lemon Test. The test has nothing to do with lemons; rather the test is based on a case in which one of the participant's last names was Lemon. The courts look at: the purpose of the support of the religion; what is the effect of the support (does the support aid or hinder a religious organization?); and does the support involve excessive government entanglement in the program. For example, say a state grinds up used car tires into a rubber mulch that can be used for playgrounds and distributes this rubber mulch to all the schools in the state, including religious schools. It could be argued that this does not violate the Establishment Clause, more commonly known as Separation of Church and State, because: the purpose of giving the rubber to the religious school is safety on playgrounds; using the rubber on playgrounds does not advance a religion; and a one-time transfer of this rubber would not excessively entangle the government in the day-to-day operations of that religious school. When it came to the Kolekole cross, I could not get past prong one. No one could tell me why the cross was on the mountaintop. Some people said it was for Easter Sunrise services while others said it was to commemorate WWII. Without knowing the purpose of why the cross was placed on federal land, I opined that under the law we had to dismantle the cross.

Fast forward 20 years and we are planning a trip to Hawaii, and Heather's dad blurts out, "Make sure you go see the Kolekole cross. It is stunning."

"Jay, the cross is gone."

"What? What happened?"

"I told them they had to take it down."

"How can you say that? You went to Catholic school."

"Yes, I went to Catholic school, and they taught me the law." (Actually, when we covered the Lemon case in law school that may have been like one of the three nights in all of law school that I was paying attention.)

The Kolekole cross cannot be mentioned ever again in my house.

"Sure, Frank, I can sub-- just let me know when you need me." For a semester, I either subbed for Frank's class or sat in on his class to watch how a college class was taught. Fortunately, a teaching position opened at the university in the Justice Law and Criminology Department, and the wonderful department chair, Joe Young, hired me first as an adjunct then in a full-time position.

The expression "It's not what you know but who you know." worked in my favor. I was able to quickly land on my feet after retirement because of Matt and Frank. If you are currently in college, or early in your career, make and keep your connections, and get onto LinkedIn. Heather actually thought LinkedIn was a dating app. "Who are all these men sending me requests to join this thing called LinkedIn? You better not be on that site."

In August 2016, in my new brown blazer, with my course textbook, which Twiggy had peed on the night before tucked under my arm, I walked into Kerwin Hall and headed to my first class as a university professor, wondering if the students would accept me, or just think of me as some retired Army Colonel. I was greeted "Good Evening, Professor." by the only student in the classroom. I thought, yes, they accept me as a professor, or at least this guy does.

This guy wound up being my favorite student ever. Kizhan Clark, at the time, a first-year student-athlete who would eventually become an All-

American in wrestling and is now a law student. Over the years, Kizhan took several of my classes and I saw him almost every day over at Bender Arena while he was at wrestling practice, and I was at track practice. Kizhan is also one of the best guest speakers in my class, giving law school hopefuls tips on preparation for law school, as well as candid talks about what law school is really like.

While coaching and teaching was going great, the allure of running, or at least running fast, was losing its luster in each passing year. As the 5K clock went from 17 minutes to 18 minutes to 19 minutes with each year after age 50, I said *no mas* to all races, limiting my running to a few minutes here and there each day along the C/O Canal. My racing was limited to include Thanksgiving mornings when Heather and I would run in the Sandbridge, Virginia, 5K Turkey Trot, justifying our big meal later that day.

Also, each year we would turn out for J&A Racing Surf-n-Santa 5 Miler in Virginia Beach. One year we even were part of a world record, "The most running Santas in one venue." J&A Racing puts on a series of fantastic races each year and in this particular holiday 5-miler, each runner received a thick, red Santa suit complete with beard, hat, pants, and top. Even though the race was held in December, those suits turned your body into a pizza oven. We may have also set the world record for most Santa suit tops removed during a race.

If you ever travel to Virginia Beach, try to find an event put on by J&A Racing. Their events are top notch. In 1990, I ran my first J&A race, the Shamrock Marathon. At the time I was in Charlottesville at the Army Law School for my initial training. It was the first time in my life I had been away from the beach, so I traveled to Virginia Beach for this event. That race was also my introduction to how strict the army can be. On the Friday night before the race, there was mandatory military dinner we had to attend called a Dining-In. They should rename it a Boring-In. I asked the leader of our group if I could skip the Boring-In as I was running a marathon the next day. I would have had a better chance asking a wall for permission.

Once the Boring-In ended at midnight, I hopped in my car and drove the two hours to Virginia Beach, in the same Buick with the two-time rebuilt engine. Upon my 2:00 a.m. arrival, I sat on my hotel balcony in the dark, hearing waves crash on the shore for the first time in months. The following morning, I used the marathon as a training run for my planned May marathon. Yes, calling a marathon "a training run" does sound like an excuse for not racing fast. However, at the time, I was constantly running up and down huge hills in Charlottesville and my May marathon was going to be totally flat, so I wanted to get a long run in on a flat course; train as you fight. The marathon and accompanying world-class five-mile race were fantastic, both finishing inside the old Virginia Beach Convention Center. I ran steady 6:30 miles and six weeks later ran 5:30 miles for my peak marathon. I don't always suggest this; however, running a marathon six to eight weeks prior to your peak marathon is not a bad idea. You do get a pace run in, plus you get all the water stops needed. Derek Clayton ran an easy marathon several weeks prior to setting his marathon world record. If it worked for the world record holder, it can't be bad.

Every semester I had to replace my brown blazer with a larger size, settling into a life of teaching in the fall and spring and fishing in the summers. I absolutely loved both. Teaching at American University is the best job I have ever had, and the tremendous support from Dean Wilkins and Dean Newman has been off the charts.

I started fishing probably before I did any other sport, catching snappers at Wantagh Park Marina with an old cane fishing pole. Every year my birthday present was a trip on the Captain Lou fishing boat out of Freeport, New York, in search of bluefish and flounders. I tried to continue to fish during my time in the army; however, I often didn't have the time or was stationed far from water, i.e., Kansas. Not only did my retirement bring me back to teaching and coaching, but it also returned me to fishing. Heather and I traveled up and down the East Coast in search of sharks, striped bass, and largemouth bass. We tried to catch any large fish we could find-- be it in the ocean, lakes, or on our favorite fishing boat, Ed Darwin's *Becky D*, where we caught rockfish under the Bay Bridge in Annapolis. On one hot August afternoon, Heather caught one of the largest black drum fish ever caught in the Chesapeake Bay. As she reeled in the almost 100-pound fish, 88-year-old Captain Ed, the saltiest, yet oddly at the same time nicest captain on the entire Eastern Seaboard, continually said, "You're stuck on the bottom, let me cut the line."

"No, I can feel it fighting."

"That's just the tide, let me cut the line."

The whole time, Jim, Ed's loyal and friendly mate, kept saying, "Cap, I'm telling you, that's a fish on there."

The fish sure was big, but one bit of advice: one hundred pounds of black drum fish fills a freezer for months and doesn't taste too great.

As the years progressed, Bass Pro Shops became my new Marathon expo; bait casters and spinning lures replaced my Nike Elites.

The calendar years continued to flip as I taught and fished. Matt left American University for Manhattan College; Chris, Edmund, and Kerri were gone, as were the runners who were first-year students when I first arrived at American University's running camp. There was a whole new crew, equally as good, but just not the same.

When he was younger, Cam enjoyed coming the meets, especially seeing the steeplechase water jump (or fall) area. However, Cam was getting older, and I didn't like to be away from him and Heather, sometimes for entire weekends under the new coach's competition philosophy. Family comes first, so I stepped away from track, focusing on teaching.

The first warm day of 2020 was the first Sunday in March. Although winters in Maryland are not harsh, the first day when hats and gloves are not needed is always a delight. Cam and I decided to take a walk. As we left our neighborhood, he said, "Do you think we can make it to the village?" To a nine-year-old who sat in the back seat of a car for all trips, the village seemed like a million miles away. "I think we can."

I called Heather and asked her to pick us up in about an hour at Sprinkles Ice Cream Parlor, Cam's favorite shop in the village. We walked and talked and walked and talked. Cam doesn't really remember my time in the Army, plus we never talk about it. He also knew that I coached track and that I would sometimes jog at the canal.

Somehow along the way, he asked how far we would walk, and I told him about three miles. (A few months later we would walk nine miles in colonial Williamsburg, his Fitbit serving as the proof.) He then asked what was the farthest I had ever walked or jogged. I told him I had done the 26-mile marathon.

Coincidentally, he was the same age as I was when I asked my dad about Frank Shorter during the Munich Olympic Marathon. I think around age nine is when children start thinking of the world beyond their neighborhood. As he asked about the marathon, I didn't tell him to run a marathon "To find out for yourself." Rather, I told him I ran my first marathon in 1979 and had done several since then but none recently. Cam is very into numbers and statistics and said, "Do you know you have done a marathon in five straight decades and its now 2020, you can make it six." After the *no mas* of the 2014 NYC Marathon, the thought of six decades didn't cross my mind.

"Do you think a lot of people have done six decades?"

"Probably not. I was pretty young when I did my first one, so I got a bit of a head start."

"Well, you should do one this year and then another one in 2030."

We made it to the village shortly thereafter and hopped in the car for the drive home. However, a spark had been lit. I thought maybe I could return to the Long Island Marathon that May-- where it all began-- but the race was only two months away. I had been able to run the 1979 Long Island Marathon with two months of training, but I had 15 straight years of swimming, track, and running around the neighborhood under my belt back then. I was now a 56-year-old, out-of-shape old man who ran maybe ten minutes at a time, three to four days a week. But I thought it would be cool to return to the scene of the original race, so I didn't totally discard the idea. Or I could do the Marine Corps Marathon eight months away at the end of October. I knew the course well, which is always comforting. Not only had I run the race several times, Ray Jackson and I had spent years at 5:00 a.m. doing runs on portions of the course. Traveling to the race would be a breeze, and this was on the plus side for keeping all pre-race preparations low-stress. And the course had many spots for Heather and Cam to see me. Finally, DC was now my home.

I was leaning toward the Marine Corps Marathon as I mulled it over the next few days. However, all my mulling became moot as the world shut down two weeks later. In mid-March, our house instantly became a multi-room schoolhouse with Cam finishing fourth grade in his bedroom, me finishing out the semester in my office, while Heather converted our dining room into a second-grade classroom. Both Dean Newman and Dean Wilkins were incredibly supportive and encouraging as our faculty had to shift our teaching platform on the drop of a dime. Each afternoon, Cam and I would hike along the C/O Canal or on the Billy Goat Trail on the banks of the Potomac River. Races were naturally canceled, and my motivation to run waned to the point where I would drive to Lock 10 of the C/O, park, and then run for just a few minutes before turning back. The world was upside down and I just didn't see the point of running.

Hope sprung eternal in spring 2021 as vaccines became widely available and restrictions eased. Once I read that the Marine Corps planned to host a live marathon in October, I revived my thoughts of running a marathon. However, the day after the semester ended in April, I realized just how much I had to train over the next six months to gain some semblance of fitness. During our American Constitution class, I was discussing police and hot pursuit and boasted to one student, "If I was a police officer, I could walk you down." On Saturday morning, April 24, my entire class showed up on the steps of Kerwin Hall on the southeast corner of American University's quad to witness for themselves if I could actually walk down that student. Somehow, my boast turned into a race challenge, and there I stood surveying the quad, trying to figure out how far I had to sprint and how much I would lose by.

"Avery, you've got to go easy on me, please keep it close," I whispered before we took off for one loop around the quad, perhaps 500 meters around. Avery didn't take it easy on me and was 50 yards ahead of me before we made the turn for home in front of Bender Library. I had walked from the library to Kerwin Hall on countless occasions, enjoying the architecture of the many buildings surrounding the quad. On those leisurely strolls, the quad didn't seem too long. This morning, the final straightway was endless as I staggered to the finish on tired legs, my knees almost buckling. Avery accepted his trophy as I continued to heave under my thick mask. Six months to go until the Marine Corps Marathon and I could barely run 500 meters. The Marines motto is "Semper Fi." I was "Simply Unfit."

Over the next month, I questioned my decision, but on May 27, I officially registered for the live version of the Marine Corps Marathon. I thought that this being one of the first large marathons held in a live format meant that registration would be difficult, but online registration was a breeze. Registration may have been easy, but the training would not be. Over the course of five months, I had to undo four years of limited training, shed lots of pounds, and even cut back on Coca-Cola.

My goal was to be running thirty minutes a day by the end of June. I ran every day in June but nowhere near thirty minutes. Each morning I would head down to the C/O Canal and start jogging, but as people walking-- yes, WALKING-- their dogs were passing me, I would get frustrated and head back to my car. I rationalized things in my head. If I get up to 30 minutes a day by the end of July, I will be OK and still have plenty of time, or if I get my legs used to running every day, even for just 15 minutes, I can just gut it out on race day.

In mid-June I came up with a brilliant plan. I would put on my old TomTom GPS watch, do a time trial, and then each week try to go farther at a faster pace. Yes, that was the ticket to give me motivation. I juiced up my trusty GPS watch, holding it up to the sun for what seemed like forever, as the watch had not synced with satellites in four years. As soon as the watch beeped, I was off for a one-mile time trial in Great Falls Park, Virginia. Except for the time I almost had a heart attack racing on the American University Quad, I had not run faster than dog walker pace for about three years. I felt like I was sprinting the entire way. My legs ached as I passed the huge Great Falls waterfall on the Potomac River on the way to my finish line at the park's visitor's center. My GPS read 13:31 for the one-mile run. I felt like I had been running all out the entire way. At least I had a baseline of where I was at, and that baseline was pretty bad. If I had to sprint to run a 13-minute mile, what type of pace would be a comfortable race pace for 26 miles? Fifteen minutes a mile? Sixteen minutes a mile? The next week, I put my GPS back on my wrist to give it another go. This time my desire to beat my previous week's time was my undoing, as I sprinted out too fast and had to jog in the final half-mile.

Clearly, my time trial system was not going to get me to the finish line. I knew what I needed to do but had been avoiding it, thinking up schemes to make my training easy. There is no realistic way to make training for, and running, a marathon easy. People say, "Let's play tennis." It's a game. You never hear people say, "Let's play a marathon."

To be ready in just three months I had to run each day and run far each of those days. But it's hard to get back in shape. It's not only hard; it's frustrating. A runner wants quick results and when they don't come, the self-doubt creeps in.

June turned into July. My scheming was not fooling anyone, most importantly myself. I was still "Simply Unfit." The land shortly inland from the banks of the Potomac River in Potomac, Maryland, and in Great Falls, Virginia, is home to numerous hilly trails with cool-sounding names like the Billy Goat Trail, The Overlook Trail, Bootleggers Trail, and The Gold Mine Trail.

Yes, there actually was a gold mine just a few miles from Washington, DC. During the Civil War, a soldier from the north was washing dishes in a stream near present-day Old Anglers Inn. In his plate appeared flecks of gold. After this find, gold mines were set up in the area and were in operation until 1940. The final mine was not fully deconstructed until fall 2020. It certainly was not the California Gold Rush, but a significant amount of gold was found in the area.

Not only do these trails have cool names, but some of them are extremely hilly, and each one is very scenic. On portions, walkers, hikers, and runners must stop to scramble over rocks. Personally, I believe the climbing on rocks during a run is extremely beneficial as it helps build arm strength. All too often, runners are focused on just running.

During my youth, swimming helped with upper-body strength. Even though I stopped competitive swimming, I did continue to swim throughout my Army career, whether in the *Schwimmbads* of Germany, arguing each morning with the lifeguard about what is considered a long enough pre-swim shower; or in the waters off Oahu's North Shore in the annual long-distance swim series of races between one and two miles in length. In Germany, the same play was acted out every morning. I woke up, showered, put on my bathing suit, walked the two blocks to the pool, took off my sweats, and headed toward the water. And each morning the *Schwimmmeister* would remind me to shower. To this day the only German phrase I can remember is *Ich habe zu hause geduscht* (I showered at home). Every day I lost the battle and ended up standing under a freezing cold shower before entering the pool.

Arm strength is incredibly important in the marathon and in running in general. Our arms are the engines that drive the legs. The last thing a marathoner wants is their weary arms dangling at their sides during the final miles of the race. In addition to the arm workout provided by the trails, the surface of the trails themselves helps build muscles that runners would not use on a road surface. Turning and climbing on dirt and uneven surfaces is great for fine-tuning muscles that would rarely be used on a flat asphalt surface.

Mr. Brynes used to have us run sprints barefoot back and forth on the football field grass to build up our Achilles' tendons. He had us run up and down sand dunes at Jones Beach. He had us run in boots. He had us sprint up and down the footbridge that crosses the Wantagh Parkway next to our school, while wearing a 35-pound weighted vest! He had us run along the Wantagh Parkway bike path holding our breath from one telephone pole to the next. Yes, it was the 1970s, but the concepts hold true today. Runners need variety in their training and training surfaces.

Running on a flat asphalt path every day is a great way to develop muscles needed to run on a flat asphalt path every day. The first slight incline in a race will be a killer to those muscles used to running every day on a flat asphalt path. Runners need to mix up terrain to fully develop leg muscles. Just watch out for roots and rocks on the trails!

On July 7, I headed out for a short jog in the woods near Old Anglers Inn. I figured I would do my usual five or six minutes out and turn around. Heck, it was early July, I had plenty of time until October. As I headed into the woods and reached my five-minute mark, I said to myself, "Enough is enough, the marathon is no party. You have to train sometime, and you may as well start today. It's going to be hard; you're going to hate it; you may have to walk a bit today, but this is it."

Or as my dad used to say, "Stop your nonsense." So, I continued running uphill on the Anglers Trail and kept running when the trail connected with the Gold Mine Loops and kept running. I use the term "running" loosely, but I never stopped to walk. When I made it back to my car, I was tired, but my legs had that nice, tired sensation and my mind had the great feeling that I had finally gone for a run.

The following Wednesday I decided to run just a bit farther. Since I would not be teaching on Wednesdays in the fall, I decided that I would start to get into the groove of Wednesday as a long run day to have my weekends free for family time. Each Wednesday I would slightly increase my "long run" on a new course. Week one, my long run on Anglers Trail and Gold Mine Loop was thirty minutes. The next week I ran forty minutes along the beautiful, long, and flat Berma Trail and around Widewater, a fabulous lake along the C/O Canal. On the other days I continued short runs. But at least I was making progress.

On week three I drove across the American Legion Bridge into Virginia and ran for an hour along the banks of the Potomac in River Bend Park prior to heading into the hills for a long, long run up Bootleggers Trail. I had not run this loop in over four years, yet I felt like I was meeting a long-lost friend-- the kind of friend who you don't see for ages but the second you see them you continue the last conversation you had years earlier. I remembered every turn, every rock formation in the river, every tree-- and yes-- every hill. And I ran and I ran for an hour, for the first time feeling like I was a runner again. I have no idea of my pace and I didn't care. For the first time, on that July morning, I honestly believed I had a realistic shot of finishing the marathon. Because pride cometh before a fall, I didn't say a guarantee of finishing the marathon, but a shot.

I also felt confident that I had come upon a system that I could use for the rest of the summer: several short runs each week, two medium-length runs slightly increasing in distance each week, and one gradually-longer run each week. It sure was better than weekly one-mile time trials. With a bit over three months to go, I felt that the runner inside me was slowly starting to reemerge. As my confidence was growing each week, I was reminded of one of Matt's sayings, "The mind leads the body."

Yes, the past few weeks were tough; yes, I was running nowhere near as fast I had previously ran, but at least I was running. All it takes is to take that first step.

I continued to run, even as we took our week-long beach vacation to Sandbridge. My runs were more difficult as I spent hours fighting on sand dunes playing King of the Hill and swimming in the pool and ocean. But it's vacation; you can't say, "I am in training for a marathon so need to rest." Your kids will look at you like you're crazy. The other thing never to say is "When I was your age . . ." You may as well just say, "Ok, now tune me out," because that's what your kids will do. First, the world was different when you were their age. Second, your child is not you. Let them live their life without pressure of your stories of how much you studied or how far you walked to school uphill.

In early August, Fred and Nicole called and said they were running in the Jersey Marathon in October and asked would I be interested in running with Fred. I was now in week four of my "training program," and figured why not register? Even though I was registered for the Marine Corps Marathon (MCM), COVID cases were creeping up. In case MCM was canceled, I could run Jersey. If MCM was still a go, I could run the first

16 miles of Jersey as a long training run. MCM would remain Plan A, but Jersey was now Plan B. Little did I know, I would eventually need Plan C, Plan D. . .

In 1985, the Norwegian pop group A-ha came out with the song and MTV video "Take on Me." In the video, a young lady is sitting in a restaurant booth reading a magazine. Suddenly, one of the characters in the magazine comes to life and reaches his hand out to her, beckoning her to join him in the magazine scene. She grasps his hand and is pulled into the world of the magazine story. In August, I renewed my interest in reading running websites, especially since I wished to keep up on the Olympics. And like the song, it was as if a hand reached through my computer and pulled me back into the running world.

Over the course of the next few weeks, my long runs got up to over two hours. I was running twice a day on my easy days; 45 minutes in the morning and 30 minutes in the evening. Back when I turned 50, my running was like treading water, running hard each day to stay at sub 18 minutes for the 5K, and each week racing about the same time, give or take a few seconds. It was fun, but the progress plateaued. Now each week I could see real progress. I was running farther and faster, and the initial pain of starting to run in early July had subsided. I was now in the A-ha video, fully immersed in running.

As my running progressed, the COVID numbers continued to climb. First, I read that the live version of the Air Force Marathon was canceled and was going virtual. Then, a few days later, the live version of the Jersey Marathon was canceled. I began to sense a trend and deep down knew way back in August that the live version of MCM would be canceled. The job of a race director is thankless and tireless. I would never question any race director for canceling a race and I know that the decisions had to be difficult.

I started to think of Plan C, Plan D . . . and I spoke to Cam and Heather about the possibility of a virtual marathon. I figured I could run 26 miles on the C/O Canal towpath with Heather on a bike and Cam at various points handing me water. Cam's elementary school holds an annual fun run. The first year we did it we ran on the roads near the school. The second year, the run was virtual due to COVID. We were down at Sandbridge on the day of the virtual run and put a line in the sand and ran for what we figured was a mile and turned back. The third year, the run was a series of loops around the schoolyard, as the school was slowly reopening.

When I mentioned a virtual marathon to Cam, the idea went over like a lead balloon.

"Remember the Carderock Elementary School Virtual Fun Run?"

"Yes, Cam."

"Did that actually feel like an official run?"

"Sort of."

"No, it didn't, it felt like us running at the beach."

Obviously, Cam was not supporting a virtual marathon. I also was on the fence about a virtual race. I had never done one before; however, I had done a "shadow run" when I was in the Army. My unit was off-island one year during the Great Aloha Run, so our brigade decided to do a shadow Great Aloha Run. After we all ran, in formation by the way, we were handed official Great Aloha Run shirts. I, in no way, not even for a second, felt that I had run the Great Aloha Run, t-shirt or not. I felt like I had run a miserable eight-mile formation run on a course that in no way, shape, or form resembled the streets of Oahu.

I found a few options. The Steamtown Marathon in Scranton became Plan C. As a child, and even now, I had vacationed in the Poconos and figured this could be a great race and vacation. We could even stay at Woodloch Pines on the shores of Lake Teedyuskung, the resort we stayed at as children, and the site of one of my first long-distance ventures. I must have been about 11 when I made the mistake of asking, "Dad, do you think someone could swim across this lake and back?"

"Let's find out tomorrow. We'll come down to the lake at 6:00 a.m. before anyone is awake and none of the resort staff is around. You can swim there and back and I will be in a rowboat next to you."

To an 11-year-old that seemed like an OK plan. Looking back, I am not so sure. First off, the lake is about three-quarters of a mile across, so a mile and a half there and back. Second, I am not sure my dad knew how to swim. He had gone in the pool and ocean with us all the time, but I always remember him standing in water up to his chest. I never actually saw him swim. He did body surf, floating like Superman face down in the water. As the washing machine of crashing waves tumbled him around, his bathing suits regularly fell off. He would emerge from the surf with his bathing suit by his knees, and all the while John and I were thinking, "Come on, use the drawstring, man."

The next morning, we set off. Me in the water, him in a canoe holding a Pall Mall. "Son, a canoe is faster, so I'll take this instead of a rowboat." Of course, he was not wearing a life jacket and there were no life jackets in the canoe. He didn't believe in life jackets. "They get all wet and weigh you down and you sink." He had the same idea with seatbelts. "You know, actually, a seatbelt will prevent the rescue workers from getting you out of the car."

It was a long swim and thinking back, if I did run into (or swim into) trouble, a potential non-swimmer in a canoe with no life jackets would be useless to me.

We never got to revisit the scene of that swim because just as quickly as The Steamtown Marathon became Plan C, it was canceled. I continued to run and increased my long runs, even running up to 2:45 hours on portions of the MCM route-- from Iwo Jima across the Key Bridge along Georgetown's waterfront, past the Kennedy Center, down around Haines Point, then around the mall and back to Iwo Jima via the Memorial Bridge.

As I ran along the mall that early September morning, I raced past the exact spot where my dad and I spoke back in 1978. We were on our annual family education trip (Williamsburg, Gettysburg, Boston, DC), and as we stood on the Mall, we saw two Marines jog by during their lunch hour.

"You know, if you join the service, you can jog down here at lunchtime every day."

At the time, I thought, what are you talking about? Well, I did join the service, and I did run around the mall a lot, but never at lunchtime; mostly at 5:00 a.m. with Ray Jackson.

I also ran many times with Ray around Haines Point. Ask any runner who has run the MCM or the Cherry Blossom 10 Miler and they will say, "I hated Haines Point." To me, Haines Point is DC at its finest. A peninsula jutting out from the southern portion of the nation's capital with the Potomac River on the west and the Anacostia River on the East, the three-mile, two-lane, traffic-free road is shared by walkers, bikers, and runners of all ages and races. Every single person greets each other with a smile or "hello" every morning. In April, bright pink cherry blossoms surround the entire three-mile loop. A mile away, thousands of tourists cram around the Tidal Basin to see the cherry blossoms while Haines Point is practically empty. It's the best-kept secret in DC.

I finished my 2:45 run right at the finish line of the MCM, in front of Iwo Jima. I tried to visualize myself crossing the line a few weeks later. But deep down, I knew that would not be happening this year.

The continued cancelations of marathons and adjustments of plans in no way affected the physical part of my preparations. I continued to increase my long runs, and now that I was in the A-ha world of the marathon, I started testing out gels. Several new ones had come on the scene since 2014. I wound up settling on CLIF Shot Energy Gel, which I loved, probably because they tasted like gummy Lifesavers, which I always buy when food shopping.

With Plan A, Plan B, and Plan C always changing, I wanted to settle in on a final plan so that I could mentally prepare and focus on a race and a course. I noticed that Long Island had a few marathons set for October, one of which was in Rockaway Beach. John Edwards, the sensational race director for the Rockapulco race series, had a marathon scheduled for early October. John was one of the first race directors in the country to hold live races after COVID, so I had no doubt that his race would go on. However, the logistics of getting to New York for an early Saturday race were too daunting.

Having lived in both Annapolis and Potomac over the years, I have traveled to Baltimore often for some fantastic races: the Zoo Zoom in the Baltimore Zoo; The Preakness 5K that used to be held the week before the Triple Crown Race; The Patterson Park New Year's race; the 9/11 race starting at the Inner Harbor and finishing at the top of Federal Hill; and the Baltimore Marathon Festival 5K.

It was clear to me that the Baltimore Marathon was the race to go to so I quickly and easily registered online. Even though the MCM had not yet been canceled, in my mind it had been, and I didn't want to miss the Baltimore race on October 9, only to have the MCM cancellation be announced in mid-October. Once I registered for the Baltimore Marathon, I was all in. Even if MCM was still on it didn't matter, my mental energy was now on Baltimore.

Yes, the constant changing of plans was annoying, but I didn't let it mentally affect me. Runners need to be flexible. If a race is canceled, there are other races or other years. Always have Plan A and Plan B and, if necessary, Plans C and D.

Having raced in Baltimore several times, I knew that the city was hilly, very hilly. Therefore, I no longer did any long runs on the flat streets of DC. Instead, I headed to Great Falls Park, Virginia, every Wednesday morning for runs up to three and a half hours on the hilly trails of that park, plus the adjacent River Bend Park. There is an endless series of interwoven trails, all of which are quite hilly. There is actually a trail called Difficult Run Trail. I have no idea of my pace on these runs, but they were incredibly enjoyable. I never wore a watch or a GPS. I simply parked my car, looked at my car clock, ran, and when I returned to my car, checked the clock. I have run along the Sydney Australia Harbor by the Opera House, along the beaches of Phuket, Thailand, and in the shadow of Table Mountain on the Southern Tip of Africa. To me, there is no more beautiful place in the world than Great Falls Park and its trail system. As I effortlessly ran up and down the hills of these trails, the agony of my July 7 run only two months ago was forgotten. Remember, no matter how you feel when you first start training, be assured that you will eventually feel better. And pick a nice place to run. Time will fly when you can enjoy the scenery.

In no time at all it was two weeks till race day. Throughout the summer and fall, I had been running in Adidas boost shoes and had worn the same shorts and same shirt every day. Yes, since I hadn't been running much over the years, I didn't have much in the way of running clothing. Plus, I was used to having only one set of running clothes when I was in the Army; black shorts, grey t-shirt, and lots of Febreze. I will admit that over many years in the Army, I would wake at 5:30 a.m. and realize I didn't have clean PT clothes, so out came the Febreze spray.

For the Baltimore Marathon I wanted very bright clothes so that Cam and Heather could see me on the course. I wound up getting neon green shorts and a bright orange muscle shirt. (To me, a running singlet will always be called a muscle shirt because that's what we wore as kids in the summer, sleeveless muscle shirts from the Sears catalog.)

As for sneakers, running shoes had changed a lot since my Puma Spikes in junior high school and my Nike Elites for my first marathon. Today, many running shoes have a carbon plate in the sole to provide a spring-like effect, propelling runners forward. I have read various runner website forums refer to these as "cheater shoes." I don't place much value on these runner forums as most of the posts these days seem to be about whether or not people should take a vaccine.

To me, there is no such thing as "cheater shoes." Technology advances in every sport. Basketball players used to shoot the ball into a peach basket. Are today's hoops now "cheater rims?" Of course not.

I decided to purchase a pair of the Nike Air Zoom Alphafly NEXT% shoes to compare them to my 1979 Nike Elites. Fortunately, when the Jersey Marathon was canceled, my entry fee could be transferred to a store credit from DC's finest running store chain, Pacers. Although these new shoes were expensive, with store credit they were very reasonable. As I walked into Pacers, I was somewhat embarrassed to purchase these shoes, figuring I would be the oldest and slowest runner to ever purchase a pair. I felt like I was fourteen years old walking into a stationary store in the 1970s as a kid to buy *Playboy*. You would get gum, baseball cards, *Sports Illustrated*, a stickball bat, and various other sundry items and place them all on the counter with the *Playboy*, hoping the cashier would not notice. In Pacers, I was at the counter like, "I'll get this gel, this pair of shorts, these socks, and throw in some Nike Air Zoom Alphafly NEXT% shoes, size 8, while you are at it." I also mumbled something about getting them for research purposes.

On my first step in them I felt as if my head was going to bounce off the store's ceiling. I had never in my life felt something so springy on my feet, aside from maybe a pogo stick growing up. As soon as I left the store I raced home, changed into my one pair of shorts and my one running shirt, put on my new, extremely snug sneakers, and drove down to the DC Tidal Basin for a test run, following the adage "Never run a marathon in shoes that you have not worn in practice." At first the sneakers felt very odd as I ran through the FDR Memorial, complete with its seven waterfalls. By the time I got to the sixth waterfall, I thought, there is no way that I am wearing these again. To me they felt like I was not connected to the ground and that I was running at a trampoline park. I carried on and by the time I got to the Jefferson Memorial, I was getting used to the sneakers and thinking, maybe I will wear them. As I rounded the Tidal Basin and headed toward the Washington Monument, I was beginning to actually like the feel of the shoes. From the Washington Monument to the Lincoln Memorial, as I raced down the path adjacent to the Reflecting Pool, I had to keep telling myself to slow down because I felt like I was flying in these shoes. By the time I reached my car parked next to the Potomac River, I was sold on the innovative technology. It took a few miles to get used to them, but I did feel as if they made the run go faster. The oddest part was when I took the shoes off; it felt like when you roller skate or ice skate for hours and feel oddly shorter when you take off your skates. It felt the same with these shoes, maybe because the sole seemed to be about two inches thick.

The final week before the race I ran less each day. My race shirt and number arrived in the mail. Since COVID, races now gave runners the option to skip the expo and have material mailed to them. To me, this is a great option, as I dislike standing on my feet for hours at expos around nervous runners. This is also a tricky week for marathoners. During the final week before a marathon runners must rest. But for many they stress that with less running they are losing fitness. It's as if they forget that they have been training for months. No one is going to lose any fitness by running a bit less for four to five days the week before a marathon.

On Friday afternoon, Cam, Heather, and I headed up to Baltimore's Inner Harbor. The last time Cam and I had been there was on March 6, 2020, for a school field trip to the aquarium. Fortunately, I was able to get a room at the Hilton, which was only blocks from the start line and finish line. A week prior to the race I watched a video of the course on YouTube. Little did I know that several changes to the course were made since that video was posted: most importantly, the start line.

After check-in we headed to the Inner Harbor, and along the way I pointed out spots to Cam and Heather where they could see me the next morning. Every single spot I told them was incorrect. Lesson learned: check the date posted on YouTube videos. Cam absolutely loved the Inner Harbor and the crepes sold there. It was a beautiful, warm evening as we sat by the water in shorts. A bit warm for the night before a marathon, but to me it didn't matter. I just wanted to finish. Before bed we downloaded the race tracker on Heather's phone so she and Cam could know when to come to various points of the race to see me.

As like every night before a marathon, I didn't sleep well. I don't think anyone sleeps well the night before a race, but that's OK. The rule of thumb is to get a good night's sleep two nights before the race because you will not be sleeping much the night before the race.

At 7:00 a.m. I headed out of the hotel in my bouncing shoes, extremely bright shorts, and muscle shirt, with my water bottle. Due to COVID, the race was to be 'cupless,' meaning runners had to carry their own water bottles and could refill them along the way. To me, this was no big deal. I rarely drink when I run, sometimes to my detriment. One year, with four miles to go, I was leading a marathon in New Jersey. It was a cloudy and warm day and I never stopped for water. I went from first place to second, to third, to fourth, to fifth, to a sixth-place finish, to a medical tent. Ever since then, my stepmom reminds me to have water in the marathon. I do drink in races now, but I still can't understand when I see runners at various races with backpacks full of water. Why would someone weigh themselves down with 15 pounds of water when they literally give out cups and cups of water on the course? In 1979, a can of Coke was all that was needed, not 15 pounds of water bouncing off your back.

As I left the hotel, I headed over to Pickles Pub a few blocks away, the start line indicated on the YouTube video I had watched. As I walked, I thought back to all my walks to marathon starts-- Honolulu in the dark, 1979 Eisenhower Park looking for Mr. Donlon . . . I arrived at an empty road and sidewalk in front of Pickles Pub, not a runner in sight. My first thought was, is the race on Sunday? To my left, I did notice a police officer.

As I approached, I stated, "This may be the dumbest question ever, but where is the start line?"

"Over by the stadium."

I quickly walked over to Camden Yards a few blocks away and mingled in with the thousands of runners waiting for the marathon and 10K start. As I waited, the start at a baseball stadium seemed very appropriate for my situation. Growing up, I had been to Yankee Stadium for some Old Timers Games. As you sit in the stands, someone like the 1948 Cy Young Awardee for pitching is driven to the pitcher's mound in a golf cart, and they amble out and throw the ball like 15 feet. In 1948 this person was winning game after game, throwing the ball 100 MPH. But age catches up to everyone. I felt like that 1948 ball player. Forty years ago, I would be in the start area thinking, I need to be at the half in 1:12, twenty miles in

1:50, etc. This morning I was thinking, the last time I timed myself I ran a mile in over 13 minutes. When you get older, you need to check your ego. You had your time in the sun. Just enjoy the fact you can still run, no matter what the pace is.

While I sat waiting for the start, I had a worm's eye view of sneakers and noticed hundreds of runners in the new Nike Air Zoom Alphafly NEXT% shoes. I didn't feel so embarrassed with my purchase.

At precisely 8:00 a.m., we were off. About 400 meters into the race, Heather and Cam were at the side of the road to cheer. I later learned that they too went to the "start" at Pickles Pub based on my faulty advice. When we compared notes, the same police officer gave them direction to the actual start area.

The city of Baltimore angles downward to the harbor, the site of the start and finish. Therefore, as we headed away from the harbor, we slowly headed uphill and then continued to head uphill and uphill. The first three miles or so were all uphill, never steep, just long, and gradual. I was shocked when I hit the first mile in eight minutes and 45 seconds. It certainly felt easier than that 13-minute time trial only about ten weeks earlier. Easy or not, I knew it was too fast and slowed down, focusing inward and not worrying about other runners. Once we reached the top of the hills, we circled through the zoo, and I thought back to running in that zoo for the Zoo Zoom 5 Miler back in 1995! Back in 1995 we had no idea what zoom would mean to us in 2020.

What goes up must go down, and after the zoo and Johns Hopkins University, we headed downhill back to the Inner Harbor. Cam and Heather planned to meet me at mile nine, and the night before we picked out a spot based on the YouTube video. Fortunately, they followed the crowd and met me at mile nine to hand me a can of Coke. Cam was so excited as he cheered, holding up a poster he had secretly made the week before.

From mile nine to the halfway point of the course, we did a flat out and back section of the course that ran along the southern portion of the harbor down to the Under Armour factory and back. By this time, reality was setting in for me. Three months ago, I had been running ten minutes a day, a few times a week. I had no doubt I would finish, but it wasn't going to be pretty.

Once we completed this out and back section, we were back at the Inner Harbor and the halfway mark of the race. The Baltimore Marathon has an accompanying half marathon that starts, you guessed it, at the halfway point of the marathon. To make it even more enjoyable for the marathoners, these half marathoners start at 9:45 a.m., just as marathoners are at the halfway point of their race. Thousands of fresh enthusiastic runners join in for the final 13 miles of the marathon. Luckily, they don't officially merge in till three miles down the road.

Earlier I said the halfway in Boston is the best in the world, then I said the halfway mark at the Seoul Marathon is even better, and later I said coming off the 59th Street Bridge in NYC is the top spot for marathon excitement. Cam at mile 13 in the Baltimore Marathon is officially the top marathon spot in the world. Heather and Cam met me halfway, handing me a fresh water bottle and CLIF shot packets.

The halfway point of the Baltimore Marathon is also at the finish line area. It was incredibly tempting to stop and call it a day and be satisfied with a half marathon finish. Going past the finish line with 13 miles to go is tough. But I was not going to drop out in front of Cam. Plus, I had already written five chapters of a book and the publisher had approved the title. Too late to change the title to *Tales and Tips from 5 and a Half Decades of Marathons.*

I continued, shortly thereafter passing the aquarium, remembering that Friday, March 6, 2020, field trip before the world turned upside down. As we turned left and away from the waterfront, we once again headed uphill like earlier in the morning. Miles 14 to 19 were the toughest in the race mentally. At miles 14, 15, and 16, runners still have double-digit miles to go, and it can take a toll on you emotionally.

Two things kept me going, the first being the thought of Cam waiting for me at mile 25.5, as he would meet me there and run to the finish with me. The second was the tremendous support from the residents as we ran by their homes. Many had music either blasting out their windows or from radios on the street. Believe it or not, one person was blasting A-ha's "Take on Me" out a second-story open window.

However, the most entertaining part of this portion of the marathon was the road crossings. At each corner, a police officer was posted to stop traffic from cross streets as runners traveled the course. At every intersection police officers kept their cool as cars blasted horns and drivers shouted that they needed to get through. I did notice two other things that seemed new to me. Several people held posters that said, "Touch here for Power Up." I think power ups are something connected to video games and certainly back in 1979, our Atari video games coated in spilled Slurpees in the 7-11 had no power ups. The second thing I noticed was how many times we were told that we were getting closer to beer at the finish line. I think the people cheering didn't understand that we were not doing this for beer. One can certainly go to 7-11 to buy a can of beer without running 26 miles beforehand.

Mile 20 took us on a flat path around a huge lake. Up until this point, the "cupless" race didn't really seem to be adversely affecting anyone. Every few miles there were water stations where runners either filled their bottles from huge orange containers of water or volunteers poured water from jugs into runners' bottles. However, by this point in the race, the sun was peeking out and runners had been on their feet for three hours or so. As I rounded this lake, a man with a full cooler of water bottles stood by the side of the path with two bottles in outstretched arms. As I reached for one bottle he yanked both back, shouting, "No, no, no, these are for Striders only." I felt like saying, "Dude, I used to live in your town, I did a bunch of your 'Striders' races, don't be a jerk." But I let it go, although I still am annoyed, he held the bottles as if he was giving them away then yanked them back. Fortunately, there was a water station a bit up the path, and the "Striders only" guy was my only issue with a "cupless" race.

Shortly after we rounded the lake, we headed downhill to the finish by the Inner Harbor. The closer we got to the harbor the thicker and louder the crowds got. Also, the sight of 10K runners and half-marathoners walking on the sidewalks headed to their homes with their finishers' medals dangling from their necks was a sure sign that we were almost at the finish. As I ran downhill, I was certain that Heather and Cam knew I was on the way, since we had downloaded the runner tracker app on Heather's phone. Little did I know they had no idea where I was. Apparently, the runner tracker app for the Baltimore Marathon presupposes that the runner has also downloaded the app and is running with a phone. Seems to me to be more of a phone tracker app rather than a runner-tracking app. I never run with a phone, so Heather and Cam were in the dark.

I did run with my phone once. During Snowzilla in January 2016, Heather made me run with a phone and ordered me to send a video every five minutes as proof that I was OK. The snow ruined my phone; hence, I never run with a phone.

As I headed downhill toward mile 26, I could see Cam on the side of the road. He ran to me and jumped into the race for the final half-mile. Both of us could not control our excitement as we raced toward the finish line, crossing with our hands above our heads. As we crossed the finish line, we shouted, "We made it!" Yes, just like my Our Town moment with my dad back in 1979 after a cross-country meet. The difference here, though, was Cam squealed, "I am not hugging you, you are gross and wet!"

A few minutes later we met up with Heather and were sitting next to the Inner Harbor eating crepes, with me drinking a can of Coke. My only thought was sitting on a picnic table bench in Eisenhower Park in 1979 with my dad, and now I was with Cam in 2021 sitting on a bench. Within an hour of the finish, we were in the Hilton pool playing pool tag, racing around waist-deep water trying to catch "A Fish Out of Water." The marathon was a memory as we enjoyed being in a pool for the first time since Labor Day weekend.

Racing around the pool, I realized I had come full circle. In 1979, my dad handed me a Coke just as Cam did in 2021. In 1978, my dad shouted, "We made it!" just like Cam and I did hours earlier.

As we walked out of the hotel later to head to dinner, Cam asked me, "If you run a marathon at midnight on January 1, 2030, does it count toward your seventh decade?"

"Well, Cam, did I ever tell you about the time I ran a marathon on December 31, 1999, the last marathon of the 1900s . . ."

EPILOGUE

By the time we arrived home Saturday evening, a mere five hours or so after the Baltimore Marathon finish, several photos of the race were sitting in my inbox courtesy of Marathon Foto. I thought, wow that is fast, so much different from 1979 when small, one-inch sample photos arrived in my house's mailbox weeks after the event.

It's not just the photos that changed, almost everything has changed since 1979. However, I am not going to lament like the owners of the Kellerman's Lodge at the end of *Dirty Dancing*. The marathon was good in 1979; the marathon is good in 2021, just different.

As I did my final long run a week or so before the Baltimore Marathon, I thought back over the past 50 years of running. At the time, as I was running along the Potomac River at River Bend Park, I realized that I have run along a lot of rivers in my life: the Missouri River when I lived in Kansas City; the Rhine River when I lived in Germany; and the Han River when I lived in Seoul. And I thought, life is always flowing like a river, not always straight and not always calm. But it is always flowing, and you must flow with life-- coping with and adjusting to the changes, rough waters, and twists and turns thrown at you.

And it is the people along the way who help you navigate this river. This marathon journey of mine has never been about the actual races, rather it's been about the great people I met along the way. I can barely remember the finish lines of several marathons I have run, let alone the actual miles I ran in those races, but I can certainly remember:

"Kick it in," as my dad handed me a can of Coke.

"We have to run over that!!!!????" as Fred, Nicole, and I stood in the dark one cold November evening under the Verrazano Bridge, Nicole staring up at the NYC Marathon starting point.

"Wind from the south again," as Mr. Byrnes did his daily weather check at track practice by tossing a handful of grass in the air and watching which direction it blew.

"We have to get started, the Yankees are on early today," as Brendan tossed a cigarette before a five-mile uphill run to the top of Carter Mountain.

"Hi, I'm Vinny!" when I first met The Champ in 1979 on the Wantagh Bike path as he mentored me for my first marathon.

"Is there a hole somewhere around here I can fall into?" running beside my college roommate, Mike Regan, at mile 5.5 of the NCAA cross-country meet-- me saying this two weeks after he had fallen in a hole at the Big East Championship.

"It's a race, isn't it?" as John tried to sprint ahead of me at the 1994 Marine Corps Marathon.

"Come on, let's get going," as my stepbrother Patrick stood in my bedroom doorway each morning at 5:00 a.m., waking me up for our summer runs through Wantagh Park as I pretended to be asleep, but he never fell for it.

"Let's meet at Key Bridge at 4 am to run."

"No, Ray, it has to start with a 5-"—daily text exchange in the early 2000s with Ray.

"Why are you doing the children's race?" every time I asked Ms. Yi to sign me up for any race less than a marathon.

"Hey, buddy," the first words Matt says every time he calls me.

"Friday runs are the best," as Brian Andes would be overjoyed that we ran at the Fort Belvior golf course on Fridays and he could change in the fancy golf club locker room.

"Remember the time you didn't drink water, remember the time he ran in brand-new sneakers, remember the time . . ." as my wonderful stepmom reminds me of all my marathon foul-ups.

"We made it," as Cam and I crossed the Baltimore Marathon finish line.

Enjoy your marathons, be flexible, and always cherish the people you meet along the way.